INSPIRE / PLAN / DISCOVER / EXPERIENCE

DELHI
AGRA AND JAIPUR

DK EYEWITNESS

DELHI
AGRA AND JAIPUR

CONTENTS

DISCOVER 6

EXPERIENCE DELHI 62

EXPERIENCE BEYOND DELHI 154

NEED TO KNOW 248

Left: Powder and flowers from Holi, Vrindavan
Previous page: View over Amber Fort in Rajasthan
Front cover: Sunrise over the Taj Mahal

DISCOVER

Bustling Paharganj in New Delhi

WELCOME TO
DELHI, AGRA
AND JAIPUR

Buzzing cities and iconic monuments. Tiger-filled jungles and epic forts. Whatever your dream trip to this part of India entails, this DK Eyewitness Travel Guide is the perfect companion.

1 Garland-making at a flower stall in Jaipur.

2 The beautiful Amber Fort in Rajasthan.

3 A tiger in Ranthambhore National Park.

4 The bustling streets of Paharganj in Delhi.

Better known as the Golden Triangle, the ancient cities of Delhi, Agra and Jaipur are among the most visited places in India. Delhi, the country's capital, is famed for its frenetic energy, colourful markets and historic monuments. Just south – and world-renowned for the incomparable Taj Mahal – Agra was heavily influenced by the region's Mughal rulers, with traces of this once-powerful empire still seen in the city's historic tombs and magnificent fort. Jaipur meanwhile is a treasure chest of ornate palaces, vibrant jewellery markets and romantic rooftop restaurants.

Beyond these three unique cities lies the region's dramatic landscapes, covering mountainous foothills, lush jungles, peaceful wetlands and barren desert. Dotted across this diverse terrain are abandoned cities, sacred towns and imposing forts, not to mention several breathtaking national parks brimming with wildlife. Throughout the year, lively festivals make the region come alive, whether it's religious celebrations like the kaleidoscopically colourful Holi or the engaging art, literature and foodie events on offer in cities like Delhi and Jaipur.

The area's sheer size and diversity can be overwhelming, but this guidebook breaks the region down into easily navigable chapters, with detailed itineraries, expert local knowledge and colourful, comprehensive maps to help you plan the perfect visit. Whether you're staying for a weekend, a week or longer, this Eyewitness guide will ensure that you see the very best this spectacular region has to offer. Enjoy the book and enjoy Delhi, Agra and Jaipur.

REASONS TO LOVE
DELHI, AGRA
AND JAIPUR

Bustling cities filled with ancient monuments; fragrant dishes bursting with spices; imposing and majestic hilltop forts. There are so many reasons to love the Golden Triangle – here are some of our favourites.

1 DELHI'S BUZZ
Delhi's chaotic cacophony can be overwhelming – but, once you find your feet, it gives you an incredible buzz. Experience this frenetic energy in the narrow streets of Old Delhi *(p104)*.

THE TAJ MAHAL *2*
One of the new Seven Wonders of the World, this exquisite mausoleum is instantly recognizable. Built by Shah Jahan for his beloved Mumtaz, it is an enduring symbol of love *(p176)*.

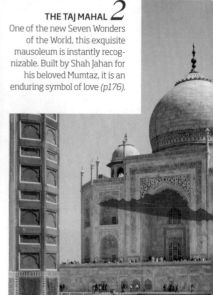

3 THE PINK CITY
Rajasthan's terracotta-hued capital, Jaipur *(p206)*, is a sight to behold. While the opulent City Palace and clifftop Nahargarh Fort are definite highlights, there are also small temples and lively markets to discover.

4 FORMIDABLE FORTS
Strongholds are scattered across the region's landscape, from the vast Red Fort *(p198)* and ancient Purana Qila *(p100)* to Amber's sprawling citadel *(p222)* and haunted Bhangarh Fort *(p245)*.

A CULINARY MELTING POT 5
North India has a rich culinary heritage with influences from Persia, Kashmir and the North West Frontier. Foodies will love sampling delicious plates of Mughal chicken, saffron-infused biryanis and hot, fluffy naan.

MODERN TEMPLES 6
Rivalling their historic siblings, Delhi's modern temples are spectacular. Find tranquillity at the monumental Akshardham Temple *(p144)* or lotus-shaped Baha'i House of Worship *(p138)*.

STREET ART 7

Murals are popping up across Delhi, bringing a splash of eye-catching colour to India's capital. Wander through Lodi Colony *(p84)* or Shahpur Jat *(p134)* to spy some of the best.

FATEHPUR SIKRI 8

This spectacular fortified city *(p182)*, once the short-lived capital of the Mughal empire, is home to ancient palaces and one of India's largest mosques, the immense Jama Masjid.

9 SIPPING A CUP OF CHAI

Served on street corners by *chaiwalas* (tea makers) and offered at roadside dhabas (tea stalls), chai is everywhere you look. Sample a steaming cup of masala chai, a milk tea flavoured with warming spices.

10 UNEARTHING ARCHAEOLOGY

Delhi's dramatic Qutb Minar complex *(p128)* and forested Mehrauli Archaeological Park *(p126)* are both filled with historic sights. Take a stroll to discover atmospheric ruins.

ANCIENT OBSERVATORIES 11

The huge open-air observatories found at both Delhi *(p84)* and Jaipur *(p212)* will leave you starstruck. Built by the stargazing king Sawai Jai Singh II, they are filled with giant astronomical instruments.

WILD NATURE 12

Encompassing some wonderfully diverse landscapes, from dense jungle to wild wetlands, the region's national parks are filled with a wealth of wildlife, including leopards, elephants and tigers.

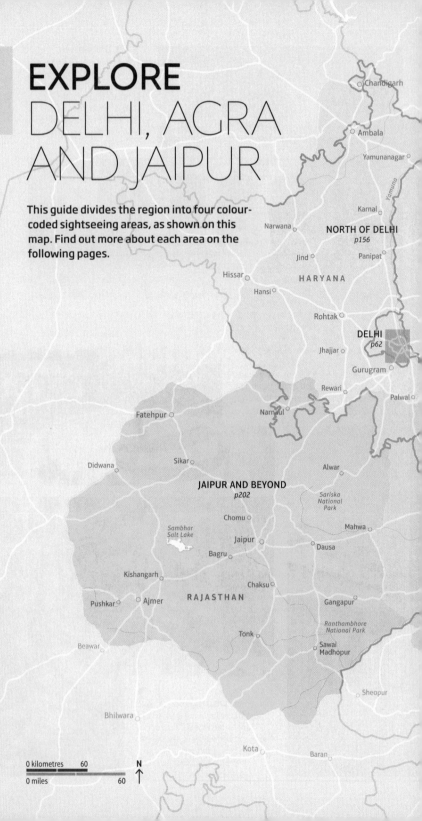

EXPLORE
DELHI, AGRA
AND JAIPUR

This guide divides the region into four colour-coded sightseeing areas, as shown on this map. Find out more about each area on the following pages.

Chandigarh

Ambala

Yamunanagar

Karnal

Narwana

NORTH OF DELHI
p156

Jind

Panipat

Hissar

HARYANA

Hansi

Rohtak

DELHI
p62

Jhajjar

Gurugram

Rewari

Palwal

Fatehpur

Narnaul

Sikar

Alwar

Didwana

JAIPUR AND BEYOND
p202

Sariska
National
Park

Chomu

Mahwa

Sambhar
Salt Lake

Jaipur

Bagru

Dausa

Kishangarh

Chaksu

Pushkar

Ajmer

RAJASTHAN

Gangapur

Beawar

Ranthambhore
National Park

Tonk

Sawai
Madhopur

Sheopur

Bhilwara

0 kilometres   60

0 miles   60

N

Kota

Baran

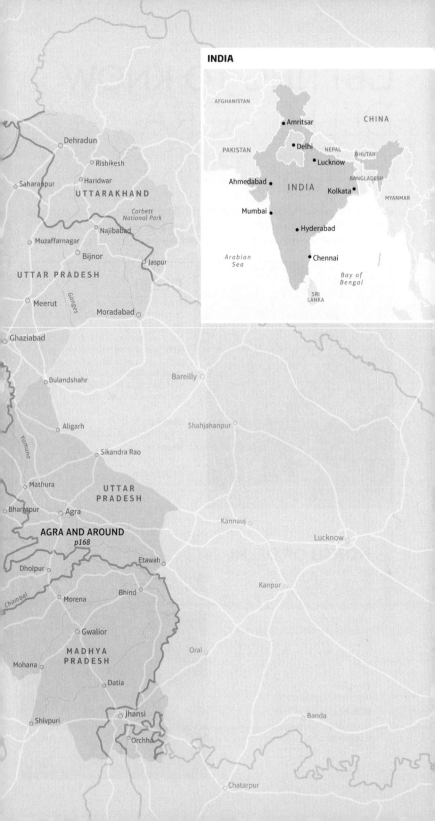

INDIA

AFGHANISTAN

CHINA

PAKISTAN

• Amritsar

• Delhi

NEPAL

BHUTAN

• Lucknow

BANGLADESH

Ahmedabad •

INDIA

Kolkata •

MYANMAR

Mumbai •

• Hyderabad

Arabian
Sea

• Chennai

Bay of
Bengal

SRI
LANKA

Dehradun

• Rishikesh

Saharanpur

Haridwar

UTTARAKHAND

Corbett
National Park

Muzaffarnagar

Najibabad

Bijnor

Jaspur

UTTAR PRADESH

Ganges

Meerut

Moradabad

Ghaziabad

Bulandshahr

Bareilly

Aligarh

Shahjahanpur

Yamuna

Sikandra Rao

Mathura

UTTAR
PRADESH

Bharatpur

Agra

Kannauj

Lucknow

AGRA AND AROUND
p168

Dholpur

Etawah

Kanpur

Chambal

Morena

Bhind

Orai

Gwalior

Mohana

MADHYA
PRADESH

Datia

Shivpuri

Jhansi

Banda

Orchha

Chatarpur

GETTING TO KNOW
DELHI, AGRA
AND JAIPUR

Better known as the "Golden Triangle", the diverse cities of Delhi, Agra and Jaipur are found in the northwest of India, a region which stretches from the foothills of the Himayalas in the north to the rocky ravines of the south.

PAGE 62

DELHI

Known for its frenetic energy, India's buzzing capital beautifully blends the ancient and the modern. At the city's heart lies spacious and leafy New Delhi, while surrounding this modern core are the city's older incarnations, from maze-like Old Delhi to the ruined forts of Purana Qila and Tughlaqabad. Find out more about Delhi on p66.

Best for
Unearthing Delhi's mosaic of historic cities

Home to
Humayun's Tomb, Red Fort, Qutb Minar

Experience
The tranquil serenity of the Jama Masjid

PAGE 156

NORTH OF DELHI

Once roamed by the heroes of epics, the vast plain north of India's capital is a land inseparably tied to Hindu heritage. Here lie towns like Kurukshetra and Panipat, once the sites of legendary battles, plus pilgrim towns such as Haridwar. Wild nature can be found at Corbett and Rajala National Parks, while holy Rishikesh is the area's adventure capital.

Best for
Holy towns on the Ganges

Home to
Corbett National Park

Experience
Whitewater rafting down the Ganges

PAGE 168

AGRA AND AROUND

Once the capital of the region's Mughal rulers, Agra is famed for the exquisite Taj Mahal. But this busy city has much more to offer, whether it's the elegant domes of the Jama Masjid or the imposing red-sandstone Agra Fort. Beyond Agra lie the holy towns of Mathura and Vrindavan, with their riverside ghats and temples, as well as the bird-filled wetlands of Keoladeo Ghana National Park, astonishing abandoned city of Fatehpur Sikri and romantic fountains of Deeg Water Palace. South lie vast plains, home to both Orchha's medieval ambience and Gwalior's hilltop fort.

Best for
Mughal monuments

Home to
Agra, Fatehpur Sikri, Deeg Water Palace, Orchha, Gwalior Fort, Keoladeo Ghana National Park

Experience
The Taj from the river in the early-morning mist

PAGE 202

JAIPUR AND BEYOND

The Jaipur region of Rajasthan is a semiarid land cut through by the craggy Aravalli Hills. Studded with hilltop and jungle forts – among them Amber's magnificent citadel – the region offers valleys and plains that glitter with palaces, pavilions, pleasure gardens and temples. It's also home to two wildlife-filled national parks, Ranthambhore and Sariska, and Shekhawati's exuberantly painted *havelis* (mansions). Rajasthan's capital, Jaipur, lies at the region's heart. This "Pink City" is filled with spectacular sights, including ornate palaces, intriguing museums and colourful, bustling markets.

Best for
Imposing forts and jewel-like palaces

Home to
Jaipur, Amber Fort, Alwar, Sariska National Park, Pushkar, Ajmer, Ranthambhore National Park, Shekhawati's Painted Havelis

Experience
Going wildlife spotting in the region's national parks

←

1 Bustling Chandni Chowk in the heart of Old Delhi.

2 The monumental yet elegant Humayun's Tomb.

3 The distinctive shape of the Baha'i House of Worship.

4 One of Hauz Khas's cool and quirky boutique shops.

A land shrouded in myth and legend, the Golden Triangle is bursting with an array of adventures. Wherever you choose to go, our handpicked itineraries will help you plan the perfect trip.

5 DAYS
in Delhi

Day 1

Morning Starting at the western end of Chandni Chowk (p112), explore bustling Old Delhi. Wander through the winding streets of this historic area, then immerse youself in the tranquility of the Jama Masjid (p110).

Afternoon Devour delicious raj kachori (deep-fried bread bursting with chickpeas and tamarind chutney) at Haldiram's (p39), before admiring the throne rooms and royal apartments of the Red Fort (p108).

Evening After a busy day exploring treat yourself to dinner at Dhaba (p80) in Connaught Place, followed by a drink on one of Q'Ba's (p83) cosy rooftop terraces.

Day 2

Morning Discover the Qutb Minar complex (p128), with its spectacular five-storeyed victory tower; a stroll through nearby Mehrauli Archaeological Park (p126) will reveal an array of atmospheric ruins.

Afternoon After a Mediterranean lunch at Olive Bar and Kitchen (p131), pay homage to Gandhi, India's renowned independence leader, at Gandhi Smriti (p84), both the site of his assassination and home to a compelling museum commemorating his life.

Evening Head over to the award-winning Bukhara (p149) for a delicious dinner of North West Indian cuisine.

Day 3

Morning Take in the heart of imperial New Delhi with a stroll down the majestic Rajpath (p79) to the monumental India Gate (p79). Spend the rest of your morning exploring the vast collection at the National Museum (p74).

Afternoon Grab a quick bite to eat in cosy Sazerac (p103), then head south to explore Humayun's Tomb complex (p92). Admire this famous emperor's majestic resting place – a precursor to the Taj – then take a late afternoon stroll through neighbouring Sunder Nursery (p95).

Evening Enjoy an evening of creative cuisine at Indian Accent (p80), where international ingredients are prepared using traditional Indian techniques.

Day 4

Morning Watch the city come to life from rooftop café India Coffee House (p83), before visiting South Delhi to discover the unique Baha'i House of Worship (p138) and colourful Kalkaji Temple (p139). Feeling hungry? Fill up on South Indian veggie dishes at Sagar Ratna (www.sagarratna.in).

Afternoon Dedicate the afternoon to unearthing the medieval monuments and boutique shops of Hauz Khas (p130), before taking a stroll around its pretty Deer Park.

Evening Hang around in Hauz Khas Village for dinner at the effortlessly cool Social (www.socialoffline.in), followed by an evening of live music at Imperfecto Hauz Khas.

Day 5

Morning Spend an energetic morning learning the basics of Bollywood dance at the Delhi Dance Academy (p132). After all that exercise, it's off to Moti Mahal Deluxe 2 (www.motimahal.in) for a calorie-fuelled lunch of butter chicken.

Afternoon Take some time to relax at the amazing Akshardham Temple (p144). After, head south to wander through the magnificent ruins of Tughlaqabad Fort (p133).

Evening Browse the boutiques of Shahpur Jat (p134). This bohemian village is full of excellent places to eat, so take your pick.

←

1 Visitors exploring the ethereal Taj Mahal.

2 A courtyard in the city of Fatehpur Sikri.

3 A vendor showcasing his wares at Kinari Bazaar.

4 One of the elegant rooms found inside Agra Fort.

2 DAYS

in Agra

Day 1

Morning There's no better way to start your Agra adventure than with a trip to the iconic Taj Mahal *(p176)*. Get there early to beat the crowds and see the rising sun illuminate the sublime beauty of this elegant mausoleum. Check the details of the pietra dura inlay work *(p178)*, carved reliefs, marble screens and Persian and Arabic calligraphy, and then wander through the beautifully landscaped *charbagh* garden *(p195)*. For lunch, head over to Pinch of Spice *(www. pinchofspice.in)* for mouthwatering curries in a modern setting.

Afternoon Speed alongside the river in a rickshaw to take in more Mughal splendour at Agra Fort *(p172)*, where you can spend the afternoon admiring its wonderful array of royal pavilions, reception halls, mosques and gateways, as well as the beautiful arcades at the Diwan-i-Aam. Then climb to the top of the fort's Musamman Burj for awe-inspiring views of the Taj Mahal.

Evening As the sun sets, stay at Agra Fort to enjoy its colourful sound and light show, recounting the history of the great Mughal emperors. Then, your tummy rumbling, take an autorickshaw down to Sadar Bazaar for a slap-up veggie supper at Zorba the Buddha *(www.zorbarestaurantagra.com)*.

Day 2

Morning Take a bus or a cab to Fatephur Sikri *(p182)* and spend the morning wandering around this abandoned Mughal capital. Admire the beautiful architecture of this palace complex, which also houses the impressive Jama Masjid, as well as the site's small but fascinating Archaeological Museum. Try some of the local *nan khatai* biscuits sold at bakeries in the village, enjoying a cup of masala chai or two with them – but don't spoil your appetite ahead of lunch at the cheerful Hotel Ajay Palace *(Agra Rd)*. Its peaceful rooftop area offers incredible views of the nearby Jama Masjid.

Afternoon Head back into Agra along the Grand Trunk Road, keeping an eye out for *kos minars* (Mughal milestones) on the way. Back in the city, take a stroll through the main souk areas such as Johri Bazaar and Kinari Bazaar, pausing to try a handful or two of toothsome *petha* (crystallized pumpkin sweets), a local speciality. After, make sure to visit Agra's own beautiful red sandstone Jama Masjid *(p174)*.

Evening After a jam-packed weekend of sightseeing, enjoy an excellent Mughal-inspired tandoori meal at the Oberoi Amarvilas Hotel's wonderful fine-dining and elegant Esphahan restaurant *(www. oberoihotels.com)*.

←

1 The giant astronomical instruments in Jantar Mantar.

2 Traders selling flower garlands in Tripolia Bazaar.

3 A colourful sari shop in Johari Bazaar.

4 An intricately decorated room at Amber Fort.

3 DAYS
in Jaipur

Day 1

Morning Begin your exploration of the Pink City with a trip to the marvellous City Palace Museum *(p208)*, an expansive complex. Found within the museum is the Chandra Mahal *(p210)* – its awe-inspiring ornate interior will demand your attention, but remember to explore the museum's other fascinating galleries, especially the Painting and Photography Gallery, filled with amazing 19th-century photographs taken by Maharaja Ram Singh II.

Afternoon Treat yourself to lunch with spectacular views at Saba Haveli *(www.sabahaveli.com)*, then wander around the Jai Niwas Bagh garden and the Talkatora water tank, stopping off at the Govind Dev Temple *(p206)*. Afterwards, check out the incredible Jantar Mantar *(p212)*, an astronomical observatory, and marvel at the huge scientific instruments built to observe the heavens back in the early 18th century.

Evening After sundown, hire a cab and head just outside of the city to Chokhi Dhani *(www.chokhidhani.com)* for some traditional Rajasthani food and entertainment; take in a folk dance and maybe an acrobatic display before tucking in to a delectable Rajasthani feast or a multi-cuisine buffet.

Day 2

Morning Devote your morning to investigating Sawai Pratap Singh's beautiful Hawa Mahal ("Wind Palace"), known for its iconic façade covered in over 900 honeycomb-shaped windows *(p206)*.

Next on your list is the fascinating Albert Hall Museum *(p206)*: filled with artistic treasures, this museum is housed in Samuel Swinton Jacob's magnificent 1886 Indo-Saracenic Albert Hall.

Afternoon By now you'll be peckish, so grab some lunch from one of the stalls at Masala Chowk, an outdoor food court. Afterwards, head down the bustling Johari Bazaar to Badi Chaupar *(p216)*; check out the Jama Masjid and take a wander along Tripolia Bazaar to immerse yourself in its many vibrant shops and markets.

Evening Spend a relaxed evening devouring delicious thali dishes at the Suvarna Mahal restaurant *(www.tajhotels.com)* in Rambagh Palace – this magical Renaissance-style restaurant is located in the palace's original dining room.

Day 3

Morning Get up early and take a bus or a Jeep to Amber, home to a spectacular 16th-century hilltop fort *(p222)*. Admire its ornate gates, and amble through its royal apartments and pleasure palaces. Refuel with lunch at the fort's cafe, then enjoy a stroll through Amber town *(p224)*, with its temples and royal cenotaphs.

Afternoon Spend the afternoon at the legendary Jaigarh Fort *(p221)*, overlooking Amber. Wander along its ramparts for a spectacular panorama over the town below and the surrounding landscape.

Evening Back in Jaipur, finish your trip at the Peacock restaurant *(p207)* for some excellent North Indian food and great views over the city.

15 DAYS
in Northern India

Northern India is sprinkled with an abundance of spectacular sights. Explore them all on this 15-day tour, from bustling cities and colourful holy towns to wildlife-filled national parks and imposing hilltop forts.

▌ Day 1

There's nowhere better than bustling Delhi to start your Golden Triangle adventure. Explore New Delhi with a wander down the regal Rajpath *(p79)*, then visit the National Museum *(p74)* to unearth ancient artifacts. Enjoy authentic Indian food at the elegant Fire *(15 Sansad Marg, Connaught Place)*, before delving into bustling Old Delhi *(p104)*. While away the afternoon wandering through its maze of narrow streets and colourful markets, stopping off at the imposing Red Fort *(p108)* and tranquil Jama Masjid *(p110)*. As evening arrives, stop in at Karim's *(p116)* for an authentic Old Delhi supper – the korma is the best.

▌ Day 2

Take the metro down to the spectacular Qutb Minar complex *(p128)* to spend an hour or so exploring its incredible architecture. Wander through the nearby forested Mehrauli Archaeological Park *(p126)*, peppered with historic ruins, on your way to a Mediterranean lunch at the Olive Bar and Kitchen *(p131)*. Then, take a tranquil post-lunch stroll past historic tombs in the peaceful Lodi Gardens *(p85)*. The rest of the afternoon can be dedicated to perusing the impressive collection at the National Gallery of Modern Art *(p80)*. Round off your day with mouthwatering North Indian cuisine at Kwality *(p80)*.

▌ Day 3

Rise early and take the morning train from New Delhi to Chandigarh *(p164)*. Refuel with healthy organic produce after your journey at AJA Fresh *(www.ajafresh.com)*. Spend a relaxing hour or two in the city's fascinating Rock Garden, with its beautiful hills, waterfalls and caves, and then – having booked ahead in advance – take the 3pm tour of the Capitol Complex. The city's pretty Rose Garden is a delightful place to wander through on your way to a dinner of traditional Punjabi food at Dera in the Taj Hotel *(p165)*. Later, as the sun sets, amble along the pretty promenade at the edge of Sukhna Lake.

1 The Rajpath and India Gate.

2 The Qutb Minar complex.

3 Statues in Chandigarh's famous rock garden.

4 Pilgrims at Har ki Pauri.

5 Rishikesh's Kailash Niketan Temple.

6 The striking interior of Agra Fort.

Day 4

Jump on a morning train to Haridwar (p167) and go for lunch at Hoshiyar Puri (Upper Road). Next, take the ropeway up to the hilltop Mansa Devi temple – this Hindu place of worship offers panoramic views. The riverside bazaar, lined with colourful stalls, is a great way to spend a few hours. As evening descends, head to the town's main ghat, Har ki Pauri, to see worshippers place small flower-filled and lamp-lit vessels onto the water. After, North Indian fare and views over the Ganges await at rooftop Haveli Hari Ganga (p166).

Day 5

It's just over an hour by train to Rishikesh (p166) from Haridwar. On arrival, make for the blessed site of Muni ki Reti on the holy Ganges, then head over the Ram Jhula suspension bridge to Swarg Ashram. Riverside Chotiwala (www.chotiwalarestaurant.com), serving delicious North Indian food, is a great lunch spot. Spend an adventurous afternoon river rafting on the Ganges; for those who'd prefer to keep their feet dry, the Swarg Ashram area is home to a number of ashrams offering yoga courses. At dinner, enjoy more river views by heading to the Sitting Elephant (Hotel EllBee Ganga View, 355 Haridwar Rd).

Day 6

Take an early morning stroll from Swarg Ashram to Lakshman Jhula – Rishikesh's other suspension bridge – for breathtaking views down the Ganges; the spectacular Kailash Niketan Temple is only a short walk away. Grab brunch at Cafe De Goa (near Laxman Jhula Bridge), then take a tour of nearby Rajaji National Park to spy elephants and sloth bears – if you're lucky, you might even spot a tiger. Back in Rishikesh, have dinner at Ramana's Organic Garden Cafe (p168) before taking the overnight train to Agra (p172).

Day 7

After your long journey, enjoy a caffeine hit and breakfast at Rumi's Cafe Agra (www. rumiscafeagra.business.site). Refuelled, it's time to be awe-inspired by Agra's most famous sight, the Taj Mahal (p176): wander through its elegantly landscaped charbagh gardens (p195) before exploring its sublime interior. Back in town, lunch at Peshwari (p175), before you wend your way to the imposing Agra Fort, home to courtly buildings and an elegantly arcaded hall, the Diwan-i-Aam; stay for the fort's magnificent sound and light show. Then, a night of pampering and delectable Mughal food await at luxury hotel the Oberoi (p173).

Day 8

Enjoy a lazy morning in your hotel, then take the train or bus to Mathura *(p196)* for a late lunch at Dosa Plaza Divinity *(Deeg Gate, Masani Road)*, which offers over 100 different types of dosa. Next, visit Krishna Janmasthan Temple and then stroll along the riverfront, lined with ghats and trees. The best way to spend the evening is gliding by boat down the river to Vishram Ghat to spy the magical *aarti* take place: this Hindu ritual sees brightly burning lamps offered to one or more deities. Your tummy rumbling, head back to Agra to sample southern Indian curries at Achman Restaurant *(86 NH Bypass Road)*.

Day 9

Hire a car for the day and journey out west to Fatehpur Sikri *(p182)*. Spend the morning exploring this epic, abandoned city before taking lunch at Jodha Restaurant in Hotel Goverdhan *(Shahcoolie, Fatehpur Sikri)*. Your next stop is Jaipur *(p206)*. When you arrive, check into the Hotel Pearl Palace *(www.hotelpearlpalace.com)*: its art-filled rooms are the perfect place to relax, while its multicuisine Peacock restaurant *(p207)* offers magical rooftop views over the city.

Day 10

Today, the sights of the Pink City await. Start with a stroll through the Jai Niwas Bagh garden, then visit the opulent City Palace Museum *(p208)*: admire its ornate Chandra Mahal, and discover royal costumes and ornate weapons in its galleries. LMB *(www.lmbsweets.com)* in Johari Bazar offers light lunches followed by mouthwatering traditional Indian sweets. On a sugar high, spend the afternoon wandering through the city's many bazaars. End the day at the elegant Bar Palladio *(p207)*, which servers soulful Italian food.

Day 11

Using Jaipur as a base, spend the next few days exploring the area. This morning, hire a car and drive to Nahargarh Fort *(p220)*, perched on a hill overlooking Jaipur. Take a walk along the battlements for expansive views over the city below, before admiring the fort's Sculpture Park. Lunch alfresco at the fort's restaurant, spectacularly situated on the battlements. After, make the short drive to Amber to explore its sprawling fort *(p222)* and historic town *(p224)*. Back in Jaipur, devour a veggie dinner at the old-world Hotel Natraj *(www.hotelnatrajjaipur.com)*.

1 Vishram Ghat in Mathura.

2 The spectacular city of Fatehpur Sikri.

3 Entrance to Jaipur's City Palace.

4 A tiger in Ranthambhore National Park.

5 A painted *haveli* in Shekhawati.

Day 12

It's an early start to drive south to the wild Ranthambhore National Park *(p236)*. Take a Jeep safari tour of this incredible area, keeping your eyes peeled for the park's most famous inhabitant, majestic tigers, while deer stir and scatter, and monkeys sound the alarm. Khem Villas *(p236)*, a luxury, ecofriendly retreat perched on the edge of the park, is a great place to spend the night – you might even spot hyenas, jackals and desert fox roaming the surrounding grasslands.

Day 13

Say goodbye to Ranthambhore and make the journey back to Jaipur. Have a long lunch in the bohemian Jaipur Modern *(www.jaipurmodern.com)*, then spend the afternoon exploring the spectacular Hawa Mahal *(p206)*, pausing before you enter to admire its honeycomb façade. If you have the time, pop into the art-filled Albert Hall Museum *(p207)* to admire intricate jewellery and Rajput miniature paintings. Dedicate your evening to devouring delicious Indo-Persian cuisine at Zarin in the Fairmont Hotel *(www.fairmont.com/jaipur)*, then hit up the regal library bar Aza to relax with a glass of wine.

Day 14

Rise with the sun and head north to explore the beautifully painted *havelis* (mansions) of the Shekhawati region *(p238)*. Stop in at Sikar to explore its busy bazaars and rural ambience, then head to Lachhmangarh to while away the afternoon visiting its Char Chowk Haveli and the fort. Enjoy a cheap and cheerful dinner at Elephant Treat (Link Road) and then make the 30-minute drive to nearby Fatehpur to bed down in the colourfully embellished 19th-century Le Prince Haveli *(www.leprincehaveli.com)*.

Day 15

Dedicate the morning to the picturesque *havelis* of Fatehpur. The rest of the day can be spent admiring the beautiful *havelis* at Mandawa, Dundlod and Nawalgarh, pausing for lunch in the latter's Bungli restaurant *(Ward No 25)*. As evening arrives, head south to the town of Samode, whose romantic, fairy-tale palace is now a luxury hotel *(p245)*. Dine on refined Rajasthani cuisine in its restaurant and treat yourself to a night in one of its mural-covered rooms before before you make the drive back to Delhi in the morning.

Get Bejewelled in Jaipur

Jaipur (p206) is renowned for its beautifully made jewellery (p215), from its iconic lac bangles – made from coloured resin – to carefully crafted *kundan* and filigree pieces. There's nowhere better to shop for these elegant items than at Johari Bazaar, the city's oldest market, home to stalls showcasing intricate jewellery.

→

A display of eye-catchingly colourful bangles at a stall in Jaipur

DELHI, AGRA AND JAIPUR FOR
MARKETS AND BAZAARS

India is famous for its colourful, bustling markets, and this area is no exception. Dotted throughout the streets of Delhi, Agra and Jaipur are nose-tingling spice markets and vibrant sari stalls, beautifully crafted jewellery shops and buzzing book markets. Just remember to save some room in your suitcase...

Travel the Spice Route

For a shot of colour and a sprinkling of flavour, head to a spice market. Running since the 17th century, Khari Baoli (p113) in Delhi is Asia's largest spice market – expect to see sacks full of vibrant chillies and piles of delicate crimson saffron fronds. Or join locals at Rawatpara Spice Market close to Agra Fort (p172) as they stock up on cardamom and turmeric. Keep your eyes peeled for bowls of mouthwatering *petha*, a boiled sweet particular to Agra made from ash gourd.

←

A stall selling spices and nuts in Delhi's historic spice market Khari Baoli

Dress to Impress

Looking for the perfect outfit? The colourful clothing markets at Janpath *(p81)*, south of Delhi's expansive Connaught Place *(p81)*, are a great place to hunt for bargains, or try Khan Market *(p83)* for upmarket India-centric shops like Fabindia *(p134)*. Outside of Delhi, Nehru Bazaar in Jaipur *(p206)* offers vibrant saris and jewel-bright textiles.

→

Embroidered garments and fabric on display at Janpath's vibrant market in Delhi

Stacks of Books

Every Sunday, bibliophiles unite at Daryaganj book market in New Delhi *(p70)*. Brand-new titles, secondhand books and even first editions are balanced in tottering piles on the pavement. No discerning book-lover should miss the chance to visit Chaura Rasta in Jaipur *(p206)*, a vast market home to a host of book shops filled to the brim with novels, non-fiction and more.

←

A bookseller shows off his wares at Delhi's Daryaganj book market

Conscious Crafts

Traditional dolls on display in Dilli Haat, Delhi ↑

If you're looking for a unique, locally made souvenir, try one of the area's craft markets. Evoking a bustling village atmosphere, Dilli Haat *(p130)* is a craft market in the heart of Delhi where you can find beautiful art, handcrafted shoes and lovingly made textiles. If you're visiting Jaipur, don't miss the intricately detailed Rajasthani textiles and colourfully attired puppets at Sireh Deori Bazaar opposite Hawa Mahal *(p206)*.

SHOP

Support local craftspeople at these Fair Trade and ecofriendly shops.

People Tree

Fair Trade clothes with pop-folk designs.

🏠 Regal Building, Connaught Place
🌐 peopletreeonline.com

Saahra

A sustainable design shop selling luxury clothes and jewellery.

🏠 New Friends Colony
🌐 saahra.com

Hansiba

Fair Trade embroidered clothes and homewares.

🏠 Baba Kharak Singh Marg 🌐 hansiba.in

Glorious Gardens

Pretty parks and gardens are peppered across the city. Hauz Khas - with its beautiful deer park and lake *(p130)* - is the perfect place for a sunset stroll, while the idyllic Lodi Gardens *(p85)*, filled with historic tombs, is ideal for a lazy picnic. If you're visiting Delhi between August and March, make a beeline for the flower-covered Mughal Gardens at the palatial Rashtrapati Bhavan *(p78)*.

The tomb-filled Lodi Gardens, an oasis of calm amid Delhi's busy streets

DELHI FOR
PEACEFUL SPOTS

While known more for its tangle of streets thronged with frenetic traffic, Delhi is in fact home to a number of wonderfully peaceful spots. From charming gardens and wild forests to tranquil temples and serene memorials, the city is full of hidden urban oases that are the perfect antidote to its hustle and bustle.

EAT

Haveli Dharampura
A charming restaurant with epic panoramas over Old Delhi.

⌖ 2293, Gali Guliyan, Dharampura
Ⓦ havelidharampura. com

Thai High
Illuminated by twinkling fairy lights, this romantic spot has views of the Qutb Minar.

⌖ Ambawatta Complex, Mehrauli Village

Ancient Oases

Delhi offers an array of architectural sites just perfect for escaping the city's frenetic energy. The paths surrounding Humayan's Tomb complex *(p92)* are great for a gentle amble, while the tree-lined trails of Mehrauli Archaeological Park's *(p126)* are perfect for escaping the crowds.

→

The peaceful gardens surrounding Humayan's Tomb

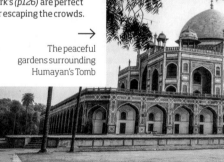

Tranquil Temples

There's no better place to find inner peace than at one of the city's temples. Found in the heart of New Delhi, the Sikh temple of Gurudwara Bangla Sahib *(p82)* has a hushed reverence - its serene *sarovar* (pool) is a beautiful place for morning contemplation. Spectacularly shaped like a lotus flower, the city's Baha'i House of Worship *(p138)* welcomes those from all faiths - seek serenity in its soothing central prayer hall.

A Nihang Sikh sitting in the tranquil Gurudwara Bangla Sahib

> 💬 INSIDER TIP
> **Inner Peace**
>
> Can't find a peaceful spot outside? Look within. Delhi offers countless yoga and meditation classes to help you find inner peace. One of the best is Seema Sondhi's Yoga Studio *(www.theyogastudio. info)* in Hauz Khas.

Peaceful Memorials

Perched on the banks of the Yamuna river, Raj Ghat *(p116)* is a tranquil memorial dedicated to the memory of Mahatma Gandhi, with a plain black marble platform set within a quiet garden. Close by is Shantivan ("the forest of peace"), the final resting place of Jawaharlal Nehru, India's first president - visit the simple memorial and well-kept, tree-lined garden.

The simple memorial to Mahatma Gandhi at Raj Ghat

Wild Areas

Probably the last place you'd associate with wilderness, Delhi is bordered to the north by the untamed Northern Ridge *(p148)*. Just one small section of the greater Delhi Ridge, this area is covered by a web of walking routes that lace through a jungle rich in biodiversity. Keep your eyes peeled for Great Horned owls, palm squirrels and leopards.

$\rightarrow$

The spectacular Great Horned Owl, found in Delhi's Northern Ridge

Getting Arty

An artistic hub, Delhi has a cultural calendar filled with cool events. The India Art Fair *(www.indiaartfair.in)* celebrates contemporary art from around the globe, while the Delhi International Arts Festival *(p55)* promotes everything from performing arts to poetry. In Agra, the ten-day Agra Taj Mahotsav *(p54)*, celebrates the crafts, cuisine and music of India's regions.

←

A contemporary art exhibition at Delhi's cutting-edge India Art Fair

DELHI, AGRA AND JAIPUR FOR
FESTIVALS

This region is bursting with vibrant festivals, whether it's the lighting of lamps at Diwali or the throwing of colour at Holi. But it's not just religious celebrations that bring this area to life: music festivals also draw the crowds, while art and literary events celebrate a rich, creative heritage.

Sacred Celebrations

Some of India's most spectacular celebrations are spiritual. During the spring festival of Holi, the region comes alive in a riot of colour – join the crowds at Govindji Temple in Vrindavan *(p196)* to throw coloured powder into the air. Celebrate Diwali, the festival of light, at Nahargarh Fort *(p220)*: perched above Jaipur, it offers awe-inspiring views of the walled city illuminated by the light of shimmering lamps.

↑ Crowds throwing coloured powder during the spring festival of Holi

National Holidays

Nowhere celebrates India's national holidays better than the country's capital, Delhi. Commemorating the constitution coming into force in 1950, Republic Day *(p54)* sees vibrant and colourful parades take place around Rashtrapati Bhavan *(p78)*, with processions of India's armed forces accompanied by rousing music from military bands. Every August, India's Independence Day *(p55)* sees the National Flag unfurled above the imposing Red Fort *(p108)*.

←

A cavalry procession and *(inset)* parade celebrating India's Republic Day in Delhi

A Musical Medley

The area offers an amazing mix of music festivals. Jahan-e-Khusrau *(www.jahan-e-khusrau.com)*, held among the historic monuments of Humayun's Tomb *(p92)* in Delhi, is a Sufi music festival infused with poetry, while the Qutub Festival *(www.seher.in/qutub.htm)* at Delhi's iconic Qutb Minar *(p128)* celebrates classical music and dance. Or head to Shekhawati *(p238)* for the cutting-edge Magnetic Fields *(p55)*, a dance-music festival held in an old *haveli* (mansion).

An energetic performance at the Magnetic Fields festival ↓

TOP 3 ALTERNATIVE FESTIVALS

Phoolwalon ki Sair in Delhi
A colourful florists' procession through Mehrauli village *(www.phoolwaalonkisair.com)*.

Vintage Car Rally in Delhi
A classic car procession from Statesman House to India Gate *(www.statesmanvintage.com)*.

International Kite Festival in Jaipur
Every January, Jaipur's skies are filled with colourful kites *(www.tourism.rajasthan.gov.in/fairs-and-festivals)*

Royal Tombs

The Mughals' royal tombs are no grey mausoleums but glorious monuments sitting in quartered *charbagh* gardens *(p195)*. Visit Humayun's grand tomb in Delhi *(p92)* to see the first instance of this style, then head to Agra to see it reach its zenith with the incomparable Taj Mahal *(p176)*, the world's most beautiful monument. Sikandra, on the outskirts of Agra, is home to Akbar's tomb *(p175)* with its intricate sandstone-and-marble façade.

The awe-inspiring Taj Mahal, the world's most famous mausoleum

DELHI AND AGRA FOR
MUGHAL MONUMENTS

Many of Delhi and Agra's greatest monuments were constructed by the Mughal emperors, whose buildings often blended the best of Hindu and Islamic traditions. Delhi and Agra both served time as the Mughal capital, and each has inherited many fabulous edifices which beg to be explored.

Marvellous Mosques

There's an arresting grandeur to Mughal mosques, especially those built to hold great congregations of worshippers. One of the most spectacular is Delhi's commanding Jama Masjid *(p110)*, designed for a whole city's communal Friday prayers. Agra *(p172)* and Fatehpur Sikri *(p182)* have their own Jama Masjids too: visit Agra's to admire its beautiful white marble *mihrab (p101)*, or head to Fatehpur Sikri to see its intricately crafted interior.

→

Visitors congregating outside Delhi's vast Jama Masjid at sunrise

KEY FEATURES OF MUGHAL BUILDINGS

A fusion of Persian and Indian styles, Mughal buildings are known for their grandeur and symmetry. Often built from red sandstone or marble, they tend to sport onion-shaped domes and slender minarets, and are surrounded by landscaped gardens. Inlay work, *jali* (filigree screens) and cusped arches give these buildings an ethereal grace.

Fantastic Forts

More like palaces than castles, Mughal forts are utterly spectacular. A national icon, Delhi's Red Fort *(p108)* dominates the old city and is full of royal apartments and reception halls. Agra's spectacular fort *(p172)*, made of eye-catching crimson sandstone, also features opulent interiors. Visit either during the evening to see them illuminated by dazzling sound and light shows. Alternatively, why not admire the atmospheric ruins of Delhi's ancient Purana Qila *(p100)*.

↑ The imposing walls of Agra Fort and *(inset)* its interior at sunset

Crafting Cities

The Mughals built whole cities from scratch – immerse yourself in their world by visiting one of these metropolises. The most impressive, Fatehpur Sikri *(p182)*, was built by the emperor Akbar *(p58)*. Time appears to stand still in this astounding city, which has been preserved almost exactly as Akbar left it.

Buland Darwaza, the entrance to Fatehpur Sikri's impressive Jama Masjid ↑

Marvellous Music

The region's diverse musical heritage is sure to captivate. Be lulled by ethereal qawwalis at one of the area's Sufi Shrines - both Delhi's tranquil Hazrat Nizamuddin Auliya Dargah *(p98)* and Ajmer's magnificent Dargah Sharif *(p234)* have weekly performances of this uplifting devotional music. Or visit Siri Fort Auditorium *(p134)* in Delhi which offers recitals of lively Hindustani music.

$\longrightarrow$

A group performing a qawwali at Delhi's Hazrat Nizamuddin Auliya Dargh

DELHI, AGRA AND JAIPUR FOR
MUSIC AND DANCE

Thanks to a rich cultural legacy, this region has a diverse performing arts scene that covers everything from traditional music to Bollywood dance. There are countless ways to experience it, too, whether that's being lulled by the otherworldly sound of qawwalis or busting some moves in a dance class.

Be More Bollywood

Made famous through film, Bollywood dancing has taken the world by storm. If you're itching to try your hand - or feet? - at this energetic style, then head to the Delhi Dance Academy *(p132)* for a fun-filled dance class. For the full Bollywood experience, visit Kingdom of Dreams *(p153)* in Gurugram, an extravagant theme park offering truly spectacular performances of Bollywood music and dance.

←

Bollywood dancers in colourful costumes undertaking an energetic dance routine

Keeping It Classical

One of northern India's most prominent forms of classical dance is the energetic kathak. Be amazed by the nimble footwork of kathak dancers at one of the performances taking place in Haveli Dharampura *(p30)* in Old Delhi; or, if you're visiting Delhi in October, don't miss the festival dedicated to this dance form run by Kathak Kendra *(www.kathak kendra.in)*. The Parsi Anjuman Hall *(p103)* showcases a whole range of classical Indian dance, with beautifully choreographed performances charting the city's history through this art form.

←

A performance of kathak, and *(inset)* the ghunghroos worn by classical dancers

KATHAK CLASSICAL DANCE

A performer of kathak is thought of as a storyteller. A typical performance of this classical Indian dance is a blend of complex footwork and facial expressions to convey a story, often from the life of Krishna. Using intricate steps, the dancer stamps out percussive rhythms, while using their arm movements and facial gestures to illustrate another melody. In order to enhance the rhythm of the dance the performer usually wears *ghunghroos* (musical anklets). Kathak was once a favourite dance at the royal courts of northern India.

Park the Kids
While children may not take much interest in the tombs and monuments at Lodi Gardens (p85) or Mehrauli Archaeological Park (p126), both of these expansive green areas are the perfect place for youngsters to burn off their excess energy. The city's wild Northern Ridge (p148) is great for young jungle explorers and zoologists – there's even a chance you could spot a leopard.

→

Families hanging out amid historic monuments in the expansive Lodi Gardens

DELHI FOR
FAMILIES

While a visit to Delhi with kids may seem challenging, don't be put off; this vibrant city offers an abundance of activities that little ones will enjoy. With things as diverse as stargazing and dinosaur-spotting on offer, there's plenty to do – plus, there are countless parks where energetic kids can let off steam.

Epic Entertainment
Delhi offers more festivals than you can shake a stick at. Twinkling lights turn the city into a wonderland during Diwali (p55), leaving both little and big people spellbound, while Dussehra (p54) sees Delhi's come to life when giant papier-mâché statues – filled with fireworks – are set alight. The colourful exuberance of Holi (p55) is perfect for older kids, who will love chucking coloured powder around. Not visiting during any festivals? Head to the Kingdom of Dreams (p153), a spectacular entertainment complex with live shows celebrating Indian culture that will delight kids.

←

A giant statue of Ravana ready to be set alight during the festival of Dussehra

Marvellous Museums

Delhi's eclectic museums are sure to be a hit with kids of all ages. Little ones will enjoy riding on the toy train at the National Rail Museum *(p131)*, while older kids can get hands on in the National Science Centre's *(p100)* "Fun Science" section or discover dinosaurs in the "Prehistoric Life Gallery". Social-media-loving teenagers should make a beeline for the Click Art Museum *(p149)*, whose optical illusions are perfect for selfies. Don't miss Bal Bhawan *(www.nationalbal bhavan.nic.in)* – created just for kids, this engaging museum covers everything from the country's rich history to scientific advancements, and offers regular activities.

←

One of the steam locomotives on display at the National Rail Museum in Delhi

EAT

The best places in Delhi to eat with the kids.

Haldiram's
Both a sweet shop and a modern canteen serving delicious lassis.
🏠 1454/2 Chandni Chowk 🌐 haldiram.com
₹₹₹

Paranthe Wali Gali
Stalls on this narrow street offer tasty, fresh-cooked paratha (flatbread) with a great choice of stuffings.
🏠 Paranthe Wali Gali, Chandni Chowk
₹₹₹

Paharganj
Delhi's backpacker mecca has loads of cafés offering omelettes and pancakes that even the fussiest eaters will readily devour.
🏠 New Delhi
₹₹₹

Be Starstruck

Are your kids captivated by the stars? Then you're in the right place – Delhi has a ton of cool astronomy stuff. The giant astronomical instruments in Jantar Mantar *(p84)*, an expansive observatory, will amaze kids, while the grounds of the Nehru Memorial Museum *(p82)* contains a planetarium offering fascinating star-filled shows in English.

Families investigating one of Jantar Mantar's instruments ↑

Time for Tea

Stop for a piping hot cup of masala chai at one of the many tea stalls peppered throughout Delhi. This delicious drink is made by a *chaiwala* (tea maker) from a mixture of black tea, milk, sugar and masala (made from spices such as cardamom, cinnamon and black pepper). For a treat, take high tea at the Taj Mahal Hotel *(www.tajhotels.com)*, which offers an extensive menu of teas from all over India.

←

A *chaiwala* carrying glasses of spicy and warming masala chai

DELHI FOR
FOODIES

Delhi's cuisine is a mouthwatering melting pot of flavours, with rich sauces, warming spices, butter chicken and tandoor all traditional staples. The city's foodie scene also takes inspiration from its neighbours, giving you the opportunity to sample a delicious assortment of dishes, including South Indian dosas and moreish Tibetan dumplings.

Street Food Specialities

Venture through Old Delhi's warren of narrow streets to discover the city's best street food. Renowned Paranthe Wali Gali *(p113)* is a narrow street lined with stalls selling portions of tummy-filling aloo paratha (deep-fried potato-stuffed bread). Nearby, Old Famous Jalebi Wala *(1795 Dariba Kalan Rd)* offers delicious *jalebi,* golden swirls of deep-fried batter soaked in syrup. Not sure where to start? Take a tour with Delhi Food Walks *(www. delhifoodwalks.com)* to smell and taste your way through a variety of finger-licking food.

→

A street food stall selling a variety of delicious dishes in Old Delhi

Foodie Festivals

Delhi's foodie festivals celebrate both regional cuisine and urban trends. At Nehru Stadium, the Grub Fest *(www.thegrubfest.com)* takes place every couple of months with chef demos, music and lots of food, while the NASVI Street Food Festival *(www. nasvinet.org)* brings together street food stalls from across India. You can also discover over a thousand varieties of mangos at the International Mango Festival *(p55)* in July.

→

Decorations adorning a tree at the International Mango Festival

Cook Up a Storm

Want to learn how to get that perfect balance of spice? Take a cooking class with Saffron Palate *(www.saffronpalate.com)*. You'll first be taken to a local market in the heart of Hauz Khas *(p130)* to buy fresh produce, before being taught how to create traditional recipes such as chicken masala - you can even try your hand at crafting a chapati.

←

Wooden bowls full of spices used in traditional Indian dishes

Did You Know?

Originally from the Americas, chillies weren't used in Indian cooking before the 17th century.

Top Tables

While known for its street food, Delhi also plays host to haute cuisine. Run by award-winning chef Manish Mehrotra, Indian Accent *(p80)* serves up inspired classic Indian dishes with a modern twist. For more fine dining, try Spice Route at the Imperial *(p79)*, a renowned restaurant which fuses together the best of Southeast Asian cuisine.

The striking courtyard at Indian Accent, housed in The Lodi hotel ↑

Take Me to Church

While Christianity is well-established in India, not many churches in the north date back very far. One of the few built in this region is St James' Church *(p115)* in Delhi – visit to see its beautiful and elaborate stained-glass windows, as well as the grave of British cavalry commander James Skinner, who founded the church. Unlike the Neo-Classical St James', Mathura's Church of the Sacred Heart *(p196)* is an unusual and distinctive blend of Indian temple and Western architecture.

→

The elegant exterior of St James' Church, found in Old Delhi

DELHI, AGRA AND JAIPUR FOR

PLACES OF WORSHIP

With its plethora of religions, India contains some truly awe-inspiring places of worship. The country's sacred buildings have been carefully crafted by the most skilled artisans, with many temples and mosques beautifully decorated.

On Sacred Ground

The holy town of Vrindavan *(p196)* – where Lord Krishna is thought to have spent most of his childhood – is peppered with Hindu temples; don't miss the seven-storeyed, red-sandstone Govind Dev Temple, the town's most famous sight. Nearby, Mathura *(p196)* is home to the Sri Krishna Janmasthan Temple, believed to stand at the site where Krishna was born. This magical town sits on the west bank of the Yamuna river – take an evening boat ride on the calm waters to see the historic ghats that line its bank lit up by glimmering lanterns.

→

Colourful temples and ghats lining the river in Mathura

Magnificently Modern

Surprisingly, some of the area's most stunning temples are modern rather than ancient. Explore the ethereal interior of Delhi's monumental Akshardham Temple *(p144)* or attend a prayer service at the city's serene Baha'i House of Worship *(p138)* – this award-winning building is shaped like a floating lotus flower. One of Delhi's most eye-catching temples is the Sankat Mochan Dham *(p82)* with its huge statue of the Hindu monkey god Hanuman: on Tuesdays and Saturdays this mechanical statue opens his chest to reveal statues of Lord Rama and Sita.

20,000

religious images are found in Delhi's Akshardham Temple.

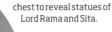

The vast Akshardham Temple, surrounded by lush green gardens

TOP 5 HINDU TEMPLE FEATURES

Garbhagriha
Literally translated as "womb chamber", this is the temple's inner sanctum.

Mandapa
The prayer hall, where public rituals are performed.

Shikara
The temple's spire, which is usually ornately carved.

Amalaka
A stone disk found at the top of the temple's spire.

Mandir Kalash
The pot-shaped finial which sits atop of the amalaka.

Majestic Mosques

Medieval mosques go back to the very beginning of the Delhi Sultanate *(p58)*. Admire the Quwwat-ul-Islam mosque at the Qutb Minar *(p128)*, with its carved pillars that were taken from destroyed Hindu temples. Stroll through the tranquil Jama Masjid *(p110)* or appreciate the Tughlaq dynasty's mosques, including South Delhi's fort-like Khirkee *(p136)*.

Admiring the intricately carved pillars at the Quwwat-ul-Islam mosque

RELIGIONS

India is a mosaic of different religions. The majority of India's population is Hindu, while around 138 million (13 per cent) are Muslims. Several other religions, such as Sikhism, Buddhism, Jainism, Zoroastrianism, Judaism and Christianity, also flourish.

HINDUISM

The bedrock of Hinduism are the four *Vedas* and the *Upanishads*, which are a holistic compilation of knowledge, philosophy and ethics. However, Hinduism is not a religion of written precepts, but a way of life that has evolved over 5,000 years. In practice, Hindus worship a huge pantheon of gods and goddesses *(p140)*.

Socially, Hindu's can be divided into four castes – the upper caste Brahmins (priests), the Kshatriyas (warriors), the Vaishyas (merchants) and the lowest caste, Shudras (workers). Families were traditionally presided over by a patriarch, but this is fast disappearing in urban areas. Yet s*anskara*, traditional values, are still instilled into children, and complicated rites mark each stage of orthodox Hindu life. One aspect of Hinduism shuns idol worship, preferring to concentrate on philosophical issues. Sadhus, who wear saffron clothes to indicate their retreat from the material world, are its most visible practitioners.

ISLAM

Islam was introduced into Western India in the 8th century by Arab traders, but only gained prominence in the north after the 12th century, when it was made the state religion under the medieval Muslim rulers.

Today, Muslims form India's second largest religious community, despite a large exodus to Pakistan after the Partition of 1947 *(p61)*. Traditional Muslim education, based on the Qur'an, is still imparted by the clergy in madrasas near mosques, which usually follow strict rules of segregation.

Sufism, a less orthodox mystic Islamic order, emphasizes direct experience of god, often through music and dance. Sufi saints like Nizamuddin Auliya *(p98)* attracted many converts from Hinduism, and the fusion of the two religious traditions led to a flowering of poetry, music and art.

Sadhus, Hindu holy men, wearing their traditional saffron-coloured clothing

SIKHISM

Sikhism is a reformist religion founded by Guru Nanak in the 15th century. Eschewing idol worship, rituals and the caste system, it believes in a formless god. The Sikhs follow the teachings of ten gurus contained in their holy book, the *Guru Granth Sahib*.

Persecution by the later Mughals led the tenth guru, Gobind Singh, to reorganize the community in 1699 as a military order (the Khalsa) based on the principles of *sangàt* (congregation), *simran* (meditation), *kirtan* (hymn singing), *langar* and *pangat* (sharing and partaking of food in a common kitchen).

CHRISTIANITY

Indian Christians believe that the apostle St Thomas brought the religion to South India in the 1st century AD. Christianity's rise in this region dates to the late 15th century when Catholic missionaries travelled to India in the wake of Portuguese traders while Christian Armenian communities also settled in Mughal India. With the coming of the East India Company, Protestant missionaries spread across the country in the 18th and 19th centuries.

↑ Catholic devotees carrying a cross during a Good Friday procession

Today, local dialects, practices and rituals have been incorporated into services.

OTHER RELIGIONS

India has other smaller though distinct religious communities. Buddhists are followers of Gautam Buddha who preached the gospel of non-violence and peace. Jains, the followers of Mahavira, are a non-violent community who respect life in every form. This small community has played a significant role in Indian industry. The first Jews came to India in about 562 BC and now live mainly in Mumbai and Cochin.

↑ A group of devotees paying their respects at the shrine of a Sufi saint on the *Urs* (death anniversary)

↑ Worshippers surrounding the Sikh holy book, the *Guru Granth Sahib*, during a colourful procession

Get Hands On

The region is perfect for releasing your inner artist. Try your hand at Rajasthani block printing at the Anokhi Museum of Hand Printing in Amber *(p223)* or take lessons from the craftspeople still practising this ancient art on a tour of Bagru *(p240)*. Photography buffs can learn how to take the perfect shot of the Taj with Photography Tours Delhi *(www. photographytourdelhi.com)*.

→

A demonstration at the Anokhi Museum of Hand Printing

DELHI, AGRA AND JAIPUR FOR
ART LOVERS

With a rich heritage of art and crafts dating back centuries, this region is a paradise for art lovers. Expect to uncover art-filled galleries, contemporary sculptures and awe-inspiring street art – plus, if you want to unleash your inner artist, the area offers plenty of opportunities to get creative.

Painted Havelis

Scattered across India are exquisitely painted *havelis*, mansions that have been ornamented with colourful murals. Admire some of the most spectacular just north of Jaipur in Shekhawati *(p238)*, a region full of ornate *havelis* that once belonged to local merchants. Tucked away amid the labyrinthine streets of Old Delhi, Naughara Gali *(p112)* is a small lane of colourfully embellished Jain *havelis*.

→

One of the spectacularly painted *havelis* found in the Shekhawati region

Take to the Streets

Vibrant, eye-catching street art is waking up sleepy residential communities and urban villages across Delhi, with murals depicting everything from Indian street life and graphic geometric prints to flora and fauna. Shahpur Jat *(p134)* is decorated with an array of awesome artworks, including a giant cat playing with a ball of wool, while just outside the Delhi Police Headquarter is a huge mural of Mahatma Gandhi. Don't miss the colourful pieces at Lodi Colony *(p84)*: thanks to an annual festival run by the St+Art India Foundation, this neighbourhood is now covered in brightly coloured, kaleidoscopic murals.

→

Some of the colourful street art found in Delhi's Lodi Colony

Did You Know?

Delhi's Municipal Council creates art installations on the city's roundabouts.

Curated Collections

India's contemporary art world has blossomed from the seeds of its traditional arts and crafts. Explore cutting-edge pieces at Delhi's National Gallery of Modern Art *(p80)* or the Kiran Nadar Museum of Art *(www.knma.in)*. In Jaipur admire intricate jewellery at the new Amrapali Museum *(p215)* or visit the Sculpture Park *(p220)* to see unique pieces dotted around the epic Nahargarh Fort.

↑ Ranjini Shettar's art installation at the Kiran Nadar Museum of Art

Forgotten History

While places like the Red Fort *(p108)* will undoubtedly be on your bucket list, there are a number of overlooked, but just as spectacular, sights here. Among them is the ruined Tughlaqabad Fort *(p133)*, once the centre of one of Delhi's earliest cities. Near Janpath you'll find Agrasen ki Baoli *(p80)*, one of the city's few remaining stepwells, while north of Old Delhi lies the bizarre Coronation Park *(p146)*, filled with the abandoned statues of former British viceroys.

→

Vistiors admiring the dramatic, hidden stepwell of Agrasen ki Baoli

DELHI
OFF THE BEATEN TRACK

Away from the crowds thronging the city's major sights, Delhi has a wealth of little-known sights. Scattered across this vast metropolis are bohemian urban villages, eccentric museums and hidden monuments, while local-led walking tours help bring a different side of Delhi to life.

Village Vibes

Hidden within the city are a number of tiny urban villages, once separate settlements that were swallowed up by the expanding capital. Still relatively unknown, Shahpur Jat *(p134)* is a bohemian urban enclave with cool street art and designer boutiques. To the north of Delhi, Majnu ka Tila *(p149)* is a colourful Tibetan neighbourhood bedecked with prayer flags - visit to devour delicious *momos* (dumplings) in one of its restaurants.

←

Prayer flags decorating the Tibetan neighbourhood of Majnu ka Tila

Quirky Museums

Delhi is home to a number of awesomely unconventional museums. Learn about lavatories through the ages at the tiny Sulabh International Museum of Toilets (p151) – try and spot the replica of the loo used by King Louis XIV of France. Equally as eccentric, Shankar's International Dolls Museum (p102) is filled with over 7,000 dolls, while the weirdly wonderful Click Art Museum features wacky 3D optical illusions (p149).

→

A replica of the toilet used by King Louis XIV of France

Memorable Mementos

After the perfect souvenir? Steer away from the usual tourist haunts and head to Khazana India in Hauz Khas (p130), an unusual shop brimming with vintage Bollywood posters, old photographs and antiques. Gulab Singh Johrimal Perfumers (www.gulabsinghjohrimal.com), has countless sweet-smelling bottles of attar, traditionally made perfumes.

←

Bottles of fragrance on display at Gulab Singh Johrimal Perfumers

→

Children talking to visitors on a walking tour run by the Salaam Baalak Trust

HIDDEN GEM
Engraved Edicts

Scattered across Delhi are three Ashokan edicts: created by the 3rd-century Mauryan Emperor Ashoka (p57), each edict is engraved with the teachings of Buddha. The two pillar edicts are found at the Northern Ridge (p148) and Feroz Shah Kotla (p102); the rock edict lies in South Delhi (p138).

Follow Your Feet

Uncover Delhi's hidden gems, discover local history and learn about the lives of its street children on a walking tour with the Salaam Baalak Trust (www.salaambaalaktrust. com). Set up with proceeds from Mira Nair's movie Salaam Bombay, the trust offers insightful and inspirational walks run by kids who formerly lived on the streets or railways.

Elephantine Inhabitants

Literally the area's biggest stars, elephants can be found roaming throughout the region. Take an early morning Jeep safari through Jim Corbett (*p160*), India's oldest national park, to try and spy these gentle giants; along the way you might also glimpse otters, crocodiles, king cobras, leopards and tigers. Bisected by the holy Ganges, Rajaji National Park (*p166*) is also ideal for spotting elephants, as well as bears, panthers and over 400 different species of birds.

→

A couple of elephants standing in Corbett National Park

DELHI, AGRA AND JAIPUR FOR
WILDLIFE LOVERS

Most famous for its bustling cities and magisterial monuments, the region is home to a wealth of wonderful wildlife. Whether it's tiger-spotting amid lush jungle or admiring regal elephants in the forested foothills of the Himalayas, there are endless ways to discover the area's flora and fauna.

Tiger, Tiger

Want to catch sight of India's most iconic – yet most elusive - resident? Ranthambhore (*p236*) and Sariska (*p228*) national parks in Rajasthan are your best bet. Jeep safaris traverse the lush jungles of both parks in search of these majestic creatures. Even if the tigers are hiding, there are plenty of other animals that you can spot, from panthers and jackals to deer and crocodiles.

→

Three tigers prowling through Ranthambhore National Park

84
—
tigers in Rajasthan – numbers are on the rise with 70 tigers in Ranthambhore and 14 in Sariska.

WILDLIFE CONSERVATION

India's Wildlife Protection Act of 1972 prohibited the hunting of wild animals and created a number of protected areas for wildlife, including many national parks. Since then a number of conservation programmes have attempted to protect the country's diverse wildlife, including the famous Project Tiger *(p160)*. Others have included schemes to protect India's elephants and crocodiles from poaching and habitat loss.

Bountiful Birdlife

The region's wetlands are brimming with birds. Leafy Sultanpur National Park *(p152)* is home to migratory birds such as grey herons and Siberian cranes, while peaceful Keoladeo Ghana National Park *(p192)* has ibises, egrets and painted storks among its resident birds – take a cycle rickshaw ride through the park, binoculars in hand, to spot them. At the spectacular Sambhar Salt Lake *(p246)* you can also spy thousands of pink flamingos.

↑ Painted storks and *(inset)* a kingfisher in Keoladeo Ghana National Park

War of Independence

Delhi was the centre of the revolt against British rule, and the city continues to bear the marks of this event. In particular, Old Delhi is filled with reminders: Chandni Chowk *(p112)* is lined with plaques commemorating the conflict's events, while Khuni Darwaza (known as Lal Darwaza or the "Bloody Gate") was the place where the sons and grandsons of the last Mughal Emperor were brutally executed *(p102)*.

→

The now-crumbling Khuni Darwaza or "Bloody Gate"

DELHI FOR
HISTORY BUFFS

As befits a city with a long and illustrious history, Delhi is bursting with historical sights. The great events of its past – from its role as the capital of both the Delhi Sultanate and the Mughal Dynasty to being the epicentre of the 1857 War of Independence – have all left their mark on this ancient city.

TOP 5 HISTORICAL FIGURES

Qutbuddin Aibak
Slave general who founded the Sultanate.

Razia Sultan
Delhi's first and last female sultan.

Shah Jahan
This Mughal emperor built the Taj Mahal.

Bahadur Shah Zafar II
Last Mughal emperor and figurehead of the War of Independence.

Mohandas K Gandhi
The eminent leader of the Indian independence movement.

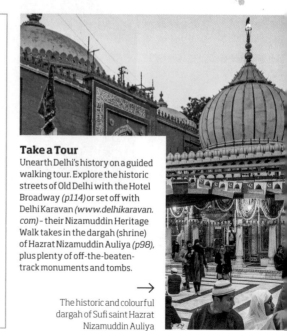

Take a Tour

Unearth Delhi's history on a guided walking tour. Explore the historic streets of Old Delhi with the Hotel Broadway *(p114)* or set off with Delhi Karavan *(www.delhikaravan. com)* – their Nizamuddin Heritage Walk takes in the dargah (shrine) of Hazrat Nizamuddin Auliya *(p98)*, plus plenty of off-the-beaten-track monuments and tombs.

→

The historic and colourful dargah of Sufi saint Hazrat Nizamuddin Auliya

Sultanate Sites

For three centuries, Delhi was the capital of the Sultanate, a dynasty that saw a wealth of impressive monuments erected. The defining image of the Sultanate is the towering spire of the Qutb Minar *(p128)*, but the ruined forts of Feroz Shah Kotla *(p102)* and Tughlaqabad *(p133)* also stand as a testament to the dynasty's power. The city is also home to majestic Sultanate tombs, such as those in Lodi Gardens *(p85)*.

→

One of the magnificent tombs in Lodi Gardens at sunrise

In Memory Of

Delhi has several sights dedicated to two of India's most beloved leaders. Gandhi Smriti *(p84)* marks the place where independence hero Mahatma Gandhi was assassianted, while Raj Ghat *(p116)* is the site of his cremation. Devoted to India's first president, Jawaharlal Nehru, the Nehru Memorial Museum *(p82)* is filled with memorabilia.

←

Path showing Gandhi's last footsteps at Gandhi Smriti

Ancient Artifacts

Delhi is peppered with captivating museums, the epitome of which is the vast National Museum *(p74)*. An immense repository of historical knowledge, this museum is full of fascinating artifacts from Delhi, across India and beyond. Learn all about the Indian freedom struggle and the man who led it at the National Gandhi Museum *(p103)*, or head to the forested Mehrauli Archaeological Park *(p126)*, essentially a huge open-air museum filled with ancient and atmospheric ruins.

→

A scultpure of the sun god Surya on display in Delhi's National Museum

A YEAR IN
DELHI, AGRA AND JAIPUR

JANUARY

Republic Day *(26 Jan)*. India's independence anniversary, with a military parade in Delhi.

△ **Beating the Retreat** *(29 Jan)*. Colourful regimental bands perform at Delhi's Vijay Chowk.

Jaipur Literature Festival *(late Jan)*. A popular literary festival with talks, interviews and readings.

FEBRUARY

△ **Surajkund Crafts Mela** *(1–17 Feb)*. This colourful handicrafts fair just outside of Delhi promotes the work of artisans using traditional skills.

Taj Mahotsav *(18–27 Feb)*. A ten-day cultural fiesta of music and dance held in Agra near the Taj Mahal, showcasing India's vibrant arts, crafts and cuisines.

MAY

△ **Buddha Jayanti, Delhi** *(around May)*. Peaceful celebrations mark Buddha's birthday, enlightenment and death. Delhi's Buddha Jayanti Park on the Ridge is a centre of these peaceful festivities.

Eid-ul-Fitr *(around May)*. Muslims celebrate the end of Ramadan with feasting and sweets.

JUNE

△ **Ganga Dussehra** *(around Jun)*. Hindu devotees celebrate the descent of the Ganges from heaven by taking a dip in its waters at towns like Haridwar.

International Yoga Day *(21 Jun)*. Held in Rishikesh on the northern hemisphere's summer solstice, this festival is celebrated with yoga classes and events.

SEPTEMBER

Janmashtami *(late Aug–early Sep)*. The birthday of Krishna is celebrated with devotional singing, and dance-drama enactments of his life. This festival is particularly big in Mathura and Vrindavan.

△ **Ganesh Chaturthi** *(early Sep)*. A ten-day event in honour of the birth of Lord Ganesha, marked by ceremonial processions of Ganesha's idols.

OCTOBER

△ **Dussehra** *(around Oct)*. A nine-day festival enacting episodes from the *Ramayana*. Celebrations in Delhi see theatrical performances and the burning of giant effigies of Ravana.

IIC Experience *(late Oct)*. Organized by Delhi's India International Centre, this festival celebrates world music, dance, theatre, film and food.

MARCH

△ **Holi** *(around Mar)*. This exuberant festival of colour marks the end of winter with lots of chucking of coloured powder. Vrindavan and Jaipur are popular places to experience this energetic festival.

Jahan-e-Khusrau *(usually in Mar)*. A three-day international Sufi music festival held in Delhi near Humayun's Tomb, which commemorates the 14th-century Sufi musician and poet Amir Khusrau.

APRIL

Mahavir Jayanti *(around Apr)*. A key Jain festival celebrating the birth of Lord Mahavira, the 24th Jain *tirthankara*. Jain temples are decorated with flags and religious processions occur.

△ **Baisakhi** *(13 or 14 Apr)*. Colourful parades take place at this Sikh festival celebrating Guru Nanak's foundation of the Khalsa (Sikh initiates) movement.

JULY

International Mango Festival, Delhi
(early Jul). Held at Dilli Haat in Delhi at the peak of the mango season, this foodie festival showcases over 1,000 varieties of delicious mangoes.

△ **Bakr-Eid** *(around Jul)*. The Muslim pilgrimage festival, celebrated with the slaughter and eating of a sheep or goat.

AUGUST

Independence Day *(15 Aug)*. National holiday where the Prime Minister addresses the country from Delhi's Red Fort and raises India's flag.

Parampara Festival, Delhi *(early Aug)*. Running for over 30 years, this three-day festival celebrates a variety of dance styles and music genres.

△ **Raksha Bandhan** *(full moon in Aug)*. Young girls tie sacred threads (*rakhis*) on their brothers' wrists as a token of love, receiving gifts in exchange.

NOVEMBER

Diwali *(Oct/Nov)*. Oil lamps and firecrackers are lit to commemorate Rama's homecoming and the triumph of good over evil.

△ **Pushkar Camel Fair** *(full moon in Nov)*. A huge fair in the town of Pushkar, with live music, a fairground, and performances from acrobats and tightrope walkers, plus a moustache competition.

Qutb Festival *(late Nov)*. Indian classical music and dance performed at the historic Qutb Minar.

DECEMBER

△ **Delhi International Arts Festival**
(early Dec). Delhi's most prestigious arts festival, celebrating dance, literature, film, theatre and more.

Tarang – Delhi International Queer Theatre and Film Festival *(early Dec)*. One of Delhi's newest festivals celebrating the Indian LGBT+ Movement. There's everything from film screenings and plays to panel discussions and debates.

Magnetic Fields *(late Dec)*. A spectacular three-day music festival held in a 17th-century *haveli* (mansion) in Rajasthan's historic Shekhawati region.

A BRIEF
HISTORY

This area's past is marked by the rise and fall of powerful rulers, from ancient empires to long-standing dynasties, as well as by foreign occupation. Delhi - built and rebuilt over the centuries - and Agra were once stongholds of Muslim rulers, while Jaipur was governed by independent Rajput rulers.

Early Civilizations

People have been living on this land for 250,000 years, with the first sophisticated urban civilization emerging in 3300 BC. Known as the Indus Valley Civilization, this culture stretched across large swathes of north India. Around 1500 BC, a group known as the Aryans moved into this region. Their Vedic religion contained the initial elements of the Hindu religion, such as caste division. This put the Brahmins (priestly class) at the top of the social hierarchy, followed by Kshatriyas (warriors), Vaishyas (traders) and Shudras (labourers). The Aryans also wrote two great epics, the *Ramayana* and the *Mahabharata*, detailing the histories of legendary heroes.

1 Map of the Delhi, Agra and Jaipur region.

2 A hunting scene from the *Mahabharata*.

3 Wedding of emperor Chandragupta Maurya to his Macedonian bride, Helena.

4 Painting of a Rajput nobleman.

Timeline of events

1500 BC
The Aryans migrate into northwest India.

3300–1700 BC
Harappan culture flourishes in the Indus Valley.

1000 BC
The use of iron is widespread during the Later Vedic Age.

486 BC
The Buddha dies in Kushinagar.

468 BC
Mahavira, the founder of Jainism, dies.

322 BC
The accession of Chandragupta Maurya, who went on to found the Mauryan empire.

Ancient Empires

In the 4th century BC, the region came under the domination of the Nanda empire. Its reign lasted barely three decades before being overthrown in 322 BC by Chandragupta Maurya who founded the Mauryan empire. His grandson Ashoka (269–232 BC) became one of India's greatest rulers, expanding the Mauryan empire from southeast Iran to Assam in the east. Around 263 BC, however, he gave up violence and converted to Buddhism, inscribing his ethical code on rocks and pillars across his empire.

The Gupta Empire and Rajput Dynasties

The decline of the Mauryans led to the rise of the Kushanas, whose empire linked the Indian Ocean to the Silk Road. Kanishka, the greatest Kushana king, was almost as great a patron of Buddhism as Ashoka had been. As the Kushanas declined, the Gupta empire (AD 320–500) emerged and presided over a cultural flowering, with developments in religion, art and science. From around the 6th century AD, a new wave of warlord clans from the Hindu Kshatriya (warrior) class arose. Nowadays referred to as Rajputs, these clans included the Chauhans, the Kachhawaha and the Tomars, who founded Lal Kot, the first city of Delhi, around 1060.

THE RISE OF NEW RELIGIONS

The 6th century BC saw the rise of two important new religions: Buddhism and Jainism. Both rejected caste, ignored the idea of a creator god and advocated ahimsa - the concept of not harming any living being. They also adhered to the Hindu idea of a cycle of birth, death and reincarnation, and of achieving spiritual liberation (moksha or nirvana) to escape it.

268–232 BC
The reign of Ashoka, the ruler of India's first major empire.

c 8th century AD
The Tomars establish Surajkund.

320–500 AD
The reign of the Gupta empire.

c 1037
Amber is taken over by the Kachhawahas.

c 1060
The Tomars found Lal Kot, the first city of Delhi.

The Advent of Muslim Rule: the Delhi Sultanate

In 1180, the Chauhans of Ajmer wrested Lal Kot from the Tomars and renamed it Qila Rai Pithora. In 1192, Muhammad of Ghur, the Muslim ruler of Afghanistan, invaded India and defeated the Chauhans. When he died, one of his generals, Qutbuddin Aibak, founded the Delhi Sultanate, which ruled much of northern India for over 300 years, although during this time many Rajput rulers stayed on as tributary rulers. The Sultanate rulers were prolific builders, erecting the second to sixth cities of Delhi.

The Great Mughals

In 1526 Babur, a central Asian prince who was a brilliant military campaigner, marched into India, overthrew the Sultanate's rulers at the battle of Panipat and established the Mughal empire. Mughal rule was briefly interrupted when Babur's son Humayun was overthrown in 1540 by an Afghan chieftain, Sher Shah Suri. Humayun regained his throne in 1555, and his son, Akbar, expanded the empire. Aurangzeb, the last great Mughal, alienated many with his religious intolerance, leading to the rise of the Maratha Confederacy, a Hindu group; they expanded their territories until, by the mid-18th century, they were the main power.

THE MUGHALS

Babur (1526-30): Founded the empire.
Humayun (1530-56): Consolidated and expanded the empire.
Akbar (1556-1605): Promoted culture and religious tolerance.
Jahangir (1605-27): Neglected politics and focused on pleasure.
Shah Jahan (1628-58): Founded Old Delhi and built the Taj Mahal.
Aurangzeb (1658-1707): Supported Islamic orthodoxy and expanded the empire.

Timeline of events

1206
The death of Muhammad of Ghur leaves Qutbuddin as ruler.

1398
Timur sacks Delhi; Sultanate Sayyid dynasty is established.

1540–55
Delhi and Agra are ruled from Bihar by the Suris.

1444
Buhul Lodi ousts the Sayyids and establishes the Sultanate Lodi dynasty.

1504
Sikandar Lodi founds Agra as his new capital.

4

The East India Company

In 1803, the British East India Company routed the Marathas and took control of the region. The Mughal emperor stayed on, but the Company were the de facto rulers. Very soon, a combination of its racism, arrogance and disregard for local religious sensibilities – in addition to the increasingly high taxes it imposed – made the Company incredibly unpopular throughout northern India.

The War of Independence

In 1857, news spread that pork and beef fat had been used to grease cartridges which sepoys (Indian soldiers in the Company's army) had to bite open. Defiance by troops in the northern town of Meerut who reacted to this event was put down with such brutality that it sparked a mutiny of sepoy troops. This was swollen by enthusiastic civilian support into a full-scale uprising against British rule, now known as the War of Independence. The British managed to hold onto Agra, but were ousted from Delhi, where the Indian troops set up the Mughal emperor Bahadur Shah II as their figurehead. The British eventually retook the city, amid much brutality on both sides.

1 Ruins of Tughlaqabad, built during the Sultanate.

2 Shajahanabad, the city built by Sher Shah Suri.

3 A colonel in the East Indian Company travels by elephant in Rajasthan.

4 Battle scene from the War of Independence.

Did You Know?

Bahadur Shah II was exiled to Myanmar (Burma) by the British.

1639
Shah Jahan founds Old Delhi.

1571
Akbar founds Fatehpur Sikri.

1737
The First Battle of Delhi, where the Marathas defeat the Mughals.

1803
The East India Company defeat the Marathas.

1857
The War of Independence against British rule.

The Raj

In 1858 following the War of Independence, the British government abolished the Company and ruled India directly as a Raj (empire) through a viceroy. Although during this period there were improvements to infrastructure, opposition to British rule continued to grow: demarcation between Indians and colonialists became more entrenched and the British ensured that the revenue from Indian produce, trade and taxation increasingly went straight to Britain, at India's expense.

The Freedom Movement

In 1885, the Indian National Congress was founded to demand self-government. Opposition to the Raj became so strong in Bengal that in 1911 the British decided to move their capital from Kolkata to Delhi – and so New Delhi was born. Britain continued to ignore the demands of the independence movement, led by Mahatma Gandhi. After World War II, Britain no longer had the strength to enforce its rule, and acceded to Indian demands for independence. On 14 August 1947, the new nation of Pakistan was born. India followed on 15 August when, from atop Delhi's Red Fort, Congress leader Jawaharlal Nehru proclaimed independence.

1 Rashtrapati Bhavan, built as part of New Delhi.

2 Mahatma Gandhi, leader of the Indian independence movement.

3 Indira Gandhi addressing a crowd.

4 Gurugram, a suburb in modern-day Delhi.

Did You Know?

Gandhi is often called *bapu* in India, a term of endearment that means "father".

Timeline of events

1885
The Indian National Congress is founded.

1931
New Delhi is inaugurated.

1858
The East India Company is dissolved and the British Crown takes power in India.

1911
The British decide to move their capital from Kolkata in Bengal to Delhi.

1947
Indian independence and partition takes place.

Independent India

Jawaharlal Nehru, India's first prime minister, laid the foundations of a modern nation state, with his Congress Party dominating parliament. After Nehru died in 1964, his daughter Indira Gandhi continued his socialist policies, but became increasingly authoritarian: in 1975, she declared a State of Emergency in reaction to political unrest, allowing her to rule by decree and override civil liberties. This was keenly felt in Delhi, where slum-clearance programmes forced the violent eviction of people living around the Jama Masjid in Old Delhi. In 1984, Indira was assassinated by her Sikh bodyguards; her son Rajiv took over on a wave of sympathy. He was assassinated by a Sri Lankan Tamil separatist during the 1991 election campaign.

Delhi, Agra and Jaipur Today

In 1998 the Hindu nationalist Bharatiya Janata Party (BJP) took power, holding it until 2004 and regaining it in both 2014 and 2019. The region continues to expand and to grow economically, in part thanks to tourism. This has helped fuel the continued growth of the country's trillion-dollar economy, with India projected to become the world's fifth-largest economy by 2020.

MILLIONS MIGRATE

Independence led to the birth of two separate countries, India and Pakistan. This partition was accompanied by mass migrations of millions of Hindus and Muslims across the borders, with communal riots in which thousands were killed. In Delhi new areas were built to house these migrants: Chittaranjan Park in South Delhi was originally named East Bengal Displaced Persons' Colony.

1948

On 30th January at 5:15pm, Gandhi is assassinated by Hindu fanatic Nathuram Godse.

1975–77

Indira Gandhi declares a State of Emergency across India.

1984

Indira Gandhi is assassinated by her Sikh bodyguards.

1992

Delhi becomes the NCT (National Capital Territory).

2002

The Delhi Metro is established.

2019

Narendra Modi and the BJP win a second term in office.

EXPERIENCE
DELHI

Sunset over Rashtrapati Bhavan

EXPLORE
DELHI

This section divides Delhi into four colour-coded sightseeing areas, as shown on this map, plus an area beyond the city *(p142)*.

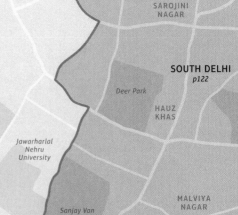

SADAR BAZAAR

JHANDEWALAN

PAHAR GANJ

Central Ridge Reserve Forest

Connaught Place

NEW DELHI
p70

Buddha Jayanti Park

The Ridge

PRESIDENTIAL ESTATE

CHANAKYAPURI

SHANTI BHAWAM

Nehru Park

Golf Course

MOTI BAGH

SAROJINI NAGAR

VASANT VIHAR

SOUTH DELHI
p122

Deer Park

HAUZ KHAS

Aravalli Biodiversity Park

Jawarharlal Nehru University

MAHIPALPUR

MALVIYA NAGAR

Sanjay Van

SAKET

MEHRAULI VILLAGE

Mehrauli Archaeological Park

0 kilometres   2
0 miles   2

N
↑

DELHI, AGRA AND JAIPUR

North of
Delhi

DELHI ■

Jaipur and
Beyond

Agra and
Around

GETTING TO KNOW
DELHI

Suffused with history, Delhi is an almost overwhelming cacophony of vibrant sights, sounds and smells. This ever-expanding metropolis has had many incarnations, with different historic settlements weaving together over time to transform into the dynamic, many-layered city we see today.

NEW DELHI

PAGE 70

With its sweeping, tree-lined boulevards and shady arcades, New Delhi is undeniably grand. Built by the British as their imperial capital, it still contains many of its Raj-era sights, including the expansive Rajpath, palatial Rashtrapati Bhavan and monumental India Gate. The area also contains some of the city's most impressive museums, including the vast National Museum and the tiny yet engrossing Nehru Memorial Museum and Library. Tucked away amid the modernity are a number of historic sights, among them the impressive Jantar Mantar observatory and the tomb-filled Lodi Gardens.

Best for
Strolling along spacious, tree-lined streets

Home to
National Museum

Experience
A tour of Rashtrapati Bhavan

PAGE 88

NIZAMUDDIN TO FEROZ SHAH KOTLA

Stretching from the medieval dargah (shrine) of Hazrat Nizamuddin Auliya, all the way to the ancient Sultanate fort of Feroz Shah Kotla, this area encompasses some of Delhi's most compelling sights. To the south lies the expansive grounds of the Humayun's Tomb complex, peppered with Mughal mausoleums, while nearby you'll find the red sandstone ruins of Purana Qila, sitting atop an ancient mound. There's also a handful of awesome museums to explore, from the art-filled Crafts Museum to the intriguing Shankar's International Dolls Museum.

Best for
Ancient forts, medieval dargahs and marvellous museums

Home to
Humayun's Tomb, Crafts Museum

Experience
The ethereal evening qawwalis at the Hazrat Nizamuddin Auliya Dargah

→

OLD DELHI

PAGE 104

Old Delhi epitomizes everything you think Delhi should be. Here you'll find a maze of winding streets packed with autorickshaws, which open up onto lively markets filled with pyramids of nose-tingling spice and reams of colourful cloth. Narrow lanes such as Paranthe Wali Gali are lined with food stalls selling a tempting array of sizzling snacks, while local haunts like Karim's offer everything from mutton kormas to butter chicken. To the west lies the epic Red Fort, with India's largest mosque, the tranquil Jama Masjid, found close by. On the outskirts sits Raj Ghat, the revered site of Mahatma Gandhi's cremation.

Best for
Bustling bazaars and Mughal monuments

Home to
Red Fort, Jama Masjid, Chandni Chowk

Experience
Shopping for tea and spices in Khari Baoli market

PAGE 122

SOUTH DELHI

South Delhi really packs a historical punch: scattered across it are the ruins of ancient cities like Jahanpanah, Siri and Tughlaqabad, as well as Mehrauli Archaeological Park, a swathe of lush forest dusted with now-crumbling monuments. Then there's the Qutb Minar complex, built on the site of Delhi's first settlement and filled with exquisitely carved buildings. But it's not all about the past, and while the area's medieval villages such as Hauz Khas, Khirkee and Shahpur Jat might be filled with an abundance of historic sights, they're also home to bohemian cafés, rooftop bars, design shops and quirky boutiques.

Best for
Checking out Delhi's oldest incarnations

Home to
Mehrauli Archeological Park, Qutb Minar

Experience
Enjoying a bit of retail therapy in Hauz Khas, Dilli Haat and Shahpur Jat

PAGE 142

BEYOND THE CENTRE

Delhi's outer areas are home to an eclectic mix of sights. The area north of Old Delhi is dotted with sights associated with British rule, including the spacious bungalows of Civil Lines, the peaceful Nicholson Cemetery and the Oxbridge-esque Delhi University, while further out you'll find abandoned statues of former viceroys at Coronation Park. Peaceful pockets can be found in the forests of the Ridge and the Northern Ridge, and at the spectacular Akshardham Temple. There's plenty to see outside the city limits, too, from migrating birds at Sultanpur National Park to Bollywood shows at the Kingdom of Dreams.

Best for
Wild areas and captivating Bollywood shows

Home to
Akshardham Temple

Experience
Wildlife-spotting on the Ridge or in Sultanpur National Park

NEW DELHI

After deciding in 1911 to move their centre of administration from Calcutta (Kolkata), in Bengal, to Delhi, the British appointed Edwin Lutyens and Herbert Baker to design their new capital. They settled on the area to the south of Old Delhi, its axis along the Rajpath, with the Viceroy's House (now Rashtrapati Bhavan) atop Raisina Hill facing Purana Qila. Some of Delhi's historic monuments, such as Safdarjung's Tomb and Jantar Mantar, were incorporated into the layout, but small villages that existed in the area were razed; only Paharganj was saved, because of its size. Roads were constructed to be wide and spacious, lined with trees and bungalows, giving the centre of Delhi a suburban feel. In a departure from the original plan, Baker moved the two Secretariat Buildings onto the top of Raisina Hill, pushing the Viceroy's House down behind it so that it no longer had a sight-line to Purana Qila. Lutyens was horrified, calling it a "colossal artistic blunder", and ended his friendship with Baker as a result.

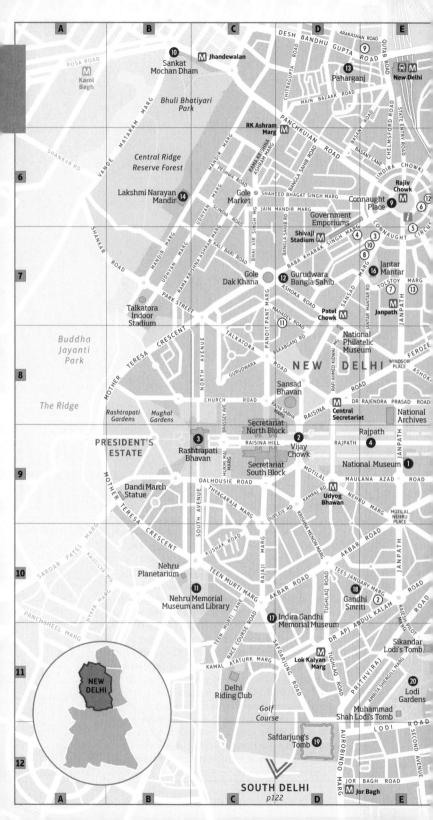

OLD DELHI
p104

NEW DELHI

Must See

❶ National Museum

Experience More

❷ Vijay Chowk
❸ Rashtrapati Bhavan
❹ Rajpath
❺ India Gate
❻ Agrasen ki Baoli
❼ National Gallery of Modern Art
❽ Mandi House Complex
❾ Connaught Place
❿ Sankat Mochan Dham
⓫ Nehru Memorial Museum and Library
⓬ Gurudwara Bangla Sahib
⓭ Paharganj
⓮ Lakshmi Narayan Mandir
⓯ Khan Market
⓰ Jantar Mantar
⓱ Indira Gandhi Memorial Museum
⓲ Gandhi Smriti
⓳ Safdarjung's Tomb
⓴ Lodi Gardens

Eat

① Indian Accent
② Dhaba
③ Kwality

Drink

④ India Coffee House
⑤ Junkyard Cafe
⑥ Q'BA

Stay

⑦ The Imperial
⑧ The Park
⑨ Hotel City Star

Shop

⑩ People Tree
⑪ Tribes India
⑫ M Ram and Sons
⑬ Central Cottage Industries Emporium

NIZAMUDDIN TO
FEROZ SHAH KOTLA
p88

NIZAMUDDIN EAST

0 metres 800
0 yards 800

N

NATIONAL MUSEUM

📍 E9 🏛 Janpath, Rajpath Rd Area, Central Secretariat Ⓜ Central Secretariat, Udyog Bhawan 🚌 501, 521, 522, 526, 531, 580, 615 🕙 10am–6pm Tue–Sun 🚫 Mon & public hols 🌐 nationalmuseumindia.gov.in

Housed in a majestic building, this vast museum is a veritable treasure trove of art and artifacts. The impressive collection, spanning five thousand years and encompassing more than 200,000 diverse objects, makes this the perfect place to uncover India's rich history.

A collection of around 1,000 artifacts, sourced from museums across India, was sent to London in the winter of 1948–9 for an exhibition at the Royal Academy. Following its return to India, the collection was meant to be temporarily exhibited in Rashtrapati Bhavan, but was such a success that plans were soon made to establish a permanent museum. The museum was moved to its current home, an imposing red sandstone building, in 1960. Over time its collection has expanded thanks to donations of artifacts from other museums and private donors.

→

A female representation of Vishnu dating from the 12th century, one of the many religious statues found in the museum's collection

The museum's expansive octagonal central foyer

GALLERY GUIDE

The museum's vast collection is displayed over three floors which radiate out from a central courtyard filled with sculptures. The first floor has displays dedicated to Harappan artifacts, Buddhist art and Indian miniature paintings. The second floor covers illustrated manuscripts, coins and Central Asian antiques, while the third floor offers exhibits on textiles, arms and armour, and tribal lifestyles in northeast India. Special exhibits are also held. Note that some exhibits may be closed due to renovation work. The museum also has a library and auditorium where film shows and lectures are held.

① The interior of the National Museum, filled with a variety of statues

② The museum's impressive red sandstone exterior

③ One of the brightly coloured Rajasthani paintings that forms part of the museum's collection

Exploring the National Museum

The museum's undoubted highlight is its collection of Harappan civilization relics, which are considered among the finest in the world. Excavations in the 1920s at Harappa and Mohenjodaro (now in Pakistan) revealed the remains of a sophisticated urban culture that existed between 2500–1500 BC along the Indus Valley (p56). Other highlights include its expansive collection of sculptures and bronzes, as well as the galleries dedicated to the lives of the country's northeastern tribes.

↑ Visitor exploring the museum's large collection of bronze statues

Statues on show in the museum's "The Body in Art" exhibition ↑

MUST SEE

Museum Highlights

Archaeological Galleries

▶ The museum's superb collection of classical sculpture dates from the 3rd century BC all the way to the 19th century AD. The collection includes pieces from Maurya, Gandhara, Kushana and Ikshvaku times, and are usually in bronze, stone and terracotta.

Harappan Civilization

◀ The museum's collection of Harappan Civilization relics includes soapstone seals, used perhaps by merchants and officials, whose pictographic script remains undeciphered. Particularly notable is the display of Harappan pottery which ranges from functional items such as pots to charming toys, beads and necklaces.

Bronzes

Covering 600 years (5th–11th centuries), the collection of bronzes is one of the museum's highlights. The gallery has a room full of Chola bronze statues of Hindu deities, including one of the most iconic images of Indian art: a pair of Shiva Natarajas.

Late Medieval Art

Outstanding examples of the sculptural arts that flourished across central and southern India during the 11th and 12th centuries feature in this excellent collection, including those from the Vijayanagara, Hoysala, Chola and Pala kingdoms.

Tribal Groups in Northeast India

This fascinating exhibit, containing over 300 items, offers a rare and compelling glimpse into the lives of India's little-known, Chinese-descended northeastern tribes. Exhibits include wood carvings, a selection of weapons, smoking pipes, a variety of household items and headgear.

Buddhist Art

A wide range of Buddhist art and artifacts from across India, Nepal, Gandhara and China are displayed here, including some rare thangkas (devotional paintings).

Decorative Arts and Textiles

▶ Dedicated to India's rich textile traditions, this gallery features a colourful display of woven, printed, tie-dyed, embroidered and appliqué-worked fabrics in silk, cotton and wool. Examples of India's varied decorative arts, including exquisite artifacts made from jade, ceramic and wood, fill the adjoining galleries.

EXPERIENCE MORE

 2

Vijay Chowk

D9 **M** Central Secretariat

The area where Rajpath meets Raisina Hill, known as Vijay Chowk, was planned as a commanding approach to the Viceroy's House. This is where the "Beating Retreat" ceremony takes place each year on 29 January (p54).

Rising from the levelled top of Raisina Hill are the two virtually identical Secretariat buildings, designed by Herbert Baker and known as the North and South Blocks. These long classical edifices house the Home and Finance ministries and the Ministry of Foreign Affairs. The stately Central Hall of the **North Block** (to the left, if facing Vijay Chowk) is open to the public.

To the north of Vijay Chowk, Baker's circular **Sansad Bhavan** (Parliament House) was a later addition following the Montagu-Chelmsford Reforms of 1919, to house the Legislative Assembly. The Constitution of India was drafted here in the early days of independence. Today,

both the Rajya Sabha (Upper House) and the Lok Sabha (House of the People) meet here when Parliament is in session. The Lok Sabha's often boisterous debates take place in the Central Hall.

North Block

🕐 9am–6pm Mon–Fri

Sansad Bhavan

🕐 11am–5pm Tue–Sat (only if Parliament is not in session)

3

Rashtrapati Bhavan

C9 🏠 Raisina Hill
M Central Secretariat
🕐 Hours vary, check website
W rashtrapatisachivalaya.
gov.in/rbtour/

Designed by Edwin Lutyens (p81) for the viceroy, the President of India's official residence stands at the crest of Raisina Hill. This 20th-century

---

| **REPUBLIC DAY PARADE**

Ever since 1950, when India became a republic, the Republic Day parade on 26 January has attracted large crowds. The president, the prime minister and other dignitaries watch as uniformed soldiers from the regiments and squadrons of the army, navy and air force march smartly past. Most popular are the Camel Corps and the floats representing different Indian states.

Rashtrapati Bhavan, situated at the end of the Rajpath

blends a typical English garden – with its charming flower beds, privet hedges and lush green lawns – with Mughal-style terraces and canals. The garden features water-courses and fountains built on three levels, and ends with Lutyens' is beautifully relaxing "butterfly garden".

Rajpath

⑨ E9 Ⓜ Central Secretariat, Patel Chowk

This 3-km (2-mile) avenue, used for parades and lined with lovely lawns, canals and fountains, is very popular on steamy summer evenings.

The **National Archives**, at the intersection with Janpath, houses a major collection of state records and private papers. Opposite is the **Indira Gandhi National Centre for the Arts** (IGNCA), with an archive of rare manuscripts. It holds many national and international exhibitions.

National Archives
🕘 9:30am–6:30pm Mon-Sat ❌ Public hols
🌐 nationalarchives.nic.in

Indira Gandhi National Centre for the Arts
🕘 9:30am–5:30pm Mon-Fri
🌐 ignca.nic.in

India Gate

⑨ F9 Ⓜ Central Secretariat, Mandi House

At the eastern end of Rajpath, the 9-m- (30-ft-) wide imposing India Gate rises high over the surrounding area. The gate commemorates the Indian and British soldiers who died

architectural masterpiece covers an area of 4.5 acres (2 ha). The cupola of its copper and sandstone dome rises 55 m (180 ft). Within are courtyards, banqueting halls, state apartments and private living quarters. The Durbar Hall is where all important Indian state and ceremonial occasions are held. Situated beneath the dome, this circular hall was originally the Throne Room and contains the two gold and crimson thrones Lutyens designed for the viceroy and vicereine. The fascinating Kitchen Museum showcases items used to cook, serve and dine at the palace, through the pre- and post-independence periods. The formal Mughal Gardens are often regarded as the "soul" of the Presidential Palace. This space beautifully

STAY

The Imperial
Housed in an Art Deco palace, Delhi's most famous hotel offers spacious rooms and every possible luxury.

⑨ E7 Ⓐ Janpath (just south of Tolstoy Marg)
🌐 theimperialindia.com

₹₹₹

The Park
Boasting a sleek, contemporary design, this opulent hotel has a pool and an excellent restaurant.

⑨ E7 Ⓐ 15 Sansad Marg (opposite Jantar Mantar)
🌐 theparkhotels.com/new-delhi.html

₹₹₹

Hotel City Star
In a backpackers' area, this hotel provides good budget accommodation, a restaurant and a gym.

⑨ E5 Ⓐ 8718 DB Gupta Road, Paharganj
🌐 hotel-citystar.com

₹₹₹

in World War I as well as those who fell in battle in the North-West Frontier Province and the Third Afghan War. An eternal flame burns in memory of the unknown soldiers who died in the 1971 Indo-Pakistan war. Facing India Gate is the sandstone canopy where King George V's statue was installed after his death in 1936. The statue now stands at Coronation Park (p146).

Found around India Gate are the stately homes of former Indian princes, including Hyderabad House, where official state banquets are held, and Jaipur, Bikaner and Patiala Houses.

EAT

Indian Accent
Fusion cuisine prepared with Indian techniques and international ingredients.

📍G11 🏠The Lodi, Lodi Road
🌐indianaccent.com

₹₹₹

Dhaba
This refined version of a Punjabi dhaba (roadside diner) serves tasty tandoori dishes.

📍E10 🏠The Claridge's, 12 Aurangzeb Road
🌐claridges.com/the-claridges-new-delhi-dine

₹₹₹

Kwality
A local favourite known for its delicious *chhola bhatura* (spicy chickpeas and deep-fried flatbread).

📍E7 🏠7 Regal Building, Connaught Place
🌐kwalitygroup.com/restaurants

₹₹₹

Agrasen ki Baoli

📍F7 🏠Off Hailey Rd, Vakil Lane, Connaught Place
🚇Barakhamba Road

This stepwell is reached by turning left on Hailey Road into a narrow lane just before the Consulate General of Malta. A little way along on the right are the remains of an old stone wall; the *baoli* is behind it and can be entered through a narrow buttressed gateway, usually locked, but the keeper will open it for you. With 103 red-stone steps and a series of

↑ Visitors admiring the impressive architecture of Agrasen ki Baoli, one of Delhi's stepwells

arches supported by columns, this is one of Delhi's finest stepwells. Its architecture suggests a 15th-century date, though popular myth holds that it was built in the 14th century by Raja Agrasen, an ancestor of the mercantile Aggarwal community, to provide water and shelter for travellers.

National Gallery of Modern Art

📍G9 🏠Jaipur House, Dr Zakir Hussain Marg, near India Gate 🚇Khan Market ⏰11am-6:30pm Tue-Fri; 11am-8pm Sat & Sun 🚫Public hols
🌐ngmaindia.gov.in

Jaipur House, the former residence of the Jaipur maharajas, is one of India's largest museums of modern art. Its vast collection includes graphics, paintings and sculptures dating from the mid-19th century to the present day. The galleries display works of British landscape painters such as the Daniells, and Indian artists such as the Tagores, Jamini Roy, Amrita Shergill and Raja Ravi Varma. Works of contemporary artists such as M F Husain, Ram Kumar, K G Subramanyam and Anjolie Ela Menon are also seen here.

Mandi House Complex

📍G7 🚇Mandi House

Mandi House, situated on the site of a princely palace, lends its name to this large cultural complex. It includes **Triveni**

Kala Sangam, with its art galleries, café and open-air auditorium, and the state-sponsored arts complex Rabindra Bhavan, which houses three national academies, one dedicated to literature (Sahitya Akademi), one to fine arts and sculpture (Lalit Kala Akademi), and the other to performing arts (Sangeet Natak Akademi). Also here is Lalit Kala, site of the international Triennale exhibition in which painters and sculptors from more than 30 countries participate. Exhibitions of photography, graphics and ceramics also take place here.

Also found within the complex, the **Shri Ram Centre for Performing Arts**, the **Kamani Auditorium** and the **National School of Drama** host a variety of theatrical, classical music and dance events.

Triveni Kala Sangam
 205 Tansen Marg
(011) 2371 8833
9:30am–5pm Mon–Sat
Public hols

Rabindra Bhavan
35 Ferozeshah Rd
(011) 2338 6626

Shri Ram Centre for Performing Arts
Safdar Hashmi Marg
shriramcentre.org

Kamani Auditorium
Copernicus Marg
kamaniauditorium.org

National School of Drama
1 Bhagwan Das Rd
nsd.gov.in/delhi

---

❾
Connaught Place
E6 Rajiv Chowk

One of New Delhi's architects, Robert Tor Russell designed this imperial plaza named after the Duke of Connaught, an uncle of King George V. Palladian archways and colonnades recall the English terraces of Cheltenham and Bath, and the first shops in 1931 had names such as "Empire Stores" to distinguish them from shops selling Indian goods nearby. Officially, the central circle is now Rajiv Chowk, the outer one Indira Chowk, but locals just call the area "CP". Connaught Place's shaded arcades offer a pleasant place to stroll around and to browse through the pavement book stalls. There are many bars and restaurants here, and a few cinemas. The park in the centre has a huge Indian flag, plus fountains and flowered lawns; it also hosts a number of annual events.

Popular markets near to the plaza include: the so-called Government Emporiums at Baba Kharak Singh Marg, each of which showcases handicrafts from its own state; Janpath Market, with its bustling clothes stalls; and Palika Bazar, a labyrinthine underground market on Rajiv Chowk, between Sansad Marg and Janpath, offering everything from books and music to clothes and accessories.

EDWIN LANDSEER LUTYENS

Architect Edwin Landseer Lutyens (1869–1944) was commissioned to design India's new capital in 1911. With Herbert Baker, his colleague, it took him 20 years to build the city in a unique style that combined Western Classicism with Indian decorative motifs. The result is classical in form and English in manner with Neo-Mughal gardens and grand vistas meeting at verdant roundabouts. Ironically, the British lived here for only 16 years.

→ The expansive streets of Connaught Place in New Delhi

10

Sankat Mochan Dham

📍B5 ⌖Dr Bhim Rao
Ambedkar Marg,
Jhandewalan
Ⓜ Jhandewalan
🕐6am–10pm daily
🌐108foot.org

Located between Paharganj
and Karol Bagh, this temple
dedicated to Hanuman (p140)
features a spectacular statue
of the monkey god standing
33-m (108-ft) high. A local
landmark, it has featured in
everything from TV adverts
to Bollywood movies. To enter
the temple you have to walk
between the jaws of another
Hanuman, found between the
larger statue's feet. At certain
times, the statue's hands
open and golden images of
Rama and Sita – the heroes,
along with Hanuman, of the
Ramayana epic – emerge from
its chest. Note that on Tuesdays
and Saturdays, the temple can
get quite packed. The metro
line between Jhandewalan and
Karol Bagh goes right past the
temple, offering great views.

11

Nehru Memorial Museum and Library

📍C10 ⌖Teen Murti Marg
Ⓜ Lok Kalyan Marg, Udyog
Bhawan 🕐9am–5:30pm
Tue–Sun (last entry
5:15pm) 🚫Public hols
🌐nehrumemorial.nic.in

Jawaharlal Nehru lived in this
house when he was India's
first Prime Minister (1947–64).
On his death, the house was
converted into a memorial
comprising a museum and a
research library. The house was
created by Connaught Place
architect Robert Tor Russell.
Its design follows Lutyens-style
classicism with a teak-panelled
interior and vaulted reception
rooms. Nehru's bedroom and
study are exactly as he left
them – the bookshelves hold
his large private collection, an
eclectic mix of English classics,
Left Book Club editions and
treatises on the Cold War.
In the grounds is the **Nehru
Planetarium**, offering shows
on the wonders of space, as
well as the square, three-
arched Kushak Mahal, a 14th-
century hunting lodge built by
the Tughlaq sultan, Feroz
Shah. On the roundabout
in front of the house,

a memorial known as Teen
Murti ("three statues")
honours the men of the
Indian regiments who died
in World War I.

Nehru Planetarium

♿ 🕐Shows: 11:30am & 3pm
Tue–Sun 🚫Public hols
🌐nehruplanetarium.org

12

Gurudwara Bangla Sahib

📍D7 ⌖Ashoka Road
Ⓜ Patel Chowk
🕐24 hrs daily

Delhi's biggest Sikh temple
was built in the 18th century.
Its sacred pond covers a well
whose waters were used in
1664 by the 8th Sikh guru,
Hare Krishna, to minister to
victims of a cholera epidemic
(to which he eventually
succumbed himself). The
temple plays devotional
music round the clock, and
it serves a simple meal to all
visitors three times a day.

Gurudwara
Bangla Sahib,
and (inset) the
↓ temple's interior

Crowds of shoppers at a nighttime bazaar in lively Paharganj

Paharganj

D5 M Ramakrishna Ashram Marg, New Delhi

Paharganj is the city's main backpacker hub, full of cheap and cheerful accommodation. This is also a vibrant market area and a great place to shop for clothes, leatherware and incense sticks, as well as souvenirs and trinkets. The Salaam Baalak Trust (*p49*), based here, offers walking tours run by former street children that show you the neighbourhood's hidden side.

Lakshmi Narayan Mandir

B6 Near Gole Market, Mandir Marg, Connaught Place M RK Ashram Marg 4:30am–1:30pm & 2:30–9pm daily

The prominent industrialist GD Birla built this temple dedicated to Lakshmi Narayan in 1938 – it is popularly known as Birla Mandir. Mahatma Gandhi attended its first *puja* as this was among the country's first temples with no caste restrictions.

Approached by a flight of marble stairs, the main shrine has images of Vishnu and his consort, Lakshmi. It is surmounted by ochre and maroon *shikharas* (temple towers). Subsidiary shrines dedicated to Radha-Krishna, Hanuman, Shiva and Durga (*p140*) are set around the courtyard. On the walls are quotations from Hindu scriptures, and paintings from the famous *Mahabharata (p163)* and *Ramayana*.

Surrounded by a peaceful park with a pleasant marble pavilion on one side and a large *dharamshala* (resthouse) on the other, this popular temple is very well maintained.

Khan Market

F10 Subramaniam Bharti Marg Sun

This market was built in the early 1940s to serve the needs of the British forces living in the barracks at Lodi Estate. It was named after the social reformer Dr Khan Sahib, the brother of Khan Abdul Gaffar Khan. Both men were revered for their role in the struggle for independence among the warlike communities of the North-West Frontier Province (now in Pakistan).

This popular market offers a wide range of Indian and Western merchandise, from crockery and cakes to exquisite jewellery and designer clothes. There are also traditional sari shops, as well as Anokhi, selling blockprinted linen and garments in both Western and Indian styles. There are also excellent places to buy shoes, as well as good bookshops, charming grocery stores and colourful flower shops. The market has a number of good places to eat, but the Iranian-Bombay-inspired restaurant SodaBottleOpenerWala is without a doubt one of the market's best.

DRINK

India Coffee House
Great coffee and simple food, plus a rooftop terrace with expansive city views and cheeky monkey visitors.

D7 2nd floor, Mohan Singh Place Shopping Complex, Baba Kharak Singh Marg (011) 2334 2994

Junkyard Cafe
A quirky bar decorated with recycled junk offering an international menu and music nightly, sometimes live.

E6 2nd floor, N-91 Connaught Place bigfishadventures.in/ junkyard-connaught. html

Q'BA
An upmarket spot offering delicious drinks from around the globe.

E6 E-42/43 Connaught Place qba.co.in

Jantar Mantar

Q E7 **A** Parliament Street, Connaught Place **M** Patel Chowk, Rajiv Chowk **O** 6am–6pm daily **W** asi.payumoney.com

Commissioned by the then Mughal emperor Muhammad Shah, Sawai Jai Singh II of Jaipur built this observatory in 1724. A keen astronomer, the maharaja felt that the existing instruments were not accurate enough to calculate the eclipses and planetary positions required to set the timings of his *pujas* and other sacred rituals. He erected new observatories here, and in four other towns, including Jaipur (*p206*), with larger and more exact instruments. They include the Samrat Yantra, a gigantic sundial, with two brick quadrants on either side which measure its shadow. The others are the Jai Prakash Yantra, Jai Singh's invention, which, among other functions, verifies the time of the spring equinox; the Ram Yantra which reads the altitude of the sun; and the Misra Yantra, a group of instruments for a variety of purposes. Today, the observatory lies obsolete, in the centre of a pleasant park, surrounded by high-rises. Tickets can be bought via the Archaeological Survey of India booking website or at the entry gate.

Indira Gandhi Memorial Museum

Q C10 **A** 1 Safdarjung Rd **C** (011) 2301 1358 **M** Lok Kalyan Marg **O** 9:30am–4:45pm Tue–Sun

This was Indira Gandhi's home when she was prime minister, and it was in the garden of the house that she was assassinated by her Sikh bodyguards after ordering an assault on the Golden Temple in Amritsar, the Sikhs' holiest site. The spot where she was killed is marked on the ground, and her blood-stained sari is displayed in the house, along with photographs and mementos.

Gandhi Smriti

Q D10 **A** 5, Tees January Marg **M** Lok Kalyan Marg, Udyog Bhawan **O** 10am–5:30pm Tue–Sun **O** Public hols **W** gandhismriti.gov.in

On 30 January 1948, at 5:15pm, Nathuram Godse assassinated Mahatma Gandhi as he was going to his daily prayer meeting in the gardens of this house, once the residence of the industrialist Birla family. A simple sandstone pillar marks the spot.

Now a museum commemorating Gandhi's life, Gandhi

→
One of the majestic tombs scattered around the verdant Lodi Gardens

Smriti offers an ambience reflecting Gandhi's philosophy of lofty political principles and down-to-earth common sense. A series of appealing dioramas tell the story of his eventful life through such defining moments as bidding farewell to his parents as he left for England and the death of Kasturba, his beloved wife. In the garden, footsteps cast in red sandstone lead to the site of his final martyrdom.

Shops in the complex sell editions of Gandhi's writings, as well as items made from khadi, the simple homespun cloth he always wore, and which became one of the important symbols of the Freedom Movement (*p60*).

LODI COLONY ART

On the south side of Lodi Road, the Lodi Colony has become an open-air gallery for street art thanks to the St+Art India Foundation (*www.st-artindia.org*). Once a residential area for civil servants, it is now covered in vibrant murals, which range from jewel-bright birds to eye-catching geometric patterns.

SHOP

People Tree
This ethical brand sells handcrafted Fair Trade clothes and accessories.

📍 E7 🏠 8 Regal Bldg, Sansad Marg
🌐 peopletreeonline.com

Tribes India
Exquisite handicrafts, including art and saris, made by indigenous craftspeople.

📍 D7 🏠 2 Rajiv Gandhi Bhawan, Baba Kharak Singh Marg 🌐 trifed.in

M Ram and Sons
Have a bespoke suit made quickly and for a fraction of department store prices.

📍 E6 🏠 E-21 Connaught Place 🌐 mramand sons.site

Central Cottage Industries Emporium
A government initiative, this shop sells handicrafts created by skilled artisans from all over the country.

📍 E7 🏠 Jawahar Vyapar Bhawan, Janpath
🌐 cottageemporium.in

 PICTURE PERFECT
Sunrise Shot

Get up early for a great shot of Safdarjung's Tomb. Facing east, the façade of this impressive marble-and-sandstone tomb, with its palm-fringed pond, is beautifully illuminated by the rising sun.

19

Safdarjung's Tomb

📍 D12 🏠 Aurobindo Marg 🚇 Jor Bagh ⏰ Sunrise-sunset daily

The last of Delhi's garden tombs was built in 1754 for Safdarjung, the prime minister of emperor Muhammad Shah. Marble was allegedly stripped from the tomb of Abdur Rahim Khan-i-Khanan in Nizamuddin (p98) to construct this rather florid example of late Mughal architecture. Approached by an ornate gateway, the tomb stands in a *charbagh (p195)* cut by water channels. Its red and buff stone façade features a number of well-preserved plaster carvings, and the central chamber itself is unusually airy, with some fine stone inlay work set into the floor.

20
Lodi Gardens

📍 E11 🏠 Entrance on Lodi Rd & South End Rd 🚇 Jor Bagh ⏰ Sunrise-sunset daily

Lodi Gardens, in the heart of residential New Delhi, was built in 1936 at the behest of Lady Willingdon, the Vicereine. Although it was originally the site of two villages, the inhabitants shifted elsewhere, and lawns and pathways were laid out around the tombs belonging to the 15th-century Sayyid and Lodi dynasties. Inside, the bridge called Athpula, literally "eight piers", near the entrance on South End Road, is said to date from the 17th century. To the west of it are the ramparts of the tomb of Sikandar Lodi (r 1489–1517) which enclose an octagonal tomb at the centre of some rather overgrown gardens. Inside, traces of tile-work and calligraphy are visible.

South of Sikandar Lodi's tomb are the Bara Gumbad ("big dome") and Sheesh Gumbad ("glazed dome"). The former is an imposing structure with an attached mosque built in 1494, while the Sheesh Gumbad is named after the glazed turquoise tiles that still cling to its outer walls.

The tomb of Muhammad Shah (r 1434–44), the third ruler of the Sayyid dynasty, is said to be the oldest in the garden. The dome of this octagonal structure is surrounded by *chhatris* (an open square or octagonal pavillion). The graves inside are said to be those of the sultan himself and some of the most favoured nobles of his court.

Today, with its tree-lined pathways and well-kept lawns, the park acts as a "green lung" for the people of Delhi. It is a favourite haunt of joggers, yoga enthusiasts and families who come here to picnic.

A SHORT WALK
AROUND VIJAY CHOWK

Distance 3.5 km (2 miles) **Nearest Metro**
Central Secretariat **Time** 40 minutes

The barren, treeless grounds around Raisina Hill were selected by the British as the site of their new capital, New Delhi. Now wonderfully verdant, the area houses India's president, ministers and officials, plus its parliament and ministries. Imperial conventions laid down by the British are still followed here, so that even today, Indian ministers and officials live in the spacious bungalows which line the area's broad tree-shaded avenues. From Vijay Chowk, Lutyens's Rajpath lies ahead – trees and fountains line the lawns of this grand avenue which leads up to the imposing India Gate (p79).

Sansad Bhavan
*is also known as
Parliament House.*

*A pair of red sandstone
obelisk-shaped fountains
flank* **Vijay Chowk** *(p78),
a forecourt that overlooks
the majestic Rajpath (p79).*

The **North Block** *of the
Central Secretariat has an
imposing Central Hall which is
open to the public.*

Iron Gates

START

DALHOUSIE ROAD

THYAGARAJ MARG

The **South Block** *of
the Central Secretariat,
a high security zone,
contains the Prime
Minister's Office and
the Defence Ministry.*

← The elegant exterior
of the South Block of
the Central Secretariat

0 metres   200
0 yards   200

N

Locator Map
For more detail see p72

←

The striking Sansad Bhavan (Parliament House) at sunset

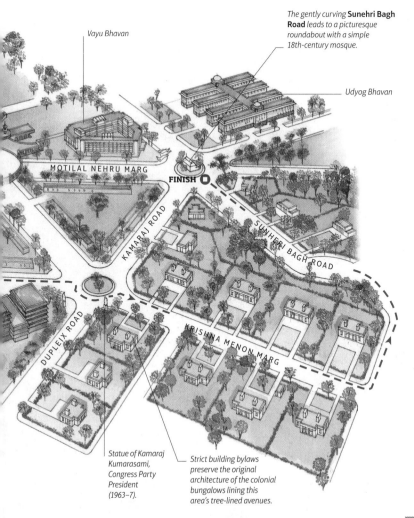

The gently curving **Sunehri Bagh Road** *leads to a picturesque roundabout with a simple 18th-century mosque.*

Vayu Bhavan

Udyog Bhavan

MOTILAL NEHRU MARG

FINISH

KAMARAJ ROAD

SUNEHRI BAGH ROAD

DUPLEX ROAD

KRISHNA MENON MARG

Statue of Kamaraj Kumarasami, Congress Party President (1963–7).

Strict building bylaws preserve the original architecture of the colonial bungalows lining this area's tree-lined avenues.

NIZAMUDDIN TO FEROZ SHAH KOTLA

Stretching from the historic village of Nizamuddin, up to the ancient fort of Feroz Shah Kotla, this diverse part of Delhi has a long history that likely dates back to the 3rd century AD. The oldest part is the area surrounding Purana Qila, believed to be the site of Indraprastha, the capital of the Pandavas, heroes of the Hindu epic the *Mahabharata (p163)*. However, this first city was lost, and it wasn't until 1533 that Emperor Humayun erected the fort of Purana Qila here, often called Delhi's sixth city. After the death of Humayun, the fort languished, although following Indian independence in 1947, it was used as a camp for Hindu refugees who had left Pakistan.

To the south of Purana Qila is the Nizamuddin area, named after the famous 14th-century Sufi saint Hazrat Nizamuddin Auliya. After his death in 1325, a dargah (tomb and shrine) dedicated to him was erected here by the Sultanate ruler, Muhammad Tughlaq; it soon became the nucleus of a medieval village. Under the Mughals, the area expanded to the east with the addition of the tomb of emperor Humayun and its surrounding complex of monuments.

To the north of both Nizamuddin and Purana Qila lies Feroz Shah Kotla. Considered the fifth incarnation of Delhi, it was built by Sultan Feroz Shah in 1354. Over the next few centuries the fort fell into disrepair, often used by subsequent rulers as a source of building materials. As the city expanded, these three areas became intertwined.

NIZAMUDDIN TO FEROZ SHAH KOTLA

Must Sees

❶ Humayun's Tomb
❷ Crafts Museum

Experience More

❸ Nizamuddin
❹ Pragati Maidan
❺ Matka Pir Dargah
❻ National Science Centre
❼ Purana Qila
❽ Khair-ul-Manazil
❾ Feroz Shah Kotla
❿ Shankar's International Dolls Museum
⓫ National Gandhi Museum
⓬ Parsi Anjuman Hall

Eat

① Café Lota
② Basil & Thyme
③ Sazerac
④ Nathu's Sweet Shop

Stay

⑤ La Sagrita
⑥ B Nineteen

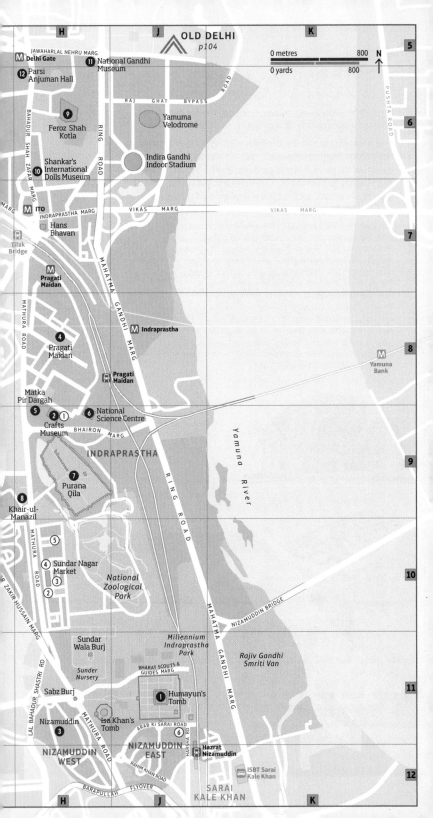

H   J   K

M Delhi Gate

JAWAHARLAL NEHRU MARG

11 National Gandhi
Museum

12 Parsi
Anjuman Hall

RAJ   GHAT   BYPASS

9 Feroz Shah
Kotla

Yamuna
Velodrome

10 Shankar's
International
Dolls Museum

Indira Gandhi
Indoor Stadium

M ITO

INDRAPRASTHA MARG

Hans
Bhavan

VIKAS   MARG   VIKAS   MARG

Tilak
Bridge

M Pragati
Maidan

M Indraprastha

M Yamuna
Bank

4 Pragati
Maidan

**Pragati
Maidan**

Matka
Pir Dargah

5

2 **1**
Crafts
Museum

6 National
Science Centre

BHAIRON   MARG

INDRAPRASTHA

Yamuna River

7 Purana
Qila

8 Khair-ul-
Manazil

5

4 Sundar Nagar
Market

3

2

National
Zoological
Park

RING   ROAD

NIZAMUDDIN BRIDGE

Sundar
Wala Burj

Millennium
Indraprastha
Park

Rajiv Gandhi
Smriti Van

*Sunder
Nursery*

BHARAT SCOUTS &
GUIDES MARG

Sabz Burj

1 Humayun's
Tomb

Nizamuddin

3

Isa Khan's
Tomb

ARAB KI SARAI ROAD

**NIZAMUDDIN
WEST**

**NIZAMUDDIN
EAST**

6

**Hazrat
Nizamuddin**

RAHIM KHAN ROAD

**ISBT Sarai
Kale Khan**

BARAPULLAH   FLYOVER

**SARAI
KALE KHAN**

H   J   K

0 metres   800
0 yards   800

N

5
6
7
8
9
10
11
12

BAHADUR SHAH ZAFAR MARG

RING ROAD

MAHATMA GANDHI MARG

PUSHTA ROAD

MATHURA ROAD

MATHURA ROAD

ZAKIR HUSSAIN MARG

LAL BAHADUR SHASTRI RD

MATHURA ROAD

MAHATMA GANDHI MARG

HARSHA RD

❶

HUMAYUN'S TOMB

◉ J11 **◨** Off Mathura Rd , Bharat Scout Guide Marg **Ⓜ** JLN Stadium
◷ Sunrise-sunset daily **ⓦ** humayunstomb.com

This magnificent tomb – the final resting place of Humayun, the second Mughal emperor – rises spectacularly above the surrounding palm-fringed gardens. The first great example of a Mughal garden tomb, it was the inspiration for several later monuments, including the impressive Taj Mahal.

Built between 1565 and 1572 by the Persian architect Mirak Mirza Ghiyas, the tomb was commissioned by Humayun's senior widow, Haji Begum. The monument is often called the "Dormitory of the Mughals", as the tomb complex houses over 150 of Humayun's Mughal family members. The graves in the tomb's chambers include those of Humayun's wives and Dara Shikoh, Shah Jahan's scholarly son. Also found in the complex are the octagonal tomb and mosque of Isa Khan, a 16th-century nobleman; the tomb of Humayun's favourite barber; and the impressive Arab ki Sarai, a rest house for the Persian masons who built the tomb. The monument is now a UNESCO World Heritage Site.

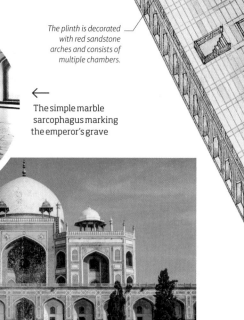

The plinth is decorated with red sandstone arches and consists of multiple chambers.

← The simple marble sarcophagus marking the emperor's grave

↑ The imposing exterior of Humayun's Tomb, one of the finest Mughal tombs

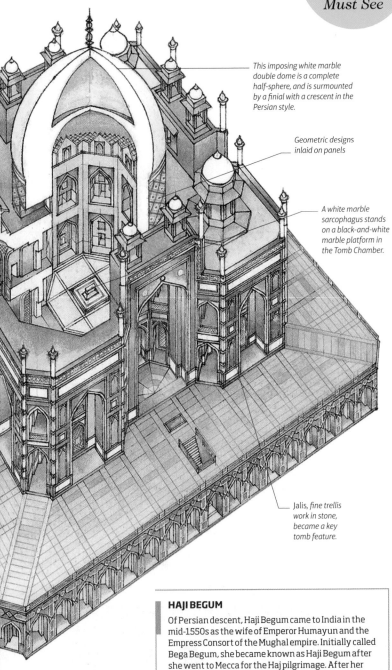

This imposing white marble double dome is a complete half-sphere, and is surmounted by a finial with a crescent in the Persian style.

Geometric designs inlaid on panels

A white marble sarcophagus stands on a black-and-white marble platform in the Tomb Chamber.

Jalis, fine trellis work in stone, became a key tomb feature.

↑ An illustration of Humayun's Tomb, showing the central chamber

HAJI BEGUM

Of Persian descent, Haji Begum came to India in the mid-1550s as the wife of Emperor Humayun and the Empress Consort of the Mughal empire. Initially called Bega Begum, she became known as Haji Begum after she went to Mecca for the Haj pilgrimage. After her husband's death, she decided to build a magnificent tomb to house his body and commissioned the Persian architect Mirak Mirza Ghiyas. Humayun's Tomb was the first majestic mausoleum in Islamic India; it was this elegant tomb, alongside others, that instigated a legacy of Mughal mausoleums.

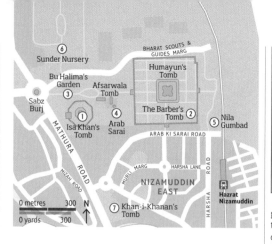

PICTURE PERFECT
Light and Shade

From within the Barber's Tomb, exquisitely carved *jali* screens make a great shot, especially when the light of the setting sun pours through the delicate stone lattice and casts patterns on the floor.

AROUND HUMAYUN'S TOMB

① Isa Khan's Tomb

Just past the entrance to the Humayun's Tomb compound, a path to the right leads to Isa Khan's Tomb, a beautiful family mausoleum, set in an octagonal garden with a mosque at its western end. Built around AD 1547–48, two decades before Humayun's Tomb, it is the resting place of Isa Khan Niyazi, a noble at the court of Afghan warlord Sher Shah, who deposed Humayun and held the throne for 16 years before Humayun

regained control. Immediately opposite this tomb, on a busy roundabout, is Sabz Burj, a beautiful blue-domed, Persian-style tomb, the grave of an unknown Mughal nobleman.

② The Barber's Tomb

A fine domed tomb of red and grey sandstone stands in the southeast corner of the *charbagh* (p195). Built in 1590–91, the tomb is known as the Barber's Tomb: it is believed to have housed Humayun's (or possibly Akbar's) barber, who was recognized as an important and trusted court official.

③ Bu Halima's Garden

The path leading in from the site entrance passes through a well-maintained enclosure known as Bu Halima's Garden. It is believed to pre-date

Humayun's Tomb, but nobody knows when it was put there or why. The raised stone platform standing north of the path seems to be a later addition, and is probably the base of a tomb, possibly belonging to the mysterious Bu Halima.

Arab Sarai

This walled compound, with its magnificent gateway, was originally a sarai, or hostel, for the many craftsmen working on Humayun's Tomb. It also apparently housed 300 Arabs whom Haji Begum recruited in Mecca to recite the Qur'an over her husband's resting place, although an alternative story attributes the name to 300 horse carts (*araba* in Persian) which were accommodated here. Just inside is a tomb and mosque belonging to a man named Afsarwala, while at the far end of the compound is a market area endowed by one Mihr Banu: the identity of both people remains a mystery.

Nila Gumbad

The beautiful blue-domed Nila Gumbad currently sits just outside the Humayun's Tomb complex, although plans are afoot to extend the compound to include it. The tomb of a Mughal noble, it was originally on an island in the Yamuna River, but now abuts the train tracks at Hazrat Nizamuddin station. The dome still has most of its original blue tiles, and many of the tiles on the outer walls also survive. Visit at dawn, when the early morning sun lights up its still-beautiful exterior.

Sunder Nursery

🕐 Sunrise–sunset daily
🌐 sundernursery.org

Just north of the Humayun's Tomb complex, Sunder Nursery was originally a 16th-century Mughal garden; it was reappropriated by the British in 1913 to be a nursery of trees and shrubs for planting in New Delhi. A haven for birdlife, it has been restored as a heritage park, with a flower garden, and nursery for trees and indigenous plants. The 90-acre park is strewn with a generous scattering of restored Mughal-era monuments, including a lotus pond, as well as trees from across the world, planted here decades ago by the British.

Khan-i-Khanan's Tomb

📍 Rahim Khan Marg
🕐 Sunrise–sunset daily

Around 400 m (1,312 ft) south of the entrance to

←

The onion-domed Isa Khan's Tomb, standing amid serene octagonal gardens

EMPEROR HUMAYUN

The second Mughal emperor, Humayun, was an endearingly irresolute figure, who alternated between bouts of utter military brilliance and total self-indulgence. After succeeding his father, Babur, in 1530, he lost his empire to the Afghan invader Sher Shah Suri, and was obliged to seek refuge in Persia for the following 15 years – that is, until he rallied enough forces to win the empire back. His luck didn't last: within a year he was dead, having fallen down a flight of steps in Purana Qila (p100).

the compound, just off the Mathura Road, Khan-i-Khanan's tomb was built by Mughal courtier Abdul Rahim Khan-I-Khana in 1598 for his wife. A well-respected poet in his day, he is best known for his Urdu couplets and his books on astrology.

At one time this striking tomb was faced with red sandstone and marble, and sat in an elegant *charbagh* garden (p195), just like Humayun's Tomb, but these have been removed over the years. Nevertheless, this imposing tomb remains an impressive sight.

❷ CRAFTS MUSEUM

📍H9 🏛Bhairon Marg, Pragati Maidan Ⓜ Pragati Maidan 🕙10am–5pm
Tue-Sun 🚫Mon & public hols 🌐nationalcraftsmuseum.nic.in

This diverse museum celebrates the rich and vibrant heritage of India's traditional arts and crafts. Filled with a wide-ranging array of handicrafts, the museum is housed in an expansive complex designed by renowned Indian architect Charles Correa.

Established in 1956, the Crafts Museum was designed to promote indigenous artisans by displaying their work in one place. By the early 1980s, over 20,000 objects had been collected; today, the museum houses over 33,000 diverse objects, including eye-catching textiles, intricate jewellery and vibrant wall murals. The exhibits, spread over two floors, are divided into separate areas by courtyards that also double up as exhibition spaces. The museum also has a tree-shaded outdoor area, which contains a number of traditional homes from across India and stalls selling hand-crafted goods; the space also hosts craft demon-strations. Inside the musuem is the Lota Shop, which sells fine Indian folk crafts and textiles.

→
An exhibit showcasing the entrance to a *haveli* (mansion)

→
A woman working on a wall mural, done in a traditional style, at the Crafts Museum

↑ One of the colourful Shekhawati-style murals found at the museum

→
A collection of terracotta statues of horses and people

EAT

Café Lota

This laid-back outdoor café offers a modern take on regional dishes from across India, all made with fresh ingredients – don't miss the delicious *palak chaat* (deep fried spinach leaves served with yoghurt and mint chutney). There's also a wide range of fine Indian teas and coffees.

⌂ Crafts Museum, Bhairon Marg
🕐 8am–10pm Tue–Sun
🌐 meltingpotfood.in/ cafe-lota

₹₹₹

EXPERIENCE MORE

3

Nizamuddin

H11 **Old Nizamuddin Bazaar, Nizamuddin East** **Jangpura**

This always-crowded, bustling medieval settlement, or *basti*, is named after Sheikh Hazrat Nizamuddin Auliya, who belonged to a fraternity of Sufi mystics, the Chishtis, respected for their austerity, piety, and disdain for politics and material desires. His daily assemblies drew both the rich and the poor, who believed that he was a "friend of God" and so a master who would intercede on their behalf on Judgement Day. Nizamuddin died in 1325, but his disciples call him a *zinda pir*, a living spirit, who heeds their pleas and alleviates their misery. His grave is found in this area at the **Hazrat Nizamuddin Aulia Dargah**. A winding alley leads to the saint's grave, and is crowded with mendicants and lined with stalls selling flowers and *chadars*, poly-chrome clocks and prints

of Mecca. The shrine's main congregational area is a marble pavilion (rebuilt in 1562). Women are denied entry beyond the outer verandah, but they may look through *jalis* into the small, dark chamber where the saint's grave lies draped with a rose-petal-strewn cloth and imams continuously recite verses from the Qur'an. The Urs, a celebration held on the anniversary of the saint's birth and death, and is celebrated by his disciples with qawwalis and offerings of *chadars*.

The complex also contains the graves of several eminent disciples, such as Jahanara Begum and Amir Khusrau. Across the western side of

the open courtyard is the red sandstone Jama't Khana Mosque, constructed in 1325. To its north is a *baoli* (stepwell), secretly excavated while Tughlaqabad (*p133*) was being built because Ghiyasuddin Tughlaq had banned all

> **INSIDER TIP**
> ### Listen to Qawwalis
>
> Visit Nizamuddin between Friday and Wednesday to hear the ethereal sound of qawwalis, devotional music sung by the followers of Hazrat Nizamuddin Auliya.

> A winding alley leads to the saint's grave, and is crowded with mendicants and lined with stalls selling flowers and *chadars*, polychrome clocks and prints of Mecca.

building activities elsewhere. According to legend, labourers worked here at night with the help of lamps lit not by oil, but by water blessed by Nasiruddin, Nizamuddin's successor.

The mid-16th-century tomb of Atgah Khan – the minister of Mughal ruler Akbar and the husband of one of his wet nurses – is found to the north. An open marble pavilion, the Chaunsath Khamba ("64 pillars"), is located nearby. Just outside is an enclosure containing the simple grave of Mirza Ghalib (1797–1869). Widely considered one of the greatest poets of his time, Ghalib wrote in both Urdu and Persian, and his verses are still recited by many today. Nearby is the Ghalib Academy, dedicated to the poet, an important repository of paintings and manuscripts.

Hazrat Nizamuddin Aulia Dargah

📍 Baoli Gate Rd 🕐 Dargah: 5am-10:30pm daily; qawwali: 5-9:30pm Fri-Wed 🌐 nizamuddinaulia.org

← Devotees in front of the Hazrat Nizamuddin Aulia Dargah

↑ Stalls at the New Delhi World Book Fair, held at Pragati Maidan

Pragati Maidan

📍 H8 🏛 Mathura Rd 📞 (011) 2337 1540 Ⓜ Pragati Maidan 🔒 For renovation

India's largest exhibition centre, covering nearly 150 acres (61 ha), Pragati Maidan is the venue for numerous exhibitions and trade fairs organized by the India Trade Promotion Organization. The work of some of India's most eminent architects can be seen here. Renowned Indian architect Raj Rewal has designed the Hall of Nations and Industries, while the World Trade Centre is by American architect Joseph Allen Stein. Among other notable buildings are those designed by Charles Correa, Achyut Kanvinde and Satish Grover. All the Indian states have their own pavilions spread across the fair's extensive grounds, which are linked by 16 km (10 miles) of roads.

A large number of exhibitions are held here throughout the year, covering a range of interesting products such as arts and crafts, textiles, electronics, jewellery, automobiles, photography, mining equipment and food products.

Every year the **World Book Fair** and the **India International Trade Fair** are held, drawing a great deal of international interest. Both fairs are incredibly popular with local people as well as visitors from overseas.

The Pragati Maidan centre is currently undergoing renovation; it is not known when it will re-open.

World Book Fair
🌐 nbtindia.gov.in/nbtbook

India International Trade Fair
🌐 indiatradefair.com

---

⑤ Matka Pir Dargah

📍 H9 🏛 Mathura Road, by Pragati Maidan 📞 (0) 97182 78786 Ⓜ Pragati Maidan 🕐 6am-9:30pm daily

The entrance to the dargah (shrine) of Matka Pir, a Sufi saint, is lined with rows of *matkas* (earthenware pots). According to legend, a man and his wife came to the saint to seek his help for the birth of a son. Being poor, they could only offer a humble pot of dal and jaggery (date palm sugar). The saint asked them to place the pot in the courtyard and leave the rest to God. A year later, their wish fulfilled, the couple returned with another pot, a tradition that has continued since then.

The *dargah* stands on a ridge overlooking Mathura Road, with nearby shops selling *matkas*, roasted grams, jaggery and dal. The biryani served here is particularly famous – the chefs trace their origins to the Delhi Sultanate era. The saint's powers still attract many pilgrims today.

Did You Know?

Devotees to Matka Pir also tie *matkas* (earthenware pots) to the trees in front of the shrine.

6

National Science Centre

📍H9 🏠Bhairon Marg, near Gate 1, Pragati Maidan Ⓜ Pragati Maidan 🕘9:30am-6pm daily 🌐nscd.gov.in

This modern science museum features dinosaur displays, nylon energy balls and interactive exhibits, plus a number of special shows. There are sections on the history of Indian science, human biology and the information revolution. Children will love the hands-on Fun Science section, while the whole family will be utterly engrossed by exhibits on the human body, pre-historic life, emerging technologies and transport. The best time to visit the museum is during the week, since it gets quite crowded at weekends.

↑ A penny-farthing bicycle on display at the National Science Centre

STAY

La Sagrita

A charming boutique hotel in a residential area off Mathura Road, with large rooms, a peaceful garden and delicious buffet breakfasts.

📍H10 🏠14 Sundar Nagar 🌐lasagrita.com

₹₹₹

B Nineteen

This upmarket B&B offers luxurious rooms, a kitchen for guests, room service and a roof terrace with views of Humayun's Tomb.

📍J11 🏠B-19 Nizamuddin East 🌐bnineteen.com

₹₹₹

7

Purana Qila

📍H9 🏠Mathura Rd, near Delhi Zoo Ⓜ Pragati Maidan 🕘7am-5pm daily 🌐delhitourism.gov.in

Purana Qila, literally "old fort", stands on an ancient mound. Excavations near its eastern wall reveal that the site has been continuously occupied since 1000 BC. It is also believed to be the place where Indraprastha, the Pandava capital mentioned in the epic *Mahabharata (p163)*, once stood.

It was here that Humayun, the second Mughal emperor, began to construct his city Dinpanah ("Asylum of Faith"), just four years after his father Babur established the Mughal dynasty in 1526 *(p58)*. His reign was short-lived, though, and in 1540, the ambitious Afghan chieftain Sher Shah Suri (r 1540–45) took possession of the citadel. He strengthened its fortifications, added several new structures and renamed it Shergarh. After his death, Humayun recaptured his domains in 1555. Purana Qila flourished as the sixth city of Delhi. Today, of the many palaces, barracks and houses that once existed, only the fort's imposing walls, Sher Shah's mosque and the building used by Humayun as a library remain.

The present fort entrance, an imposing red sandstone gate on the western wall called the Bara Darwaza, is one of the three principal gates. Its double-storeyed façade,

→ The dramatic ruins of the 16th-century Purana Qila fort, surrounded by a moat

surmounted by *chhatris* and approached by a steep ramp, still displays traces of tiles and carved foliage. The Yamuna once flowed on the fort's eastern side and formed a natural moat: a small lake to the west, facing busy Mathura Road, is all that remains today.

Humayun's Gate, on the southern wall, has an inscription bearing Sher Shah's name. To the north, the Taliqi Darwaza (the so-called "forbidden gate") has carved reliefs, and across the road is the red sandstone Lal Darwaza, or Sher Shah Gate, one of the entrances to the town that grew around the fort.

The single-domed Qila-i-Kuhna Mosque, built by Sher Shah in 1541, is an excellent example of pre-Mughal design. Its prayer hall inside has five elegant arched niches or *mihrabs* set in its western wall. Marble in shades of red, white and slate is used for the calligraphic inscriptions and marks a transition from Lodi to Mughal architecture. A second storey provided space for female courtiers to pray, while the arched doorway on the left wall, framed by ornate

jharokhas, was reserved for members of the royal family.

The Sher Mandal stands to the south of the mosque. This double-storeyed octagonal tower of red sandstone was built by Sher Shah and later used as a library by Humayun. The tower is topped by an octagonal *chhatri*, supported by eight pillars and decorated with white marble. Inside, there are remnants of the decorative plasterwork and stone shelving. This was also the spot where, in January 1556, on hearing the muezzin's call, the devout Humayun hurried to kneel on the stairs, missed his footing and tumbled to his death. His tomb can be seen from the southern gate.

The small **Purana Qila Museum** at the entrance of the fort displays items excavated from the site, while **Delhi Heritage Walks** offer fascinating tours of the fort.

Purana Qila Museum
⊗ ⊗ 🄲 (011) 2435 5387
🄾 10am–5pm Sat-Thu

Delhi Heritage Walks
🆆 delhiheritagewalks.com

 GREAT VIEW
Reflecting The Past

Visit Purana Qila at night to see this ancient fort magically illuminated. Its dramatic ruined walls are beautifully reflected in the tranquil, fountain-dotted lake on its western side.

8

Khair-ul-Manazil

🄾 H9 🄰 Mathura Rd
🄼 Pragati Maidan
🄾 Sunrise-sunset daily

This mosque was constructed in 1561 by Akbar's wet nurse, Maham Anga, and a courtier, Shiha-bu'd-Din Ahmed Khan. An imposing red sandstone gateway leads into a large courtyard ringed by cloisters, one of which was used as a *madrasa*. The prayer hall with its five-arched openings is topped by a single dome. Inside, the central mihrab is decorated with bands of blue and green calligraphy.

 9

Feroz Shah Kotla

⚐ H6 🏠 Bahadur Shah Zafar Marg Ⓜ Pragati Maidan 🕐 10am-7pm daily

Only some ramparts and ruined structures remain of Feroz Shah Kotla. This was once the palace complex of Ferozabad, Delhi's fifth city erected by that indefatigable builder, Feroz Shah Tughlaq. Entry to this expansive site is from the gate next to the Indian Express Building. Towards the very end of the walled enclosure stand the partial ruins of the Jama Masjid. Roofless, with only the rear wall still extant, this was at one time Delhi's largest mosque, where, as

---

 PICTURE PERFECT
Panorama From a Pillar

For some truly great photos of Feroz Shah Kotla's hauntingly atmospheric ruins, make the short climb up to the impressive Ashokan Pillar, which surveys the crumbling fort from on high.

---

legend says, Timur the Lame, the Mongol conqueror who sacked Delhi in 1398, came to say his Friday prayers. Next to the Jama Masjid is a rubble pyramidal structure topped by one of the Mauryan emperor Ashoka's polished stone pillars *(p57)*, brought from the Punjab and installed here in 1356 by Feroz Shah. It was from the inscriptions on this pillar that James Prinsep, the Oriental linguist, deciphered the Brahmi script, a forerunner of the modern Devanagari, in 1837.

Khuni Darwaza (also known as the "bloodstained gate"), opposite the Indian Express Building, was built by Sher Shah Suri as one of the gates to his city *(p58)*. This was where Lieutenant Hodson shot the sons of Bahadur Shah Zafar – the figurehead of the 1857 War of Independence – after the war was over. It is said that, at the monsoon, the gate drips blood in their memory, although this could also be rusty water from the gate's iron frame. Across the road is Delhi's main cricket stadium, Feroz Shah Kotla Ground. Almost 140 years old, it was built in 1883 and named after the fort complex which forms its backdrop.

Did You Know?

Pillai started collecting dolls in 1950 after being given one as a gift by the ambassador of Hungary.

10

Shankar's International Dolls Museum

⚐ H6 🏠 Nehru House, 4 Bahadur Shah Zafar Marg Ⓜ ITO 🕐 10am-6pm Tue-Sun 🌐 childrens booktrust.com/dolls museum.html

Definitely one of the city's quirkier attractions, Shankar's International Dolls Museum was set up by the famous political cartoonist Shankar Pillai. This truly fascinating museum houses an incredible collection of nearly 7,000 different dolls from around the world. Many of them are in the national costumes of the countries they come from, and several were presented by visiting heads of state. There are 150 dolls dressed

← Eid prayers at the ruins of the Jama Masjid mosque, part of Feroz Shah Kotla

in traditional costumes from around India – each of these dolls has been meticulously crafted to ensure that every detail is completely correct. The museum also has an eclectic collection of dolls of famous people, among them Louis Armstrong, John Wayne and Henry VIII.

National Gandhi Museum

Q H5 **A** Jawaharlal Nehru Marg **M** Delhi Gate **C** 9:30am–5:30pm Tue–Sun **W** gandhimuseum.org

Just across the road from Raj Ghat *(p116)* is the National Gandhi Museum, which houses a small collection of exhibits about the life of Mahatma Gandhi, including photographs, press cuttings and some of his possessions. Among these are his spectacles, and the clothes and watch he was wearing when he was assassinated. The museum also displays one of the bullets that killed him.

A framed plaque on the stairs explains his simple philosophy: "Non-violence is the pitting of one's whole soul against the will of the tyrant… it is then possible for a single individual to defy the might of an unjust empire." The museum also contains a library and a bookshop. On Saturdays at 4pm, an hour-long documentary about Gandhi in English is shown.

Parsi Anjuman Hall

Q H6 **A** Bahadur Shah Zafar Marg, near Delhi Gate **C** (0) 9999211610 **M** Delhi Gate

Every night at 7pm the Parsi Anjuman Hall puts on a show of classical Indian dance. Beautifully choreographed, with colourful and lavish costumes, the two-hour show explores Delhi's fascinating and compelling history, and its continuing place as a seat of power. The performance is typically followed by a traditional Indian barbecue meal, served hot from the fire. It's the perfect place to discover the rich history of both classical Indian dance and of Delhi itself.

EAT

Basil & Thyme
This airy and stylish restaurant offers great European cuisine.

Q H10 **A** 28 Sundar Nagar Market **C** (011) 4378 7722

₹₹₹

Sazerac
A cosy USA-style diner serving up all-American classics alongside creative cocktails.

Q H10 **A** First floor, 21 Sundar Nagar **W** passcodehospitality.com/sazerac

₹₹₹

Nathu's Sweet Shop
Set up in 1939, this traditional shop sells a variety of delicious speciality sweets from across India.

Q H10 **A** 2 Sundar Nagar Market **W** nathusweets.com

₹₹₹

→ Mural illustrating the life of Gandhi, National Gandhi Museum

OLD DELHI

What is known as Old Delhi today was originally the Mughal capital of Shahjahanabad, built by Shah Jahan when he moved the imperial court here from Agra. Construction began in 1638, and ten years later the Red Fort, Jama Masjid, Chandni Chowk and the surrounding residential and mercantile quarters were ready for occupation. The city was surrounded by a rubble wall pierced by 14 gates of which three – Delhi, Turkman and Ajmeri – survive. An elegant, mannered lifestyle flourished, enriched by the courtiers and merchants, artists and poets who lived in the lanes and quarters, called *galis* and *katras*, of the walled city. In 1739, the Persian freebooter Nadir Shah came to plunder the city of Shahjahanabad and left a bleeding ruin behind him. The final death-blow was dealt when the British troops moved into the Red Fort after the 1857 War of Independence, turning it into a military garrison, while a railway line cut the walled city in half. Yet, the spirit of the place has survived these upheavals, and its busy *galis* continue to support a vibrant life. Modernity has brought a new urgency to the pace of the traditional traders who still live and operate from here.

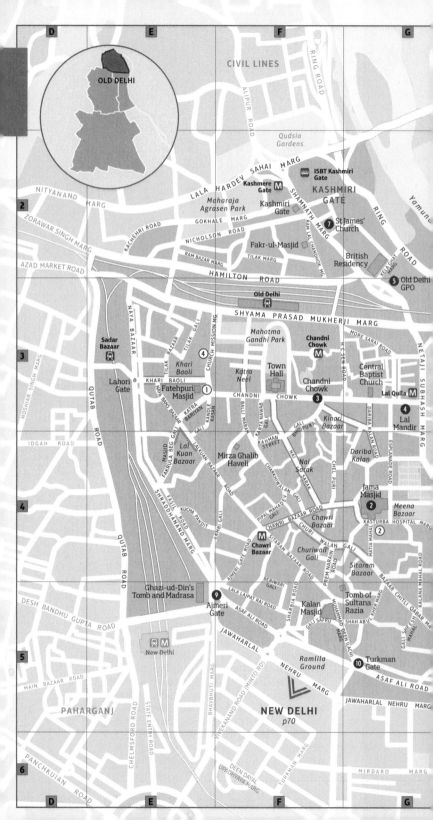

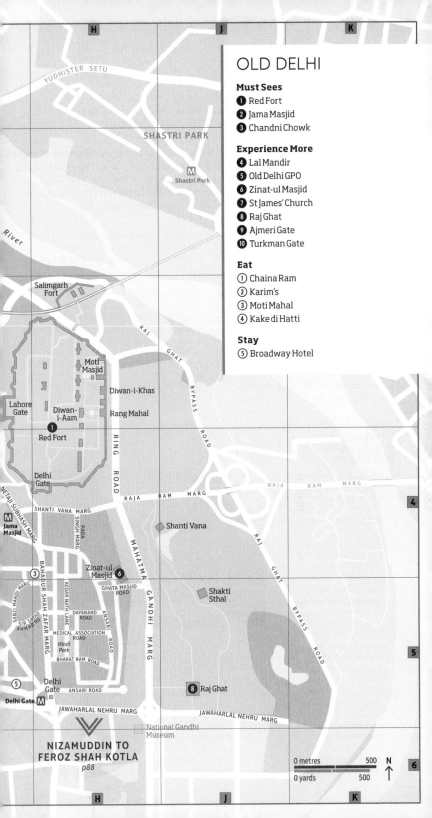

OLD DELHI

Must Sees
1 Red Fort
2 Jama Masjid
3 Chandni Chowk

Experience More
4 Lal Mandir
5 Old Delhi GPO
6 Zinat-ul Masjid
7 St James' Church
8 Raj Ghat
9 Ajmeri Gate
10 Turkman Gate

Eat
1 Chaina Ram
2 Karim's
3 Moti Mahal
4 Kake di Hatti

Stay
5 Broadway Hotel

YUDHISTER SETU

SHASTRI PARK

M Shastri Park

River

Salimgarh Fort

Moti Masjid

Diwan-i-Khas

Lahore Gate

Diwan-i-Aam

Rang Mahal

1 Red Fort

RING ROAD

RAJ GHAT BYPASS ROAD

Delhi Gate

RAJA RAM MARG

NETAJI SUBHASH MARG

SHANTI VANA MARG

M Jama Masjid

PADAM SINGH MARG

Shanti Vana

RAJA RAM MARG

RAJ GHAT BYPASS ROAD

4

BAHADUR SHAH ZAFAR MARG

SABZI MANDI MARG

3

SIR SYED AHMAD RD

KEDAR NATH LANE

DAYANAND ROAD

MEDICAL ASSOCIATION ROAD

Hindi Park

BHARAT RAM ROAD

ANSARI ROAD

Zinat-ul Masjid 6

GHATA MASJID ROAD

MAHATMA GANDHI MARG

Shakti Sthal

5

5 Delhi Gate

ANSARI ROAD

Delhi Gate M

JAWAHARLAL NEHRU MARG

8 Raj Ghat

JAWAHARLAL NEHRU MARG

National Gandhi Museum

NIZAMUDDIN TO FEROZ SHAH KOTLA
p88

0 metres 500
0 yards 500

N

6

H   J   K

❶ ✍ 🅜

RED FORT

📍H3 🅐Chandni Chowk Ⓜ️Lal Quila, Chandni Chowk 🕐Complex: sunrise-sunset
Tue-Sun; Son et Lumière: Feb-Apr, Sep & Oct: 8:30-9:30pm daily; Nov-Jan: 7:30-8:30pm
daily; May-Aug: 9-10pm daily 🚫Mon & public hols 🌐delhitourism.gov.in

Red sandstone battlements give this imperial citadel its name, Lal Qila, or Red Fort.
Commissioned by Shah Jahan in 1639, it took nine years to build and was the seat
of Mughal power until 1857, when the last Mughal emperor, Bahadur Shah Zafar,
was dethroned and exiled. It was here that the national flag was hoisted for the
first time when India became an independent nation on 15 August 1947.

One of Delhi's most famous and visited monuments, the Red Fort is iconic. Entry to the complex is through one of two main gates: the Delhi Gate and the Lahore Gate. The latter leads to the covered bazaar of Chatta Chowk, filled with paintings and trinkets. Beyond this lies the Naqqar Khana, a pavilion where ceremonial music was played.

Also found within the fort is the Diwan-i-Aam – a 60-pillared, red sandstone hall, where the emperor gave audiences to the public beneath the lavishly carved stone canopy – and the Rang Mahal, which has a lovely lotus-shaped marble fountain inside its gilded chambers. Don't miss the spectacular Khas Mahal, the emperor's royal apartments, or the Tosh Khana (Robe Room), with its superb marble *jali* screen carved with the scales of justice (a motif seen in many miniature paintings). One of the Red Fort's most impressive sights, the Diwan-i-Khas is constructed completely of white marble. The walls and pillars of this exclusive pavilion, where the emperor met his most trusted nobles, were once inlaid with gems. Close by lie the Hamams (Royal Baths), with inlaid marble floors and three enclosures. The first chamber provided hot vapour, the second scented rosewater, and the third cold water. To the west of the baths is the elegant Moti Masjid (Pearl Mosque), built in 1659.

THE LAST OF THE MUGHAL EMPERORS

The majestic Red Fort was the seat of power of the Mughal empire until its fall in 1857. William Dalrymple tells the tale of the empire's final days in *The Last Mughal,* a beautifully written history of Delhi under Bahadur Shah Zafar II. A gifted poet and calligrapher, Bahadur reluctantly took on the mantle of the King of India just as the Mughal empire was failing. His reign culminated in the ultimately tragic Siege of Delhi, one of the bloodiest uprisings in India's history. The book is a fantastic and gory read, offering valuable insight into the Mughal world.

↑ The battlements of the Delhi Gate, one of the fort's main gateways

→ Brass relief of a figure riding an elephant on one of the Red Fort's doors at the Delhi Gate

⬛ PICTURE PERFECT
Pretty Pillars

Every angle provides a great photo op in the Diwan-i-Aam, the majestic reception hall of the Red Fort. Head there late afternoon for exquisitely sculpted archways and long languid shadows.

↑ The intricately carved red sandstone arches of the Diwan-i-Aam

JAMA MASJID

G4 **Off Netaji Subhash Marg** **Chawri Bazaar, Jama Masjid**
Sunrise–sunset daily **To visitors during prayer hours**

Built on the orders of the Emperor Shah Jahan, the architecturally eager Mughal ruler whose other famous commission was the Taj Mahal, this grand mosque took six years and a force of 5,000 workers to construct. It is an imposing sight, with three large black-and-white marble domes and towering twin minarets framing its great central arch. Completed in 1656, what turned out to be the emperor's final architectural flourish is still considered to be India's largest mosque.

Did You Know?

It took a whopping million rupees to build the Jama Masjid.

Perched on top of a hillock, the Jama Masjid was also given the name Masjid e Jahan Numa, suitably meaning "mosque with a view of the world". A magnificent flight of sandstone steps leads to the arched entrances of the mosque (also known as the Friday Mosque). Entry can made through either of the north, south or east gates. The mosque's huge square courtyard can accommodate up to 25,000 devotees at the communal Friday prayer sessions and at Eid, when a sea of worshippers fills out the vast space. The south minaret is a popular with visitors for its great views; however the 120 steps leading to the top are narrow and can get crowded.

Ensure that you cover up appropriately before attempting to enter, and remove your shoes (unofficial "shoe minders" will offer look after them for a fee).

TOP 5 ARCHITECTURE FEATURES

Foundation stone
This was laid on Friday 6 October 1650.

Sundials
Two in the central court-yard show prayer times.

Central arch
Inscribed on the central arch are the words "Ya-Hadi" (one who shows the right path).

Motifs
The mosque is decorated with a lotus flower motif.

Domes
Three domes in black-and-white marble strips adorned with gold top the mosque.

Strolling through the ↑ courtyard before the main façade of Jama Masjid

Panoramic view across Delhi from the Jama Masjid's south minaret

GREAT VIEW
South Minaret

The south minaret has one of the best views in the city – visitors are rewarded with a panoramic look over both the new and old cities of Delhi. Particularly worth spotting are Connaught Place, Parliament, and the Jama Masjid itself.

High cusped arches above the mosque's prayer hall

→

The lively Chandni Chowk, filled with cycle rickshaws and motorbikes

3

CHANDNI CHOWK

Ⓟ F3 **Ⓜ Chandi Chowk**

This bustling street lies at the heart of Old Delhi. Lined with colourful stalls and sacred shrines, and crammed full of rickshaws and bicycles, it is a constant hub of activity. Spiralling off from this thoroughfare are narrow lanes which open up onto treasure-filled bazaars.

EAT

Chaina Ram
This traditional sweet shop sells the absolute best *halwa* in Delhi.

**Ⓟ E3 Ⓐ 6499
Fatehpuri Chowk
Ⓒ (011) 2395 0747**

The now frenetic Chandni Chowk was once the most elegant boulevard of the 17th-century city of Shahjahanabad *(p135)*. It gets its name ("moonlight place") from a pool found here during Mughal times that was said to reflect the glowing light of the moon. This wide avenue, extending from the Red Fort *(p108)* to Fatehpuri Masjid, is bordered by stalls, restaurants and religious places of worship.

Surrounding Chandni Chowk are a number of maze-like alleyways and streets, each peppered with street food stalls and historic eateries beloved by locals. The area is also home to the city's legendary bazaars, which offer an astounding variety of goods. Here, wares spill out onto the pavement and the air is filled with the sound of vigorous haggling. Just off Kinari Bazaar, keep an eye out for Naughara Gali, a narrow alley containing nine colourfully painted 18th-century Jain *havelis* (mansions) and a Jain temple. Nearby is the restored Haveli Dharampura, now a luxury hotel with a rooftop restaurant *(p30)*.

Dariba Kalan

Delhi's oldest market for gems and jewellery, Dariba Kalan is a glittering lane where artisans have worked for over two centuries. Here, twinkling shops overflow with delicate gold necklaces and sparkling silver bangles. During Shah Jahn's time, ladies of the court would come here to buy their jewels.

Nai Sarak

Bursting with books, Nai Sarak is packed with a huge variety of secondhand titles; the market is very popular among students, as school and college textbooks are sold on this street. There are also a number of stationery stores.

Paranthe Wali Gali

Found close to Nai Sarak, this little winding alley has three parathawalas, each with their own regular clientele, and each selling freshly cooked parathas stuffed with a variety of fresh veggies.

Khari Baoli

◄ Colourful mounds of nose-tingling spices line the steet at Khari Baoli, Asia's biggest spice market. Dating back to the 17th century, the market derives its name from a stepwell that no longer exists. Alongside sacks full of spices like cinnamon, cumin, tumeric and cardamon, are bowls of dried fruit, piles of nuts, and bags of rice.

Churiwali Gali

Popularly called the "lane of bangle-sellers", Churiwali Gali has garlands upon garlands of glass bangles strung along rods to match every sari or *lehenga* (long skirt).

Katra Neel

Straddling a narrow lane, Katra Neel is reminiscent of Middle Eastern *souks*. At this market, tiny shops sell a wide variety of textiles, such as brocades from Varanasi, silk, cotton and voile.

Kinari Bazaar

▶ This market specializes in tinsel accessories, and attracts many wedding shoppers.

Chawri Bazaar

This bazaar has every conceivable variety of paper, plus brass and copper items.

> **Here, wares spill out onto the pavement and the air is filled with the sound of vigorous haggling.**

↑ Chandni Chowk, lined with bustling stalls, in the early evening

EXPERIENCE MORE

 4

Lal Mandir

📍 G3 🏠 Netaji Subhash Marg, Chandni Chowk Ⓜ Lal Quila, Chandni Chowk ⏰ Summer: 5:30–11:30am & 6–9:30pm daily; winter: 6am–noon & 5:30–9pm

Delhi's most important Jain temple, Lal Mandir is located

directly opposite the Red Fort, at the southern end of Chandni Chowk. Founded under Shah Jahan for the Jain soldiers in his army, the present building dates from the 1870s. The colourful interior is adorned with dozens of diminutive statues of Jain *tirthankaras* (spiritual leaders). The temple's well-known bird hospital, the Charity Birds Hospital, stands next door, caring for hundreds of hungry and injured pigeons and other birds.

 5

Old Delhi GPO

📍 G3 🏠 Lothian Rd (Netaji Subhash Marg) Ⓜ Kashmiri Gate ⏰ 10am–6pm Mon–Fri, 10am–5pm Sat

To the south of Kashmiri Gate is the Old Delhi General Post Office, an old fashioned establishment caught in a time warp. This stucco-fronted

colonial edifice is significant because it faces a traffic island on which stand two structures dating to the War of Independence of 1857. The Telegraph Memorial is a memorial obelisk dedicated to the officers of the Telegraph Department. The inscription on it honours the telegraph operators Brendish and Pilkington who flashed news of the Indian rebellion to the British garrison at Ambala. Nearby lies the ruined British Magazine. It was blown up by a Captain Willoughby on 11 May 1857 to prevent it from falling into the hands of the rebelling sepoys.

 6

Zinat-ul Masjid

📍 H4 🏠 Ansari Rd, Daryaganj Ⓜ Delhi Gate ⏰ 7am–5pm daily

This mosque was built in 1707 by Princess Zinat-un-Nissa

> # STAY
>
> **Hotel Broadway**
> Comfortably old-fashioned and handy for both Old and New Delhi, with a restaurant serving Kashmiri food.
>
> 📍 G5 🏠 4/15A Asaf Ali Road 🌐 hotel broadwaydelhi.com
>
> ₹ ₹ ₹

The distinctive towers of Lal Mandir, rising above Old Delhi's bustling streets

Begum, one of Emperor Aurangzeb's daughters. The gracefully proportioned red sandstone mosque features a spacious courtyard built over a series of basement rooms. Its impressive seven-arched prayer hall is surmounted by three domes, each with alternating stripes of black and white marble. The locals who worship here have a more lyrical name for this structure, the Ghata ("Cloud") Mosque, because its striped domes simulate the monsoon sky.

7

St James' Church

Q F2 **Ω** Lothian Rd (Netaji Subhash Marg) **M** Kashmiri Gate **C** 9:30am-12:45pm & 2:30-4:30pm daily; services: 9am Sun **W** stjameschurchdelhi.com

A tablet in the church founded by Colonel James Skinner and

JAMES SKINNER

One of the British empire's most famed mercenaries, Skinner was the son of a Scotsman and a Rajput. Rejected by the British Army because of his mixed parentage, he raised his own cavalry regiment, Skinner's Horse, whose flamboyant yellow uniforms gave rise to the name Yellow Boys. His troops fought with distinction and are still part of the Indian Army. On his death he was honoured as a Commander of the Order of the Bath. His descendants still live on an estate in Mussoorie, Uttar Pradesh.

completed in 1836 explains: "This church is erected at the sole expense of Colonel James Skinner" in fulfilment of a vow he had made on the battlefield when he was badly wounded. Built at the cost of Rs 80,000, the church (now the oldest in Delhi) is in Renaissance-Revival style and matches the shape of a Greek cross, surmounted

by an imposing eight-leafed dome. The two elaborate stained-glass windows were installed in the 1860s. Skinner died at Hansi *(p165)* in 1841. A marble tablet, in front of the altar, marks the location of his simple grave.

The 19th-century St James' Church, and *(inset)* a choir performing during a service

→

The black granite platform at Raj Ghat, a memorial to Mahatma Gandhi

EAT

Karim's

This is the place to come for kebabs, grills and mutton curries.

 G4 🏠 16 Gali Kababian, near Jama Masjid 🌐 karim hotels.com

₹₹₹

Moti Mahal

This venerable spot claims to have invented the butter chicken.

📍 G4 🏠 3703 Netaji Subhash Marg, Daryaganj 📞 (011) 2327 3661

₹₹₹

Kake di Hatti

This place draws flocks of locals to mop up its legendary dal makhni.

 E3 🏠 654 Church Mission Rd, Fatehpuri, Chandni Chowk 📞 (0) 99107 22254

₹₹₹

❽
Raj Ghat

📍 J5 🏠 Mahatma Gandhi Rd 🚇 Delhi Gate 🕐 6am-7pm daily (prayer meetings 5pm Fri)

Raj Ghat, the most revered symbol of Indian nationalism, is the site of Mahatma Gandhi's cremation. A sombre black granite platform inscribed with his last words *Hey Ram* ("Oh God") now stands here, surrounded by a tranquil garden. The only splash of colour comes from the bright garlands of orange marigolds draped over this simple monument. Visiting devotees sing *bhajans* (spiritual songs), and the steady beat of *dholak* drums lends the scene a dolorous melancholy.

All visiting heads of state are taken to this *samadhi* ("memorial") to pay their respects and lay wreaths in memory of the "Father of the Nation". On Gandhi's birthday (2 Oct) and death anniversary (30 Jan), the nation's leaders congregate at Raj Ghat for prayer meetings.

The National Gandhi Museum *(p103)*, crammed with memorabilia connected with the Mahatma's life, including his letters and diaries, is located nearby on Jawaharlal Nehru Marg.

❾
Ajmeri Gate

📍 F5 🏠 Ajmeri Gate Rd 🚇 New Delhi

This is one of the 14 gates that once encircled Shahjahanabad, the seventh city of Delhi. Having survived more than 300 years, it now stands in the midst of the city's congested commercial centre. Diagonally opposite Ajmeri Gate is Ghazi-ud-Din's Tomb and Madrasa. Ghazi-ud-Din Khan was an eminent courtier during the reign of the sixth Mughal emperor Aurangzeb, and his son, Mir Qamar-ud-Din, established the dynasty that was to rule the southern state of Hyderabad until independence in 1947.

The imposing red sandstone *madrasa* has several arcades and a mosque on its western side. Founded in the late 17th century, this was at one time Delhi's foremost *madrasa* and after 1824 came to be known as the Anglo-Arabic School.

Husain College, was also located on the premises.

A cycle rickshaw from Ajmeri Gate will take you past tiny shops to the teeming lanes of Lal Kuan Bazaar where the Zinat Mahal is situated. Built in 1846, this was the eponymous home of the favourite wife of the last Mughal emperor Bahadur Shah Zafar. Today, it houses a school, lawyers' offices and shops. The original façade was wonderfully carved and arcaded with an oriel window. The beautiful verse by Bahadur Shah Zafar that was inscribed over the arched gateway can still be seen.

English classes were held here, and British teachers also introduced mathematics and science texts to students, which were then translated into Urdu. Ghazi-ud-Din's grave is in a marble enclosure at the mosque's southern end. Athough this complex is surrounded by today's urban congestion, it still performs the noble function it was meant to. The three-domed mosque is in regular use and students crisscross the courtyard, while striped towels hang from the hostel balconies where glorious silks may once have billowed. Until recently, the esteemed Delhi College, now the Zakir

Turkman Gate

G5 **Asaf Ali Rd**
New Delhi, Delhi Gate

The solid, square-shaped, red sandstone Turkman Gate stands in splendid isolation among the modern high-rise buildings of busy Asaf Ali Road. It marked the southern boundary of Shahjahanabad and was named after a Muslim *pir*, Hazrat Shah Turkman Bayabani, whose 13th-century tomb and dargah stand to the east. The serpentine lanes behind the gateway are home to two medieval monuments. Kalan Masjid ("black mosque"), in the Bulbulekhan area, was

RAZIA SULTAN

The ruler of the Delhi sultanate from 1236, Razia Sultan was India's only female monarch until Queen Victoria. Loved by the people, she was hated by the aristocracy, who resented being ruled by a woman. During her brief reign she established schools and public libraries, minted coins and wore men's clothes. Overthrown after a reign of only four years, she was killed at Karnal in 1240 while fleeing from Delhi. The tomb next to hers is thought to be her sister's.

built in 1387 by Khan-i-Jahan Junan Shah, Feroz Shah Tughlaq's prime minister. This is one of the seven mosques he built in Delhi; the others are at Khirkee (*p136*) and Begumpuri (*p133*). A short walk away, at the end of an alley off Sitaram Bazaar Road, lies what is believed to be the grave of Razia Sultan, Delhi's only medieval female ruler. Her plain rubble-stone grave lies open to the sky in a cramped enclosure amidst houses and shops.

The artist studios and workshops of the last practising craftsman of Delhi's blue pottery, Hazarilal, are situated in the bustling and congested alleys of Hauz Suiwalan, located behind Turkman Gate.

↑ The impressive red-sandstone façade of Turkman Gate, once the southern gate of Shahjahanabad

A SHORT WALK
CHANDNI CHOWK

Distance 2 km (1 mile) **Nearest Metro** Chandni Chowk
Time 30 minutes

Once the most elegant boulevard in the Mughal capital of
Shahjahanabad, Chandni Chowk ("Moonlit Square"), laid out
in 1648, had a canal running through it, and was lined with
grand shops and mansions. Today, Chandni Chowk is the
heart of Old Delhi, which built up around it. It is a bustling
area where religious and commercial activity mix easily.
At the entrance to Chandni Chowk is the Digambar Jain
Temple. Built in 1656, it is the first of many shrines along
the boulevard's length.

*There is a box for
donations at the
Bird Hospital.*

Sunehri Masjid
*("Golden Mosque"),
built in 1722, is
famous for its three
gilt domes. On 22
March 1739, Persian
invader Shah Nadir
stood on its roof
as Delhi's citizens
were massacred.*

*In 1675, Guru Tegh
Bahadur, the ninth Sikh
guru, was beheaded at
Sisganj Gurdwara.*

*Old Famous
Jalebi Wala (p40)*

START

CHANDNI CHOWK

KINARI BAZAAR

DARIBA KALAN

*Tightly packed stalls in
Kinari Bazaar sell all
manner of glittering gold
and silver trimmings, such as
braids, tinsel garlands and
turbans for festivals.*

CHEL PURI

BAZAAR GULIYAN

Shiv Temple

← A bustling street filled
with people and rickshaws,
just off Chandni Chowk

Old Delhi's iconic Jama Masjid, filled with visitors and the devoted

Locator Map
For more detail see p106

Chandni Chowk

OLD DELHI

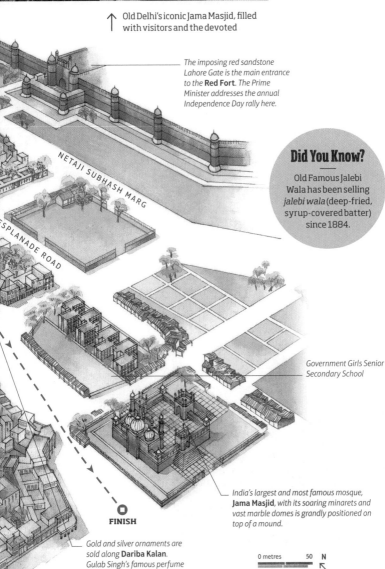

The imposing red sandstone Lahore Gate is the main entrance to the **Red Fort**. *The Prime Minister addresses the annual Independence Day rally here.*

NETAJI SUBHASH MARG

ESPLANADE ROAD

Did You Know?

Old Famous Jalebi Wala has been selling *jalebi wala* (deep-fried, syrup-covered batter) since 1884.

Government Girls Senior Secondary School

India's largest and most famous mosque, **Jama Masjid**, *with its soaring minarets and vast marble domes is grandly positioned on top of a mound.*

FINISH

Gold and silver ornaments are sold along **Dariba Kalan**. *Gulab Singh's famous perfume shop is located here.*

0 metres   50
0 yards   50

N

A SHORT WALK
AROUND KASHMIRI GATE

Distance 0.65 km (0.4 miles) **Nearest Metro**
Kashmiri Gate **Time** 15 minutes

Kashmiri Gate is the northern entrance to the historic
city of Shahjahanabad (Old Delhi). The area surrounding it resonates with memories of the 1857 War of
Independence. Many of the dramatic events between
May and September took place on the short stretch
between Kashmiri Gate and the Old Delhi GPO (p114).
In the 1920s, this area was also a favourite watering
hole of the British residents living in nearby Civil Lines,
and was home to grand shops and restaurants.

Did You Know?

The Mughals used to
set off from Kashmiri
Gate to spend the
summer in Kashmir –
hence its name.

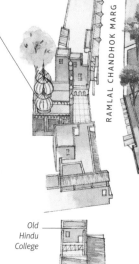

*The grand old shops
of the Raj era are now
shabby and derelict.*

START

During the 1857 War of Independence,
Kashmiri Gate *was the scene
of a bitter battle – a plaque on the
western side of the gate honours
"the engineers and miners who died
while clearing the gate for British
forces on September 14, 1857".*

NICHOLSON RD

The domes and minarets of **Fakr-ul-
Masjid**, *a small mosque, rise above
the rows of shops and offices along
this busy street. Local residents
come here to worship every Friday.*

RAMLAL CHANDHOK MARG

*Old
Hindu
College*

↑ The crumbling red sandstone Kashmiri Gate, once
the northernmost entrance to Shahjahanabad

↑ The impressive yellow-and-white St James' Church, founded by Colonel James Skinner

Locator Map
For more detail see p106

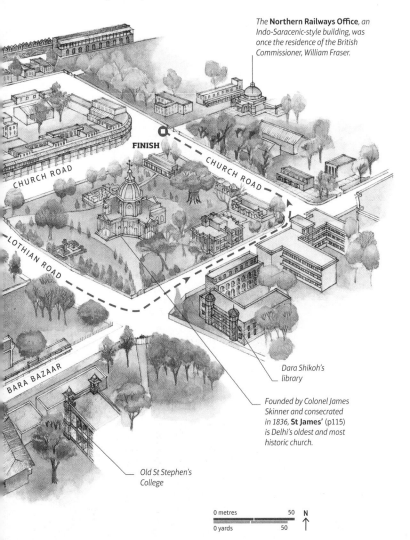

The **Northern Railways Office**, an Indo-Saracenic-style building, was once the residence of the British Commissioner, William Fraser.

FINISH

CHURCH ROAD

CHURCH ROAD

LOTHIAN ROAD

BARA BAZAAR

Dara Shikoh's library

*Founded by Colonel James Skinner and consecrated in 1836, **St James'** (p115) is Delhi's oldest and most historic church.*

Old St Stephen's College

0 metres 50
0 yards 50

N ↑

SOUTH DELHI

The history of South Delhi has been one of gradual expansion: here, multiple adjoining cities were built over hundreds of years by successive rulers. Lal Kot, a fort established by the Tomar Rajputs in 1060, was the first of these cities. In the 12th century the fort came briefly under the control of the Tomars' rivals, the Chauhans of Ajmer, who renamed it Qila Rai Pithora, before it was conquered by the Afghan ruler, Muhammad of Ghur. To celebrate this victory and the advent of Muslim rule, Muhammad's general, Qutbuddin Aibak, built the magnificent Qutb Minar complex here in 1193. Successive Sultanate dynasties also added to the Qutb Minar, as well as building their own fortified outposts surrounding it, first at Siri, and then at Tughlaqabad and Jahanpanah. South Delhi grew again during the 14th century when two further Sultanate rulers, Muhammad bin Tughlag and Feroz Shah, established walled villages at Chiragh Delhi and Kirkee. Following first the building of New Delhi, and then particularly after Indian independence, these historic villages and ancient cities were absorbed by Delhi's ever-expanding residential areas.

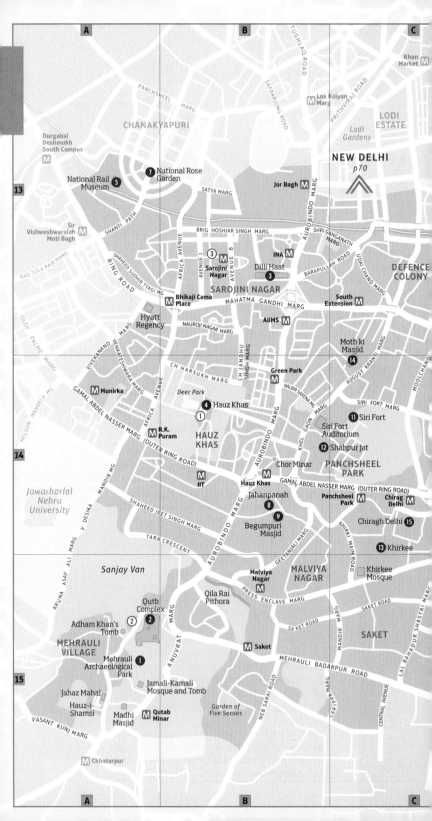

SOUTH DELHI

Must Sees
1. Mehrauli Archaeological Park
2. Qutb Complex

Experience More
3. Dilli Haat
4. Hauz Khas
5. National Rail Museum
6. Delhi Dance Academy
7. National Rose Garden
8. Jahanpanah
9. Begumpuri Masjid
10. Tughlaqabad Fort
11. Siri Fort
12. Shahpur Jat
13. Khirkee
14. Moth ki Masjid
15. Chiragh Delhi
16. Baha'i House of Worship
17. Ashoka's Rock Edict
18. Kalkaji Temple

Drink
1. Kunzum Travel Café
2. Olive Bar & Kitchen

Shop
3. Sarojini Nagar Market
4. Saahra
5. Fab India

❶

MEHRAULI ARCHAEOLOGICAL PARK

📍A15 🚌Anuvrat Marg, Mehrauli Ⓜ️Qutab Minar 🕐Sunrise-sunset daily
ℹ️Conservation Assistant's Office; www.delhitourism.gov.in

Surrounded by lush forest, the Mehrauli Archaeological Park is a
spectacular collection of ancient ruins, imposing tombs and striking
stepwells. There are over 400 historic buildings scattered throughout
this expansive park, which span the Sultanate, Mughal and British periods.

Now the most historically rich area in Delhi, Mehrauli was established as an archaeological park in 1997. The earliest buildings here date from the Rajput era, although more significant buildings are from the 12th century, when this area was the centre of the Delhi Sultanate, a kingdom founded by Qutbuddin Aibak who also started building the neighbouring Qutb Minar (p128). Later, Mughal princes came here to hunt, and they also built tombs and shrines in the area. During the British Raj in the 19th century, British officials built weekend houses in Mehrauli, attracted by its orchards, ponds and game. Now a popular place for an evening stroll, Mehrauli can also be explored on a guided walking tour.

The spectacular Jamali-Kamali Mosque and Tomb surrounded by trees ↑

METCALFE'S FOLLY

Mehrauli witnessed one of the stranger episodes in Anglo-Indian history when Sir Thomas Metcalfe (1795–1853), British Resident at the Mughal Court, decided to establish a summer residence in the area. Rather than build a new house, Metcalfe made the decision to convert the tomb of Quli Khan into an English-style country residence, which he christened Dilkusha (Heart's Delight), although it is generally known as Metcalfe's Folly. He also built a string of Indian-style follies around it. As fate would have it, Metcalfe's love of all things Mughal did him little good: he died slowly, allegedly poisoned by one of the emperor's queens.

Jahaz Mahal

Venue of the Phoolwalon ki Sair (a colourful flower procession), this square pleasure pavilion, built during the Lodi era (1451–1526), seems to float on the Hauz-Shamsi tank, a reservoir built in the 11th century.

Madhi Masjid

▶ Surrounded by bastions and a high wall, this fortress-like mosque, dating back to 1200, has a large open courtyard and a three-arched, heavily ornamented prayer hall.

Dargah Qutb Sahib

Both the 13th-century dargah of Sufi saint Qutbuddin Bakhtiyar and the nearby Moti Masjid ("Pearl Mosque") attract many pilgrims.

Jamali-Kamali Mosque and Tomb

◀ The tomb of Jamali (the court poet during the late Lodi and early Mughal age) is inscribed with some of his verses. Its well-preserved interior has coloured tiles and richly decorated painted plasterwork.

Balban's Tomb

The 13th-century tomb of Balban, Qutbuddin's successor, lies in a square rubble-built chamber.

Rajon ki Baoli

This dramatic three storeyed stepwell is also known as Sukhi Baoli (dry well). Nearby is the five-storeyed Gandhak ki Baoli, named after its strong sulphur (*gandhak*) smell. These *baolis* once supplied fresh water to the area.

Adham Khan's Tomb

▶ The son of Emperor Akbar's wet nurse, Adham Khan murdered a rival and was executed by the emperor for his crime. Akbar later built this large tomb for mother and son.

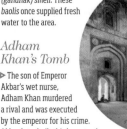

Did You Know?

The Iron Pillar next to the Qutb Minar grants wishes – if you can get your arms around it backwards.

The towering Qutb Minar, soaring high above the surrounding ruins ↑

② 🚴 Ⓜ 🍴

QUTB COMPLEX

🔵 A15 ⌂ Mehrauli, Delhi-Gurugram Rd Ⓜ Qutab Minar
🕐 Sunrise–sunset daily 🌐 delhitourism.gov.in

One of the most spectacular sites in Delhi, the Qutb Complex houses a number of historical buildings, including the city's oldest mosque. It is, however, most famous for the Qutb Minar, an impressive sandstone-and-marble minaret standing 73 m (240 ft) high, a monument to Islamic victory in Delhi.

Qutbuddin Aibak, founder of the Delhi Sultanate, started to build the Qutb Complex in the late 12th century to celebrate his victory over Delhi's last Hindu kingdom. The two main structures of the complex are the Quwwat-ul-Islam ("Might of Islam") Mosque and the Qutb Minar, which were built using elements of razed temples that had previously stood here.

The mosque is a fusion of decorative Hindu panels from the destroyed temples, and Islamic domes and arches. The Qutb Minar, also known as Victory Tower, is a five-storey monument that was completed in the reign of Aibak's successor, Iltutmish. Other Mughal emperors continued to add more structures to the area. One such building is Alai Darwaza, the complex's gateway, erected in 1311 by the emperor Khilji, which established a new Islamic architectural style, marked by arches and panels carved with verses from the Qur'an.

↑ Intricate wall carvings at the complex

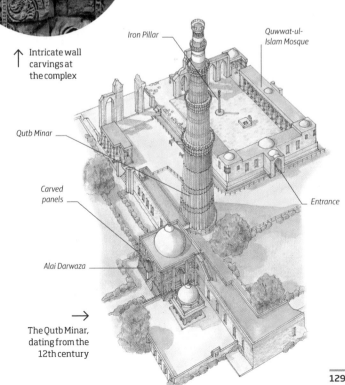

Iron Pillar

Quwwat-ul-Islam Mosque

Qutb Minar

Carved panels

Entrance

Alai Darwaza

→ The Qutb Minar, dating from the 12th century

↑ Textiles stalls under a colourful tent at Dilli Haat market

EXPERIENCE MORE

3

Dilli Haat

📍B13 🚇Laxmi Bai Nagar, Aurobindo Marg 🚇INA
🕐11am–10pm daily 🌐delhi tourism.gov.in

This lively bazaar retains all the trappings of a traditional Indian village market, with acres of landscaped gardens, handicraft shops and regional food stalls. Everything you can imagine can be found at Dilli Haat – ready-made garments, spices, bags, brass artifacts, jewellery, shawls, pottery and much more.

There are about 17 food stalls, each representing a different state in India. Run by their respective tourism authorities, the stalls offer delicious authentic dishes from distant and diverse regions, such as Tamil Nadu, Manipur and Kashmir. If you are lucky, you may even experience a state-organized cultural event, complete with puppet shows, dances, regional cuisine, paintings and a lot of shopping. Often, themed bazaars are organized during festivals, such as Teej, Diwali and the Mango festival (*p55*).

4

Hauz Khas

📍B14 🚇W of Aurobindo Marg 🚇Hauz Khas

Once the site of Delhi's oldest university (*madrasa*), Hauz Khas village is a vibrant, easy-to-navigate area. There are gems like the Delhi Art Gallery, housing modern art from across India, and restaurants celebrating global tastes, from Italy to the Middle East. The area's tree-shaded deer park comes alive in the early morning and at sunset with joggers, yogis and drum circles, while its peaceful lake is popular for a relaxed evening stroll.

The village has many medieval monuments from Feroz Shah Tughlaq's reign, including the double-storeyed *madrasa*, built so that the tank and lower storey were at the same level, while the upper floor was at ground level. The low domes, colonnades and *jharokhas* (an enclosed, over-hanging balcony) relieve the severity of its façade, while plaster carvings and deep niches for books embellish the interior. The tomb of Feroz Shah lies at one end of the

madrasa. Wine-red painted plaster calligraphy decorates the interior of the austere tomb. The complex is best viewed in the afternoon when sunlight filters through the *jalis* carved into the linteled archway, covering the graves of the sultan, his sons and grandson with delicate star-shaped shadows.

FEROZ SHAH TUGHLAQ'S BUILDING PROGRAMME

Feroz Shah Tughlaq (r 1351–88) was responsible for the most ambitious building programme of any of the Delhi sultans. Contemporary accounts claim that he ordered the construction of 30 Qur'anic schools, 40 mosques, 50 dams, 100 towns and 150 bridges. His constructions include a number of the buildings around Alauddin Khilji's tank at Hauz Khas, as well as the fifth city of Delhi, Feroz Shah Kotla (*p102*).

East of Hauz Khas, off Aurobindo Marg, is a small rubble-built tapering structure called Chor Minar ("tower of thieves"). This dates to the 14th-century Khilji period and its walls, pockmarked with holes, are said to have held the severed heads of thieves to deter others from crime. Close by, to the northwest, is the Nili Masjid ("blue mosque"), named after the blue tiles above its *chhajja*. Nearby is an Idgah, whose remaining long wall is carved with 11 mihrabs and an inscription proclaiming that it was built in 1404–5 by Iqbal Khan, a Tughlaq noble.

National Rail Museum

📍 A13 📌 Shanti Path, Chanakyapuri Ⓜ INA ⏰ 10am–5pm Tue–Sun 🚫 Public hols 🌐 nrm india.com

India's extensive railway network gives rise to astonishing statistics. It has a route length of 65,436 km (40,660 miles) and tracks that cover about 115,000 km (71,458 miles). There are around 7,150 stations, 12,617 passenger trains and 7,421 goods trains that run every day. As many as 23 million passengers travel by train each day.

This museum encapsulates the history of Indian railways. Steam locomotive enthusiasts will appreciate the collection that traces the development of the Indian railways from 1849, when the first 34 km (21 miles) of railway between Bombay (now Mumbai) and Kalyan was planned. Items on display include the skull of an elephant which collided with a mail train at Golkara in 1894, and a realistic model of an 1868 first-class passenger coach with separate compartments for accompanying servants. Outside, are several retired steam locomotives built in Glasgow, Manchester and Darlington in the late 19th century, and the splendid salon that carried the Prince of Wales (later King Edward VII) on his travels during the 1876 Royal Durbar.

A "toy train" offers rides around the compound.

DRINK

Kunzum Travel Café
A pay-what-you-feel café where people can hang out, read the books and magazines littered about the place, and use the free Wi-Fi.

📍 B14 📌 T-49, Hauz Khas Village 🌐 kunzum. com/travelcafe

Olive Bar and Kitchen
Housed in an old *haveli*, this pretty spot has an airy courtyard and the Qutb Minar as a backdrop. The food, mainly Mediterranean and Indian, is delicious, too.

📍 A15 📌 One Style Mile, Haveli 6, Mehrauli 🌐 olivebarand kitchen.com

Steam train outside the National Rail Museum, and *(inset)* a 19th-century locomotive ↓

6 Delhi Dance Academy

 C14 ⚐ E-238/239, Amar Colony, Lajpat Nagar 4 Ⓜ Kailash Colony ⏰ 6am–9pm daily 🌐 delhidance academy.in

The Delhi Dance Academy offers workshops and classes for both adults and children. A lot of Delhiites come here to keep fit, but most foreign visitors come to learn some Bollywood-style dance moves. It is possible to take part in group classes, or to have individual tuition.

7 National Rose Garden

⚐ A13 ⚐ Satya Marg, Chanakyapuri Ⓜ Dhaula Kuan ⏰ 8am–5:30pm daily

Situated in Delhi's diplomatic enclave, the National Rose

↑ Strolling among colourful blooms in the National Rose Garden

Garden, also known as the National Indo-Africa Friendship Rose Garden, doesn't just look lovely – it smells lovely, too. The garden is home to myriad rose varieties from both India and abroad, including green and black roses. And in case the vibrant rose bushes aren't a strong enough draw, there are other flowers too, plus a cohort of busy butterflies to add even more colour. The garden is at its best around the turn of the year.

8 Jahanpanah

⚐ B14 ⚐ S of Panchsheel Park Ⓜ Hauz Khas

Delhi's fourth city was built by Muhammad bin Tuglaq as his capital. At its heart lies Begumpuri Masjid. Nearby, to the north, is the palace of Bijay Mandal, a derelict, brooding octagonal structure rising from a high plinth. It is worth climbing the broken stone-cut stairs to the upper platform to get a sense of its size. According to the famed 14th-century Arab traveller Ibn Batuta, it was from these very bastions that Muhammad bin Tughlaq held public audience and reviewed his troops. Later, in the early 16th century, the palace is believed to have been used as a residence by Sheikh Hasan Tahir, a much revered saint who visited Delhi during the reign of Sikandar Lodi. Panoramic views of the city of Delhi, extending from the Qutb Minar to Humayun's Tomb and beyond, can be seen from its upper platform.

 TOP 5 BOLLYWOOD DANCE FILMS

ABCD: Any Body Can Dance (2013)
Featuring contestants from the TV show *Dance India Dance*.

Kalpana (1948)
A classical dancer struggles to open an academy.

Naache Mayuri (1986)
The true story of a dancer who loses a leg in an accident.

Taal (1999)
Aishwarya Rai in some of her greatest and most famous dance scenes.

Dil Se (1998)
Not strictly speaking a dance film, but famous for its classic dance scene filmed on the roof of a moving train.

The dramatic ruins of the monumental 14th-century Tughlaqabad Fort ↑

9
Begumpuri Masjid

📍 B14 🏠 Begumpur, off Guru Govind Singh Road Ⓜ Hauz Khas 🕐 Sunrise-sunset daily

Built by Khan-i-Jahan Junan Shah, Begumpuri Masjid is the finest of the Sultanate-era mosques in the city, and a perfect example of the austere, monumental style favoured by the Tughlaq dynasty. With its huge, thick walls, the mosque appears almost fortress-like, raised high above the surrounding streets. At its entrance, a single doorway opens onto a flight of stairs leading to a vast courtyard, where arched cloisters are topped by 44 domes. The mosque's prayer hall has 24 arched openings, the central one surmounted by a large dome. When asking for directions, ask specifically for the old mosque, as a new one is located nearby.

10
Tughlaqabad Fort

📍 D15 🏠 Off Mehrauli-Badarpur Rd Ⓜ Govind Puri 🕐 7am–5pm daily

This spectacular fortress, built by Ghiyasuddin Tughlaq in the 14th century, was completed in just four years. It was so sturdy that the rubble-built walls clinging to the shape of the hill survive intact all along the 6.5 km (4 mile) perimeter. To the right of the main entrance is the citadel from which rise the ruins of the Vijay Mandal ("tower of victory"). To the left is a rectangular area where arches are all that remain of a complex of palaces and halls. Beyond these, houses were once laid out in a neat grid pattern. Legend has it that when Ghiyasuddin tried to prevent the building of the *baoli* at Hazrat Nizamuddin Auliya's dargah (*p98*), the saint cursed him by saying that one day only jackals and the Gujjar community would inhabit his capital. Perhaps the saint forgot to add tourists and monkeys to that list!

A good view of the fort and of the adjoining smaller fort of Adilabad is possible from the walls. Adilabad was built by Muhammad bin Tughlaq (r 1325–51), who is believed to have killed his father Ghiyasuddin by contriving to have a gateway collapse on him. They are both buried in Ghiyasuddin's Tomb, joined to the Tughlaqabad Fort by a causeway that crossed the dammed waters of a lake.

The tomb was the first in India to be built with sloping walls, a design that was repeated in all subsequent Tughlaq architecture. Its severe red sandstone walls, relieved by white marble inlay, are surmounted by a white marble dome. The red sandstone *kalasha* (urn) that crowns it and the lintel spanning the arched opening, decorated with a lotus bud fringe, are influenced by Hindu architecture.

> ### Did You Know?
> ---
> When it was first erected, Tughlaqabad Fort had over 50 gates; now there are only 13 left.

11 Siri Fort

📍C14 🏛Asiad Village Complex, August Kranti Marg & Siri Fort Rd Ⓜ Green Park ⏰ Sunrise–sunset daily

Crumbling ramparts are all that remain of Alauddin Khilji's 14th-century city of Siri, built as protection against foreign, and in particular Mongol, attack. The ruins of mosques and tombs can be found in the adjoining village of Shahpur Jat. The nearby **Siri Fort Auditorium** regularly hosts concerts and film festivals. It is adjacent to the Asian Games Village complex where speciality restaurants serve Indian, Chinese and Mexican cuisine.

Siri Fort Auditorium
🏛August Kranti Marg
🌐dff.nic.in

Did You Know?

Legends say that Khilji used the heads of 8,000 Mongols to build the foundations of Siri Fort.

12 Shahpur Jat

📍B14 🏛Shahpur Jat Market, Siri Fort Ⓜ Panchsheel Park ⏰ 10am–8pm Mon–Sat

A cool little urban village next to Siri Fort, Shahpur Jat (meaning "Royal Town of the Jats") is home to designers' studios, quirky shops and good places to eat. In the 14th century, when the fort was abandoned, this area was taken over by members of a pastoralist ethnic group called the Jats who, over the years, transformed it into a handsome urban district. Today it's a trendy market area full of concept stores and fashion boutiques, a great area to browse for modern Indian designs in clothes, accessories and home furnishings. A store worthy of mention is Anand Prakash, which sells cool ornamental stationery such as elegant writing paper, envelopes and pens.

The area is also home to some wonderfully vibrant street art, not to mention a number of restaurants and cafés that serve an amazing variety of cuisines, including Bihari dishes, Australian food, and British-style tea and cakes.

SHOPS

Sarojini Nagar Market

A bustling clothes market famous for its low prices, where haggling is the order of the day.

📍B13 🏛Sarojini Nagar ⏰10am–9pm Sun–Tue

Saahra

This designer boutique specializes in fair-trade, sustainable fashion for women. All its clothes are ethically made using natural, often organic, fibres.

📍D13 🏛C-16 Hotel Suryaa, New Friends Colony 🌐saahra.com

Fabindia

Fabindia stocks everything from furniture and natural cosmetics to organic food and clothes.

📍C14 🏛7 N Block Market, Greater Kailash I 🌐fabindia.com

The atmospheric crumbling ruins of the 14th-century Siri Fort ↓

↑ The Red Fort, the centre of power in Shahjahanabad, Delhi's seventh city

THE SEVEN CITIES OF DELHI

Delhi's famous "seven cities" range from the 12th-century Qila Rai Pithora, built by Prithviraj Chauhan, to the imperial Shahjahanabad, constructed by the Mughals in the 17th century. Each of these cities comprised forts erected by powerful sultans and the settlements that grew up around them. Today, Delhi is a medley of the ruins of these cities and an ever-expanding, modern concrete jungle.

QILA RAI PITHORA

Qila Rai Pithora, the first of Delhi's seven cities, was erected by the Chauhans in about 1180. In 1192, it was captured by Qutbuddin Aibak.

SIRI

Delhi's second city, situated near the Siri Fort Auditorium and the adjacent Shahpur Jat village, was constructed by Alauddin Khilji around 1303.

↑ The ruined walls of Delhi's first city, Qila Rai Pithora

TUGHLAQABAD

Tughlaqabad, a dramatic fort (p133) on the foothills of the Aravallis, was Delhi's third city, built during Ghiyasuddin Tughlaq's four-year reign (1321–5).

JAHANPANAH

Jahanpanah (p132) was erected by Muhammad bin Tughlaq (r 1325–51) as a walled enclosure to link Qila Rai Pithora and Siri. The ruins stand near Chiragh.

FEROZABAD

Stretching north from Hauz Khas (p130) to the banks of the Yamuna, Ferozabad is Delhi's fifth city, established by Feroz Shah Tughlaq (r 1351–88).

↑ The well-preserved remains of Siri, near Hauz Kaus

DINPANAH

Purana Qila (p100), the citadel of Delhi's sixth city, Dinpanah, was raised by Humayun, but captured by Afghan chieftain Sher Shah Suri (r 1540–45).

SHAHJAHANABAD

Delhi's seventh city was built between 1638 and 1649 by Shah Jahan and became the Mughal capital.

↑ The striking main gate to the sixth city's fortress

→ The dramatic fortress-like exterior of Khirkee Masjid

13

Khirkee

C14 **N of Press Enclave Marg** **M Malaviya Nagar**

This village has been named after the huge mosque built by Feroz Shah Tughlaq's prime minister, Khan-i-Jahan Junan Shah, in the mid-14th century. Standing today in a declivity and surrounded by village houses, the unusual two-storeyed Khirkee Masjid has a sombre fortress-like appearance with bastions on all four corners. Its severe façade is broken by rows of arched windows that are covered by dramatic portcullis-like *jalis*;

HIDDEN GEM
Khirkee's Murals

Murals covering subjects as diverse as Bollywood movies and women's football adorn Khirkee's buildings. They were created by KHOJ *(www.khojworkshop.org)*, a group aiming to bring art into public areas.

---

these are what give the mosque its name – "khirkee" translates as "windows". Built on a high plinth, flights of stairs lead up to imposing gateways on the north, south and east sides. The inner courtyard is partly covered, its roof supported by monolithic stone pillars, and crowned by nine sets of nine small domes. Only four courtyards remain open to the sky. This was the first example of this type of mosque design; however, the division of open space by pillars was found to be unsuitable for large congregations, so this design was never repeated.

During cleaning and renovation work in 2018, members of the Archaeological Survey of India (ASI) uncovered a hoard of over 250 coins. Found near the entrance to the mosque, the coins were believed to date from Delhi's medieval period, specifically the reigns of Afghan chieftain Sher Shah Suri *(p58)*, and his son and successor, Islam Shah Suri. An earlier discovery had been made in 2003, when

81

The number of domes that crown the roof of Khirkee's mosque.

a collection of over 60 coins was unearthed, again during renovation work.

Satpula ("seven-arches"), the dam and stone weir built by Muhammad bin Tughlaq in 1326, is located just down the same road. It formed part of the reservoir which was once used for irrigation, and the grooves, meant for sliding the shutters that regulate the flow of water, can still be seen on the seven arches. The weir also formed a portion of the fortified wall enclosing the city of Jahanpanah *(p132)*. Its upper storey was previously used as a *madrasa* (university) during the reign of Delhi sultan Muhammad bin Tughlaq.

⑭ Moth ki Masjid

📍 C14 🅰 Behind South Extension, Part II Ⓜ Moolchand

This atmospheric mosque was built in 1505 by Miyan Bhuwa, the prime minister of Sikander Lodi, who was one of Delhi's sultans. Legend tells that Sikander Lodi picked a *moth* (lentil seed) which he then gave to Miyan Bhuwa. The crop from this single seed was apparently so fruitful and reaped Bhuwa such rich returns that he was able to build this beautiful mosque. Unfortunately for Bhuwa, however, he later annoyed Sikander's successor, Ibrahim Lodi (r 1517–26), so much that Ibrahim had him put to death.

The design of this elegant and graceful red sandstone, structure with its five-arched, three-domed prayer hall, was developed further in later Mughal mosques. Over the central arch is a fine *jharokha* (an enclosed and overhanging balcony) that still boasts traces of the original plaster decoration. Both the red sandstone gateway and the ornate decorations that are found on the mosque's façade are also noteworthy.

> Its severe façade is broken by rows of arched windows that are covered by dramatic portcullis-like *jalis*; these are what give the mosque its name - "khirkee" translates as "windows".

⑮ Chiragh Delhi

📍 C14 🅰 Bordered by Outer Ring Rd and LB Shastri Marg Ⓜ Chiragh Delhi

The dargah of the Sufi saint Nasiruddin Mahmud (died 1356), who succeeded Hazrat Nizamuddin Auliya (*p98*) as spiritual leader of the Chishti sect, lies in the once secluded village of Chiragh Delhi. This saint, known as Raushan Chiragh-i-Dehlvi ("illuminated lamp of Delhi"), was buried here and the village that grew around his tomb was named after him. Muhammad bin Tughlaq, the sultan at that time, built the original village walls in the 14th century.

The shrine itself is small and is approached on foot through the narrow, congested village lanes, past rows of tailors establishments and shops selling *mithai* ("sweetmeats"), flower garlands and other religious offerings. Some ruined *havelis*, which must have once been very beautiful, also line the street. A huge arched doorway leads to the dargah, a quieter and simpler shrine than that of Hazrat Nizamuddin. Well-shaded by trees, the tomb is set in a 12-pillared square chamber, enclosed by *jali* screens and surmounted by a large plastered dome rising from an octagonal drum. The roof inside has been embellished with fine painted plaster carvings set with mirrors, clearly a recent addition. Within the enclosure are several smaller mosques and halls, added over the years for religious discourses.

At the far end from the gateway is a partially ruined tomb that is locally claimed to be that of Bahlol Lodi (r 1451–89), the founder of the Lodi dynasty. The *chhajja* has collapsed, but the square chamber is still surmounted by five domes, the central being the largest. The arches have engraved inscriptions.

Entrance to the shrine of Sufi saint Nasiruddin Mahmud, at Chiragh Dehli ↓

9

All Baha'i temples have nine sides because this number symbolizes perfection.

16

Baha'i House of Worship

Q D14 **A** Bahapur, Kalkaji **M** Kalkaji Mandir **O** Apr-Sep: 9am–6pm Tue–Sun; Oct–Mar: 9am–5pm Tue-Sun; prayer services: 10am, noon, 3pm & 5pm **R** Public hols **W** bahai houseofworship.in

The arresting shape of its unfurling 27-petalled white marble lotus has given the Baha'i House of Worship its more popular name, the Lotus Temple. Located just opposite the Kalkaji Temple, this edifice – spectacularly encircled by nine pools and 27 acres (92 ha) of lush green manicured lawns – is one of Delhi's most innovative modern structures. It is the main temple of the Baha'i faith in India, which believes in the unity of all religions and all human beings. It is also one of the most visited monuments in the world.

This temple was designed by the Iranian-Canadian architect Fariborz Sahba. Construction began in 1980 and was completed in 1986. Composed of a total of 27 "petals" this eye-catching structure stands 34 m (112 ft) high. The temple's elegant petals are clad with Pentelikon marble, the same type of marble that was used to build the Pantheon in Greece. Inside, the lofty auditorium can seat 1,300, and visitors from all religions are welcome to meditate there and attend the daily 15-minute services.

Concerts with a social message are held here often. There is an Information Centre as well, designed for those interested in learning more about the Baha'i faith.

The Lotus Temple looks particularly awe-inspiring after dark when the lighting gives its gently curving marble panels a luminous and wonderfully ethereal quality.

17

Ashoka's Rock Edict

Q D14 **A** Off Raja Dhirsain Marg **O** 24 hrs daily

Not far from the Baha'i House of Worship lies a large boulder, carved with a faint tracery of fading Brahmi script. This is one of the city's three monuments dating from the time of the Mauryan Emperor Ashoka (p57). Ashoka converted to Buddhism early in his reign, and erected across

the country a series of pillars and rock edicts on which his various proclamations were recorded. Unlike the city's two Ashokan columns, this rock edict stands on its original site. It was discovered in 1966 by the Archaeological Survey of India (ASI). While the edict has become a place of pilgrimage for many Buddhists, it remains a little visited sight for tourists.

Kalkaji Temple

☑D14 ☐Lotus Temple Rd ☐Kalkaji Mandir ☐4am–10pm daily ☐skmpsc.org

This colourful temple is a good place to experience Hinduism in bustling, popular practice. Kalkaji Temple is approached through a narrow winding alley, lined with an abundance of stalls selling everything from

> **Kalkaji Temple is approached through a narrow winding alley, lined with an abundance of stalls selling everything from laminated religious prints and bangles to *sindoor* (vermilion powder) and fruit.**

laminated religious prints and bangles to *sindoor* (vermilion powder) and fruit, while devotional hymns blast from rival cassette stalls. The dramatic red-and-yellow 12-domed temple, with a heavily decorated pillared pavilion, was built in the mid-18th century on an older site by Raja Kedarnath, prime minister of Emperor Akbar II.

Thereafter, many contemporary additions, financed by rich merchants, have been made to the temple. Inside, the goddess Kali *(p140)* or Kalka, draped in silks, sits under silver umbrellas and a marble canopy. Legend has it that a farmer, on discovering that his cow regularly offered her milk to the goddess, built this temple in her name.

↑ Visitors exploring the Baha'i House of Worship, with its unique lotus-like design, and *(inset)* the building's lofty and peaceful interior

HINDU GODS AND GODDESSES

The great pantheon of Hindu gods and goddesses is a bewildering array, ranging from anthropomorphic symbols and shapes to exotic half-human, half-animal forms. Although community worship takes place in temples, especially on festivals, for most Hindus, the home with its own shrine and personal deities is where the daily *puja* (prayer) is conducted.

Did You Know?

All deities have their own vahanas (animal mounts) as their vehicles for travel.

THE HOLY TRINITY

This sacred *trimurti* (triumvirate) is made up of Brahma the Creator, Vishnu the Preserver and Shiva the Destroyer. The four-headed Brahma brought the world and all its creatures into existence. Vishnu mediates between Brahma and Shiva to preserve life. He is the protector of the universe and is believed to returns to the earth during periods of adversity, assuming a different avatar (incarnation) each time in order to save the world from destruction. The final deity is Shiva, whose role is to eventually destroy this world so that it can be remade again. The present age *(Kaliyuga)* is seen as only one stage of the unending cycle of life.

GODDESSES

Every major god has a corresponding goddess. Saraswati, the goddess of wisdom, learning and music, is the consort of Brahma and is seen as the embodiment of purity. Lakshmi, the goddess of wealth and prosperity, is the consort of Vishnu. She always accompanies Vishnu when he manifests himself on earth in human form, taking on her own earthly avatar: when he was Rama she became Sita, and when he was Krishna she was incarnated as Rukmini. Shiva's wife is Parvati, the goddess of love and devotion. She lives in the Himalayas and is the mother of Ganesha.

OTHER HINDU GODS AND GODDESSES

Hinduism features countless other deities. One of the most important is Ganesha, the elephant-headed son of Shiva and Parvati, who is regarded by Hindus as the remover of obstacles. He is usually invoked at the start of any auspicious task. There's also the monkey god, Hanuman, who is a faithful attendant of Rama, one of Vishnu's avatars. He is often invoked by those in need of courage and fortitude.

Other goddesses include the fierce Durga, who rides a tiger and has a deadly arsenal of weapons to help her destroy evil, often in the form of the buffalo-demon Mahishasura. The ten-handed goddess Kali, wearing a garland of skulls, also annihilates evil. Along with Durga, she is the patron goddess of many Rajput clans who lived by the sword.

↑ Colourful painting of Ganesha, the elephant-headed god

BOTH MANY AND ONE

While the myriad gods and goddesses of Hinduism mean it is often regarded as a polytheistic religion, it could also be seen as being monotheistic. This is because Hinduism's abundance of deities are all believed to personify aspects of a single reality, Brahman. Constrained by neither form nor limits, Brahman is the ultimate divine reality of the universe: all life originates from it and eventually returns to it. One school of Hindu thought, Advaita Vedanta, holds that atman (the self) is the same as Brahman, while all material objects are mere illusions (maya).

TOP 5 RELIGIOUS SYMBOLS

The Om
A symbol of the primal sound, is recited to start all religious ceremonies.

The Swastika
A symbol of divinity and auspiciousness commonly used during pujas, rituals and festivals.

The Kamal
The lotus flower is a Vaishnavite symbol for purity.

The Trishul
The trident is a Shaivite symbol of asceticism.

The Shankh
The conch shell is a Vaishnavite symbol of the life-giving ocean.

↑ A representation of Vishnu's first incarnation, Matsya

→ Bronze statues of the Hindu goddesses Kali and Durga

Ferris wheel at Surajkund's famous craft fair

BEYOND THE CENTRE

In the 8th century, the first permanent human settlement in the area was erected by the Rajput Tomars. Named Surajkund, it was built near the southern end of the Ridge, an ancient stretch of wooded hills. In the 11th century, the Tomars left the area and moved to Lal Kot, now in South Delhi. Following the decline of Tomar rule in the 12th century, Surajkund fell into disrepair – it wasn't rebuilt until the reign of Delhi sultan Feroz Shah. The area north of the city was used by Feroz Shah as a base for hunting expeditions – he erected several lodges here. It was developed further by the Mughals, who built pleasure gardens, and then by the British in the 19th century, when they constructed the residential area known as Civil Lines. During the War of Independence in 1857, the Ridge and the Northern Ridge were used by the British East India Company as a base for their forces.

Must See
❶ Akshardham Temple

Experience More
❷ Coronation Park
❸ Nicholson Cemetery
❹ Qudsia Gardens
❺ Civil Lines
❻ Delhi University
❼ The Ridge
❽ The Northern Ridge
❾ Click Art Museum
❿ Sultan Ghari
⓫ Delhi Cantonment
⓬ Kumhar Gram and Prajapati Colonies
⓭ Sulabh International Museum of Toilets
⓮ Sanskriti Museums
⓯ Sultanpur National Park
⓰ Surajkund
⓱ Kingdom of Dreams

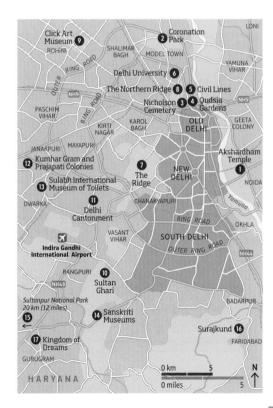

❶

AKSHARDHAM TEMPLE

🏠 NH 24, Akshardham Setu Ⓜ Akshardham 🕐 9:30am–6:30pm Tue-Sun
🌐 akshardham.com

Rising out of shady green gardens, this modern temple complex – Delhi's largest – is unrepentingly opulent. Its pink sandstone façade is adorned with intricate carvings that depict Hindu deties, flowers and animals.

Perched on the east side of the Yamuna River, Akshardham Temple was built in 2005 by the Sri Swaminarayans, followers of a 19th-century Hindu saint from Gujarat. The complex was built using traditional methods, without any iron or steel. The main shrine is surrounded by a dynamic frieze of elephants on its plinth, while inside is a 3-m- (10-ft-) high golden statue of the Swaminarayans' founder, Bhagwan Swaminarayan. Subsidiary shrines honour the divine couples of Lakshmi and Vishnu, Radha and Krishna, Sita and Rama, and Parvati and Shiva.

Around the main shrine are spacious grounds, with a large lotus-shaped fountain. A smaller fountain contains marble images of Bhagwan Swaminarayan's footprints, watered by four golden conches. Photography is not allowed and clothing must cover the upper arms and come down to below the knee.

> 💬 INSIDER TIP
> **The Circle of Life**
>
> The Sahaj Anand Water Show takes place every evening at the main fountain. Depicting the cycle of life, the show features multicoloured lasers, underwater flames and spurting jets of water. Buy tickets from the visitors' centre.

8,000

volunteers spent around 300 million hours helping to build the temple.

↑ The breathtaking Akshardham Temple, illuminated at dusk

The area surrounding
the main temple, dominated
by friezes of elephants ↑

→ One of the tranquil
carved corridors
found inside
the temple

EXPERIENCE MORE

2
Coronation Park

📍 KB Hedgewar Rd,
S of NH1 Bypass
Ⓜ Vishwa Vidyalaya
🕐 Sunrise–sunset daily
🌐 delhitourism.gov.in

Also known as the Coronation Memorial, this park was the site of the Royal Durbar held in 1911 to proclaim the accession of George V as King Emperor of India. A red sandstone obelisk records that the King Emperor proclaimed his coronation to the "governors, princes and peoples of India" (in that order) and "received their dutiful homage". He also announced the transfer of the capital from Kolkata to Delhi and two days later laid the foundation stones for the new city (p60). On 12 December 1911, more than 100,000 people thronged the site where the King Emperor and Queen Empress sat beneath a golden dome mounted on a crimson canopy. Today, the site is filled with the statues of former viceroys, ranged in a semi-circle, that were evicted from their perches in the city to make way for later Indian leaders. Towering over them all is the 22-m (73-ft) statue of the King Emperor himself, which was removed from the canopy at India Gate (p79) and installed here in the 1960s.

3
Nicholson Cemetery

📍 Club Rd, Lala Hardev
Sahai Marg, Civil Lines
Ⓜ Kashmiri Gate 🕐 6am–
6pm daily

In the walled cemetery named after him, surrounded by traffic and overlooked by the Inter State Bus Terminus (ISBT), lies the flamboyant Brigadier General John Nicholson, the British commander. The head-stone on his grave, which is to the right of the entrance, records that he "led the assault on Delhi but fell mortally wounded and died 23rd September 1857, aged 35". The surrounding graves belong to others like him who died at the time of the War of Independence, between 10 May and 30 September 1857. The saddest are the tiny graves of children, such as the headless angel mourning over Alfred and Ida Scott's little daughter: "We gave her back to bloom in heaven".

To enter the cemetery, knock on the gate and the chowkidar (gatekeeper) will open it. A small tip (10–20 rupees) to the chowkidar and a donation to the Church of North India will be welcome. Monkeys are rampant in the cemetery and are dangerous if teased.

4
Qudsia Gardens

📍 Railway Colony,
Shamnath Marg, Civil
Lines Ⓜ Kashmiri Gate
🕐 Sunrise–sunset daily

Qudsia Begum, the dancing girl who became the wife of Emperor Muhammad Shah (r 1719–48), laid out these gardens in around 1748, and although the Inter State Bus Terminus and the Tourist Park

The grand and well-preserved gateway leading to the Qudsia Gardens

The obelisk at Coronation Park commemorating the 1911 accession of George V

now occupy much of the original site, the imposing gateway still stands. The rest of the present park is more modern with a children's playground and a rather formidable statue of the great Rajput king, Maharana Pratap. North of the gardens is the children's home run by Mother Teresa's Missionaries of Charity, where abandoned children are cared for.

STAY

Maidens Hotel

Established in 1903, this is one of Delhi's oldest hotels, with classic style, tip-top service and great views of the Delhi Ridge (p148). Surrounded by lush gardens, its garden terrace is perfect for dining alfresco or for after-dinner drinks.

🏠 7 Sham Nath Marg, Prema Kunj, Civil Lines
🌐 maidenshotel.com

₹₹₹

Civil Lines

🏠 Bounded by Shamnath Marg and Mahatma Gandhi Marg Ⓜ Civil Lines

Old Delhi's Civil Lines were inhabited by British civilians. They lived in spacious bungalows, shopped at the Exchange Stores, dined at Maidens Hotel and worshipped at St James' Church. The old "temporary" Secretariat (built in 1912) is also located here on Mahatma Gandhi Marg. This long white building with its two towers, where the former Legislative Assembly once sat, also housed the offices of the Delhi Administration at one time. When the British moved into New Delhi, established Indian professional and merchant families settled here. Several old bungalows have been redeveloped as modern blocks of flats, yet some areas, such as Rajpur Road, still retain their colonial character.

To the east of Civil Lines, near the Delhi-Chandigarh bypass, is Metcalfe House, a sprawling mansion built in the 1830s by Sir Thomas Metcalfe. This house, once the hub of British social life, can be seen from the highway.

Delhi University

🏠 Vishwavidyalaya Marg Ⓜ Vishwavidyalaya 🌐 du.ac.in

The university area runs parallel to the Northern Ridge, and colleges dot the vast campus. Among the most attractive is St Stephen's College, designed by Walter George in 1938. With its long corridors built in quartzite and its well-kept gardens, the college has some deliberate Oxbridge associations. At one time this was one of India's premier institutions, with renowned scholars such as the historian Percival Spear on its staff. The office of the Vice Chancellor is now the registrar's office. It was here that the young Lord Louis Mountbatten proposed to Edwina Ashley. They eventually became India's last viceroy and vicereine.

> With its long corridors built in quartzite and its well-kept gardens, the college has some deliberate Oxbridge associations.

7

The Ridge

◩ Upper Ridge Rd
Ⓜ Central Secretariat
🕒 Sunrise–sunset daily

Delhi's Ridge, the last outcrop of the Aravalli Hills extending northwards from Rajasthan, runs from southwest to northeast. The area was originally developed by Feroz Shah Tughlaq, some 600 years ago, as his hunting resort. He erected many lodges, the ruins of which can still be seen here and also at the Northern Ridge (p148). This green belt of undulating, rocky terrain is covered by dense scrub forest consisting mainly of laburnum (Cassia fistula), kikar (Acacia arabica) and flame of the forest (Butea monosperma) trees, interspersed with bright splashes of bougainvillea.

A large portion in the southwest is now the **Buddha Jayanti Park**, a peaceful, well-manicured enclave, criss-crossed with paved paths. Pipal (Ficus religiosa) trees abound, and on a small ornamental island is a simple sandstone pavilion shading the large gilt-covered statue of the Buddha, installed by the 14th Dalai Lama in October 1993. An inscription nearby quotes the Dalai Lama: "Human beings have the capacity to bequeathe to future generations a world that is truly human". Every May, Buddhist monks and devotees celebrate Buddha Jayanti here.

Buddha Jayanti Park
🕒 5am–7pm daily

8

The Northern Ridge

◩ Rani Jhansi Rd, Ridge Rd, Magazine Rd
Ⓜ Vishwavidyalaya
🕒 Sunrise–sunset daily

The northern end of the Ridge is a forested park cut through by Ridge Road and Rani Jhansi Road, with the small clearing of Bara Hindu Rao in the middle. This area still resounds with memories of the War of Indepdendence of 1857. It was around Flagstaff Tower, to the far north, that British women and children took shelter before they were evacuated to Karnal near Panipat (p162).

The Mutiny Memorial (known locally as Ajitgarh), at the southern end, is a red sandstone Victorian Gothic spire built by the British to commemorate "the soldiers, British and native… who

→
The Northern Ridge's Mutiny Memorial, honouring British soldiers

Serene golden Buddha statue encircled by a pond, at the Ridge

were killed" in 1857, and lists separately the names of those who died. At the entrance is a plaque, dated 1972, which points out: "The enemy of the inscriptions were those who fought bravely for national liberation in 1857". There are panoramic views of Old Delhi from the platform at the base of the tower. Nearby is a 3rd-century Ashokan Pillar, one of the two Feroz Shah Tughlaq brought from Meerut in 1356. Faint inscriptions in Brahmi, extolling the virtues of practising *dhamma* (the Buddhist Way of Truth), are still visible. Feroz Shah also had a large hunting estate here where he built a lodge called Kushak-i-Shikar, a mosque, as well as a double-storeyed mansion, the Pir Ghaib, now in the grounds of the Hindu Rao Hospital (enter the main gate and turn right at the Cardiac Unit). The name Pir Ghaib derives from the tale of a resident *pir* who, one day, simply vanished (*ghaib*) while meditating at this site. A cenotaph in one of the rooms marks the spot.

 9

Click Art Museum

🏠 Block C, Adventure Island, Metro Walk, Sector 10, Rohini Ⓜ Rithala Ⓒ 11am–8pm daily 🔤 clickartmuseum.com

This two-hall exhibition is the Delhi branch of a popular museum chain. Its theme is 3D trick art, and the installations are specifically designed so that you can have your picture taken with them. The *trompe-l'oeil* paintings look like 3D art in photographs and show you apparently interacting with them, for example being a

 Decorated doorway at the 13th-century Sultan Ghari tomb

puppet on strings held by a giant hand, or shaking hands with the Mona Lisa. Selfie-lovers will have a field day, but it's better if you have someone else to take your pictures – although the staff may well oblige you on this.

 10

Sultan Ghari

🏠 C-9, Vasant Kunj, off Mahipalpur-Mehrauli Rd Ⓜ Chattarpur Ⓒ Sunrise–sunset daily

Sultan Ghari was the first Islamic tomb to be built in Delhi and among the earliest in India. The ruler of the sultanate Slave dynasty, Iltutmish erected this tomb in 1231 for his eldest son and heir Nasiruddin Muhammad, who was killed in battle. Today, its fortress-like exterior appears out of place in the midst of one of the city's largest residential complexes, Vasant Kunj. Inside is a raised courtyard, and the tomb itself is an octagonal platform, forming the roof of the crypt (*ghar*) below. Like many monuments of this early medieval period, Sultan Ghari was constructed from pillars and stones taken from temples nearby. Fragments

EAT

Majnu ka Tila
Delhi's "Little Tibet" is packed with places offering *momos, thukpa* (noodle soup) and other tasty Tibetan fare.

🏠 Aruna Nagar

Punjabi by Nature
A pioneer of modern Punjabi cuisine, with dishes such as *murgh makania* (chicken in a creamy sauce).

🏠 T-305, 3rd Floor, Ambience Mall, Nelson Mandela Marg, Vasant Vihar 🔤 punjabibynature.in

Bukhara
Succulent kebabs and super-creamy dal are among the specialities at this top-class restaurant.

🏠 Maurya Hotel, Sardar Patel Marg, Chanakyapuri 🔤 itchotels.in/hotels/new-delhi/itcmaurya/dining/bukhara.html

of these are visible in the surrounding colonnades, which may have once housed a *madrasa* (university). The mihrab on the west side has some fine calligraphic decoration and, interestingly, there is a marble *yonipatta*, the base of a Shiva *linga* (phallic statue), embedded in the floor.

The tomb, located on the road from Andheria More to Delhi Airport, is reached after turning left from the Spinal Injuries Centre and taking the next left after that.

①

Delhi Cantonment

🏛 Bounded by NH8, M G Rd and Sadar Bazaar Marg
Ⓜ Dhaula Kuan

The cantonment in Delhi was planned by John Begg and built by the Military Works Department in the 1930s. With its straight roads, neat, whitewashed walls, well-clipped hedges, parade ground and shooting-range, it epitomizes the quintessential spit and polish of the military.

The garrison **Church of St Martin's**, probably the most original modern church in India, was designed by Arthur Gordon Shoosmith (1888–1974), the close associate of the famous British architect Edwin Lutyens. Consecrated in 1931 and built from three and a half million bricks, it rises straight-walled with small, recessed windows and a 39-m (128-ft) tower, the lines between the bricks being the only ornamentation. Within is a stark classical interior with a plaque in honour of the architect and a haunting tablet in memory of the three children of Private Spier, who died within days of each other at Abbottabad

Monument honouring the military forces in the Delhi Cantonment

---

CANTONMENT TOWNS

Following the 1860s, more than 170 cantonments (pronounced "cantoonment") were built on the outskirts of major towns to impress Indians with the seriousness of British military might. Each of them was a self-contained world, with symmetrical rows of barracks, finely graded bungalows, clubs and regimental messes, bazaars, hospitals and churches. Military hierarchies, too, were rigidly followed. Even after independence, the military remained mostly stationed in cantonment areas.

(now in Pakistan) in 1938. If the church is locked, contact the Presbyter-in-Charge who lives in the adjacent cottage.

A short distance from Dhaula Kuan Circle is the **Delhi War Cemetery**, where lie the Commonwealth soldiers and airmen who died on the Eastern Front in World War II. A monument at the entrance proudly declares: "Their Name Liveth Evermore". The graves are set in neat rows with matching headstones; only the regimental insignia and biblical texts are different. On every Remembrance Day (11 November), wreaths are laid at the Memorial Column, followed by a short prayer.

Church of St Martin's
🏛 Church Rd, Delhi Cantonment 🕐 Hours vary, check website
🌐 stmartinschurch delhi.com

Delhi War Cemetery
🏛 Brar Square 🕐 7:45am–5pm daily 🌐 cwgc.org

---

⑫

Kumhar Gram and Prajapati Colonies

🏛 Prajapati Colony, Rani Bagh Ⓜ Uttam Nagar East
🕐 6am–8pm daily

On the western outskirts of Delhi are Kumhar Gram and Prajapati, two colonies of potters set up by migrants originally from Rajasthan. The artisans in these enclaves still make pottery the traditional and time-honoured way, and they welcome visitors who come and watch them at work, especially if they want to purchase as well. There's a pleasant rural atmosphere here, as villagers sift and make up the clay, throw and form it on potters' wheels, carefully incise and decorate it, and fire it in kilns fuelled with cow dung.

↑ Assortment of sanitation facilities on display at the Museum of Toilets

The pottery made at Kumhar Gram is unglazed terracotta earthenware, and is for practical rather than decorative use, but it has its own charm. Sometimes the rejects from the potters work are used in the construction of the walls of the surrounding buildings.

 13

Sulabh International Museum of Toilets

⌂ Sulabh Bhawan, Palam Dabri Marg, Mahavir Enclave I **Ⓜ** Dashrath Puri **🕒** 8am-8pm Mon-Sat, 10am-5pm Sun **🌐** sulabhtoilet museum.org

This quirky but genuinely interesting little museum has an exhibition on toilets and sanitation devices through the ages, from the ancient Harappan culture's sewer system through to the latest technological developments in the field. The Sulabh Movement, which runs it,

campaigns for – and helps to provide – good public sanitation in both urban and rural communities. The museum grounds have examples of ecofriendly, non-polluting toilet facilities, including those designed for use where there is no running water or sewerage. There's also the replica of a toilet used by France's Louis XIV. The museum is even home to a machine for converting human excrement into methane gas, which can be used as bio-fuel, with fertilizer as a by-product.

 14

Sanskriti Museums

⌂ Anandgram, Mehrauli, Delhi-Gurugram Rd **Ⓜ** Arjan Garh **🕒** 10am-5pm Tue-Sun **🔒** Public hols **🌐** sanskriti foundation.org

These three unusual museums are set amid beautifully landscaped spacious grounds

where exhibits are displayed both in the garden and in specially constructed rural huts. The collections, too, are equally unusual. They are devoted to traditional objects of everyday use, exquisitely crafted by an unknown, unsung, rural artisan. O P Jain, whose personal collections gave birth to this museum, has donated exquisite combs, nutcrackers, lamps, foot scrubbers and kitchenware. A variety of terracotta objects from all over India are also on display. The pots are especially dazzling, particularly as their production techniques have not changed for centuries.

> **This quirky but genuinely interesting little museum has an exhibition on toilets and sanitation devices through the ages.**

Visiting egrets nesting at tranquil Sultanpur National Park

Sultanpur National Park

🏠 46 km (27 miles) W of Delhi ⏰ 7am–4:30pm Wed–Mon ℹ Haryana Tourism, Chanderlok Building, Janpath, Delhi; www.haryanatourism.gov.in

This sanctuary, located a two-hour drive from Delhi, has been developed around a low-lying marshy area that is dry in summer, but fills up during the monsoon to form a shallow lake (*jheel*). Sultanpur is at its best in the winter months, when this shallow sheet of water provides a haven for a wide variety of migratory birds.

Several pleasant walks, including a paved pathway which runs around the small lake, allow visitors to explore the 35-km (22-mile) area, while the many hides or *machans*, mounted on stilts, provide a good view of the birdlife on the lake. The Sarus crane, the world's tallest flying bird, breeds in the mud spits covered with reeds that rise above the waters. Often, on winter evenings, noisy flocks of demoiselle cranes descend on the lake. The other birds that visit the lake include egrets, herons, kingfishers, pelicans and painted storks.

The rolling tree-shaded lawns are home to herds of friendly deer and have beautifully sited picnic spots, ideal for lunch breaks. The sanctuary shop has a good selection of informative books and posters on Indian birdlife.

Surajkund

🏠 21 km (13 miles) S of Delhi ℹ Haryana Tourism, Chanderlok Building, Janpath, Delhi; www.haryanatourism.gov.in

King Surajpal of the Rajput Tomar dynasty (*p57*), hero of many legends, built this reservoir some time in the late 10th or early 11th century. An embankment of stone terraces was built round a pool which trapped rain water running down from the hills. A sun temple is thought to have stood on the western side. Tomar Rajputs trace their descent from the sun, hence the name: *suraj* (sun) *kund* (pool). Today, the embankment is more or less intact, though there is no trace of the temple, and the pool itself is none too clean. The nearby artificial lake is

SURAJKUND CRAFTS MELA

For two weeks in early February, Surajkund comes alive with one of India's largest arts and crafts fairs. Mirrorwork from Gujarat, puppets from Jaipur and Madhubani paintings from Bihar can be found under thatched canopies. Food stalls and a giant ferris wheel give the mela a carnival air, while folk dancers and musicians in colourful costumes weave in and out of the crowds. Evenings are given over to folk theatre, dance and music performances.

picturesque and is best enjoyed from the paddle or rowing boats on hire. You might even glimpse a pale green water snake swimming alongside you.

About 2 km (1 mile) to the west is Anangpur Dam built by the Tomar king, Anangpal. A rather impressive quartzite stone stucture, it blocks a narrow ravine to create an artificial lake. The dam is reached on foot, but it is an extremely brambly and rocky walk and best avoided in rainy weather.

This area is a popular picnic spot for Delhi's residents. Haryana Tourism and the Delhi Transport Corporation run special daily buses to Surajkund during the annual crafts mela (fair).

Kingdom of Dreams

◨ Sec 29, Gurugram Ⓜ IFFCO ⏱ 12:30pm–midnight Tue-Sun ⓦ kingdomofdreams.in

An extravagant entertainment complex similar to Disneyland®, the one-of-a-kind Kingdom of Dreams is home to a near-constant carnival atmosphere. This live entertainment hub allows you to visit all corners of India without leaving the city – so be sure to experience it all, from the backwaters of Kerala and the beaches of Goa to the ancient temples of Chennai. The complex contains 14 state pavilions, with live arts and crafts activities, and village-themed restaurants where you can sample the wealth of Indian cuisine. As you stroll through the complex, you'll see energetic Bollywood dance performances taking place on nearly every street corner.

The complex's undisputed highlights are the sensational immersive Bollywood-style shows, all supported by cutting-edge technology. The huge main auditorium, which seats over 800 people, has regular Bollywood-esque shows, as does the complex's other, smaller, amphitheatre. Book ahead for a variety of fantastic performances, including *Zangoora* – the first original live Bollywood musical telling the tale of a gypsy who falls in love with a princess.

There's also the fun-filled Bollywood-themed IIFA Buzz Lounge, showcasing a wealth of memorabilia from Bollywood films, including posters, props and costumes.

DRINK

Soi 7
Sample delicious Thai food and great beer at this microbrewery in Guragon's Cyber City mall.

◨ 205-208 Cyber Hub, DLF Cyber City, Phase 2, Gurugram ⓦ facebook.com/soi7pub

Vapour Pub
This classy pub has great beer and good bar snacks, as well as a full food menu.

◨ 2nd Floor, MGF Mega City Mall, MG Rd, Gurugram ⓦ pub mgroad.vapour.in

Ministry of Beer
Among the many awesome draught beers on offer at this steampunk-themed microbrewery is a "basmati blonde" rice beer.

◨ Ground Huda Complex, Leisure Valley Rd, Sector 29, Gurugram ⓦ mobbrewpub.com/gurugram

Downtown Diners & Living Beer Café
This is one of Gurugram's first microbrewery bars, with great food and beer, plus a rooftop eating area.

◨ 34 Leisure Valley Road, Sector 29, Gurugram ⓦ facebook.com/downtowndiners

← The Kingdom of Dreams, renowned for its live Bollywood shows

EXPERIENCE BEYOND DELHI

Pushkar's sacred lake and ghats

NORTH OF DELHI

Lying between the Ganges and Yamuna rivers, this agriculturally prosperous region is held to be the cradle of Indian civilization. From about the 2nd millennium BC onwards, this vast plain has been one of India's most densely populated areas. First populated by the Harappan civilization around 2500 BC, it was then dominated Vedic peoples in 1500 BC, who founded settlements across the region. Descended from these Vedic peoples were the Pandavas, heroes of the Hindu epic of *Mahabharata*. This group are believed to have fought a mighty battle against their rivals the Kauravas on the plains of Kurukshetra, and to have erected the town of Panipat.

Around the 7th century BC, holy towns such as Haridwar and Rishikesh came into existence, quickly becoming places of religious pilgrimage for the devout. As time went on, the region became dominated by fortified city states that then developed into medieval walled towns surrounded by prosperous agricultural lands and containing flourishing markets. In the 16th century the region fell under Mughal control; during this time Panipat was the scene of epic battles. As Mughal power declined in the early 18th century, the area became dominated by the Marathas, then by the Durranis, and finally by the British. In 1857, troops in the town of Meerut rebelled against British rule, an event which served to ignite the War of Independence. The 1960s saw the establishment of a brand-new city, Chandigarh, built by the French architect Le Corbusier; it is now one of the area's major hubs.

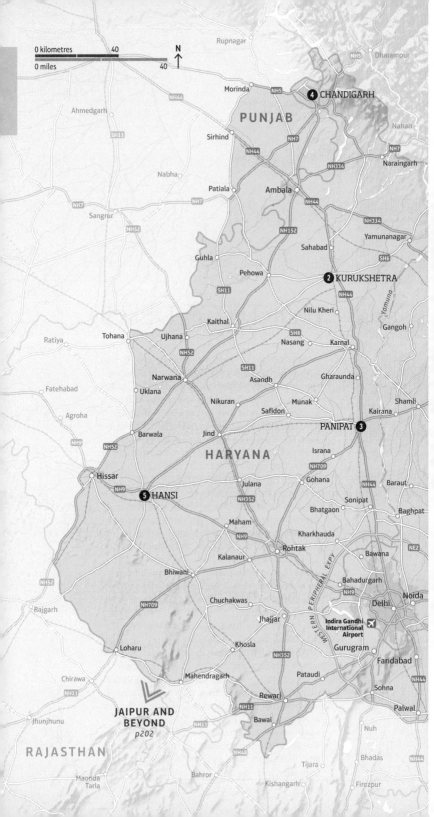

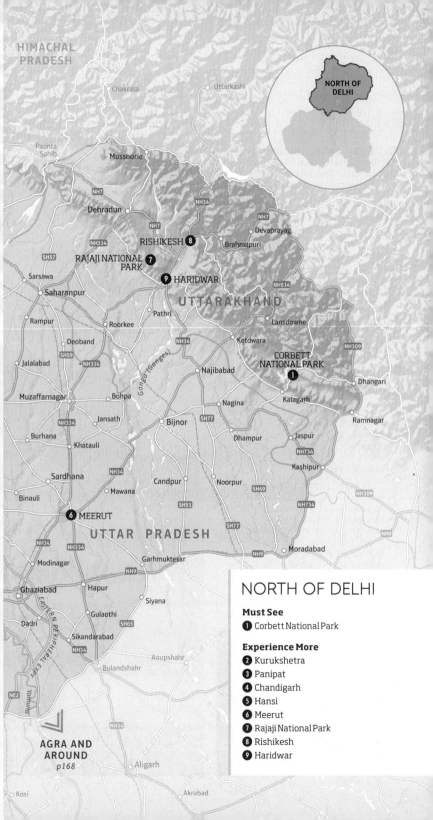

HIMACHAL
PRADESH

Chakrata

Uttarkashi

Paonta
Sahib

Mussoorie

NH7

Dehradun

NH7

NH334

RISHIKESH **8**

NH34

Devaprayag

Brahmapuri

RAJAJI NATIONAL **7**
PARK

SH57

Sarsawa

9 HARIDWAR

Saharanpur

UTTARAKHAND

NH534

Rampur

Pathri

Roorkee

Lansdowne

Deoband

Kotdwara

SH59

NH34

NH336

Jalalabad

Najibabad

CORBETT
NATIONAL PARK

NH309

Muzaffarnagar

Bohpa

Nagina

Kalagarh

1

Dhangari

Jansath

Dhampur

Jaspur

Ramnagar

Burhana

Khatauli

Bijnor

SH77

NH734

NH334

Kashipur

Sardhana

Candpur

Noorpur

SH49

Binauli

Mawana

SH51

NH734

NH309

6 MEERUT

SH77

NH9

UTTAR PRADESH

Moradabad

NH9

Modinagar

Garhmuktesar

Ghaziabad

Hapur

NH34

NH9

Siyana

Dadri

Gulaothi

Sikandarabad

SH65

Anupshahr

NH34

Bulandshahr

NE2

NH34

**AGRA AND
AROUND**
p168

Aligarh

Kosi

Akrabad

Ganga (Ganges)

Yamuna

EASTERN PERIPHERAL EXPY

NORTH OF
DELHI

NORTH OF DELHI

Must See

1 Corbett National Park

Experience More

2 Kurukshetra
3 Panipat
4 Chandigarh
5 Hansi
6 Meerut
7 Rajaji National Park
8 Rishikesh
9 Haridwar

CORBETT NATIONAL PARK

🅰 F2 ⬛ Pauri Garhwal & Nainital districts, Uttarakhand; 110 km (68 miles) SE of Haridwar; entry points at Dhangarhi & Kalagarh ⬛ Hours vary, check website 🛈 Tourist Rest House, Ramnagar; www.corbettonline.uk.gov.in

This national park was India's first, and is home to a spectacular array of wildlife, including elephants, tigers and more than 600 species of birds, in an equally diverse natural setting.

Situated along the valley of the Ramganga river and fringed by the Himalayan foothills in the north, the park encompasses varied terrain, from savannah grasslands to hilly ridges of deciduous forest with chir pine and sal (Shorea robusta). It is considered one of India's finest wildlife sanctuaries, and is one of the most popular places in Uttarakhand, mainly visited by people on safari hoping to catch a glimpse of an elusive tiger.

The 1,288-sq-km (497-sq-mile) reserve was a hunter's paradise during the British Raj. In 1936, it became India's first national park, largely due to the efforts of the British hunter-turned-conservationist Jim Corbett, after whom the park is named. Corbett advocated for the establishment of a national park, photographed local animals and educated people about conservation – although he never stopped shooting tigers. Today, the park is renowned for its remarkable variety of wildlife.

> **Did You Know?**
>
> Jim Corbett killed the Champawat Tiger, which was responsible for killing at least 436 people.

PROJECT TIGER

Launched in Corbett National Park in 1973, Project Tiger is a government-backed programme to save India's tigers from extinction using a network of protected reserves. From nine reserves when it started, the project now has over 50. It has had to surmount all kinds of problems, particularly poaching. Despite this, the project has been very successful, and has seen India's tiger population increase from fewer than 1,500 in 2006 to around 3,000 today.

1 The sambar deer is native to India, and is now considered a vulnerable species.

2 There are five zones within Corbett National Park, only one of which is open to visitors on safari tours. This group has just spotted a tiger in the wild.

3 The colourful Indian roller bird is one of hundreds of bird species in the park.

↑ Elephants drinking from a waterhole in the national park

EXPERIENCE MORE

 EXPERIENCE North of Delhi

❷
Kurukshetra

🅰D2 🏛Kurukshetra district, Haryana; 175 km (109 miles) N of Delhi on NH1 🚌🚋 ℹwww.haryanatourism.gov.in

The *Mahabharata*'s epic battle between the Pandavas and Kauravas was fought on the plain surrounding Kurukshetra. The town also marks the start of a 128-km (80-mile) pilgrimage circuit, undertaken at the solar eclipse or at Gita Jayanti when lighted clay lamps are set afloat on the sacred waters of the bathing tanks during a ceremony called *deepdan*.

The main bathing tanks are the Brahmasar, with a small temple on an island, and the smaller, more sacred Sannahit Sarovar, lined with ghats and temples. A dip in the Sannahit Sarovar during the solar eclipse is believed to be especially holy.

The town's **Sri Krishna Museum** displays a large collection that brings out the pervasiveness of the Krishna cult in Indian art.

Sri Krishna Museum
 🏛Off Sannihit Sarovar Rd ⏲10am–5pm daily 🌐srikrishnamuseum.com

---

❸
Panipat

🅰D2 🏛Panipat district, Haryana; 85 km (53 miles) N of Delhi on NH1 🚌🚋 ℹwww.haryanatourism.gov.in

The three "Battles of Panipat" fought on the flat, dusty plains surrounding this town, changed the course of Indian history. In 1526, Babur's defeat of Delhi sultan Ibrahim Lodi led to the establishment of Mughal rule; 30 years later, in 1556, Babur's grandson Akbar subdued the Mughals' Suri challengers under the Hindu general Hemu. Finally, in 1761, an Afghan army halted the expansion of the Maratha empire, leaving a power vacuum that the British were able to exploit.

Today, Panipat is a busy and bustling town that is known for its fabrics and carpets. A number of *kos minars* (Mughal milestones) on its outskirts mark the Grand Trunk Road that once linked Kolkata to Kabul. The 700-year-old Sufi dargah (shrine) of Qalandar Shah is here, as is the tomb of Ibrahim Lodi, moved and rebuilt by the British when they paved over its original location on the Grand Trunk Road. Babur's 1557 Kabuli Bagh Mosque – built to commemorate his victory at the First Battle of Panipat – is India's oldest Mughal monument; nearby is the Mughal fort of Purana Qila. South of town, the Panipat Museum displays items from the town's three important battles, and at Shodapur, 2 km (1 miles) west of town, there is a monument to the Suri general Hemu, built after his defeat and death in the Second Battle of Panipat.

> **Did You Know?**
>
> Thanks to its thriving textile industry, Panipat has become known as the "City of Weavers".

> The *Mahabharata*'s epic battle between the Pandavas and Kauravas was fought on the plain surrounding Kurukshetra. The town also marks the start of a pilgrimage circuit.

Sculpture depicting Lord Krishna with Arjuna, Brahmasar, Kurukshetra

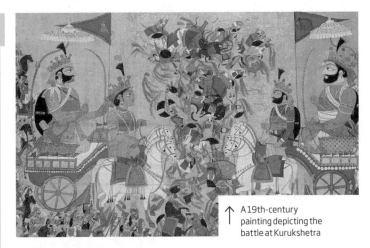

↑ A 19th-century painting depicting the battle at Kurukshetra

THE MAHABHARATA

Considered an inexhaustible fount of knowledge and ideas, the *Mahabharata* is about an eponymous battle between the Pandavas and Kauravas. Said to be first narrated by a sage, Ved Vyas, the Hindu epic was written down only between the 6th and 7th centuries BC. The subtle moral subtext of its legends and stories codifies notions of theology and statecraft that inspired rulers down the ages. The text also charts the evolution of Hinduism from around 400 BC to 200 AD.

↑ Painting of Arjuna, one of the five Pandava princes

The *Mahabharata* follows the story of the Pandavas, the five sons of the king of Hastinapur. The Pandavas were banished from their father's kingdom by the Kauravas, their jealous cousins. During their exile the Pandavas met and jointly married Draupadi, the daughter of the king of Panchal. However, upon their return to the kingdom of Hastinapur they were tricked by the Kauravas in a game of dice, losing both the kingdom and their wife, Draupadi. After a long exile, the heroic Pandavas fought a huge battle against the Kauravas at Kurukshetra, just north of Delhi. Despite being outnumbered by the hundred Kauravas, the Pandavas were led to victory by their ally Lord Krishna.

The epic's didactic tone made it an authoritative manual on moral rules and righteous conduct. The battle is an allegory for the war between right and wrong, with Lord Krishna seen as the divine charioteer who steers the mind (chariot) and five senses (the five horses that pull the chariot) to follow the right path through life.

BHAGAVAD GITA

A later insertion to the *Mahabharata* of 700 stanzas, the *Gita* records a conversation between Lord Krishna, the divine charioteer, and Pandava prince Arjuna on the battlefield of Kurukshetra. Arjuna is troubled at the idea of causing so much death on the battlefield, particularly of family members. However, Lord Krishna condones the use of violence against injustice and extols the virtues of performing one's moral duty without seeking reward. The *Bhagavad Gita*'s philosophy of righteous living and the importance of one's *dharma* (duty) continues to guide the lives of millions of Indians.

Visitors strolling in Chandigarh's Rock Garden, and *(inset)* a series of statues

4

Chandigarh

🅰 D1 🏛 Chandigarh district, Punjab & Haryana; 248 km (154 miles) N of Delhi 🚇🚌🚍 ❼ Interstate Bus Terminal, Sector 17; www.punjab tourism.gov.in

The capital of both Haryana and Punjab, Chandigarh was designed in the 1950s by the architect Le Corbusier. A city of concrete blocks and straight arterial roads, it is laid out on a grid of 57 rectangular sectors modelled loosely on the human body. Its "head" is the **Capitol Complex**, which includes the Secretariat, Assembly and High Court buildings, as well as a 13-m- (43-ft-) high sculpture of an Open Hand, the city's emblem.

> **Le Corbusier Centre is where the famous architect oversaw Chandigarh's construction. Models and photographs showcase his work.**

The main shopping area, Sector 17, is the "heart" of Le Corbusier's plan, set around a central plaza and fountain. Adjoining it, in Sector 16, is a gently undulating stretch of green, the city's "lungs".

Chandigarh's main tourist sight is the **Rock Garden**. Created illegally on waste ground by road inspector Nek Chand as a hobby, it was discovered by the authorities in 1975. Recognizing it as a work of art, the city council allowed Chand to continue adding to it. There's a labyrinth with hills, waterfalls and caves, and sculptures crafted from neon lights, broken crockery and glass.

Chandigarh's **Government Museum and Art Gallery** houses sculptures and miniature paintings, including a serene 6th-century *Standing Bodhisattva* and an 11th-century Kashmiri statue of Vishnu, plus watercolours by Bengali art pioneer Abanindranath Tagore.

Le Corbusier Centre is where the famous architect oversaw Chandigarh's construction. Models and photographs showcase his work.

Capitol Complex

🕸 🏛 Sector 1 🕐 Tours: 10am, noon, 3pm daily (book online; bring photo ID) 🌐 admser. chd.nic.in/capitolcpermission

Rock Garden

🕸 🏛 Sector 1 🕐 9am–7:30pm daily (to 6pm Oct–Mar) 🌐 nekchand.com

Government Museum and Art Gallery

🕸 🏛 502, Sector 10C 🕐 10am–4:30pm Tue–Sun 🌐 chdmuseum.gov.in

Le Corbusier Centre

🏛 Old Architect Building, Sector 19B, Madhya Marg 📞 (011) 172 277 7077 🕐 10am–5pm Tue–Sun

⑤ Hansi

🄰 C3 🄰 Hisar district, Haryana; 137 km (85 miles) NW of Delhi 🚌🚆 𝐟 www.haryanatourism.gov.in

One of Northern India's most ancient towns, Hansi is surrounded by a defensive wall with five gates leading into the old city. Perched atop the old city is Asigarh Fort, originally built in the 7th century, but refortified in 1798 by George Thomas, an Irish soldier of fortune. Thomas ran an army for the Marathas before breaking away to create his own kingdom here, which he ruled for three years.

As a brutal reprisal, after the War of Independence the British crushed over 100 people with a road roller on Lal Road ("Red Road", for their blood), found just below Asigarh Fort; a monument stands on the road to commemorate the atrocity. The town is also scattered with monuments from the 12th century, including the shrine called Char Qutbs, a Sufi dargah of the Chishtiya order.

Hissar, 26 km (16 miles) west of Hansi, was the favourite retreat of Feroz Shah Tughlaq. He had palaces built here, now in ruins.

⑥ Meerut

🄰 D3 🄰 Meerut district, Uttar Pradesh; 72 km (44 miles) NE of Delhi 🚌 𝐟 www.uptourism.gov.in

Meerut is better known as the place where the sepoys first mutinied on 10 May 1857, igniting the War of Independence (p59). Today, this bustling town swirls around monuments dating to the 11th and 12th centuries, such as the Jama Masjid (1019), Salar Masa-ud Ghazi's *maqbara* (1194), the tomb of Makhdum Shah Wilayat and the *maqbara* of Shah Pir (1620). Meerut's colonial heritage is preserved in its manicured cantonment to the north of the old city. This is one of the country's best-planned cantonments with a broad, tree-lined main road and colonial bungalows with sprawling gardens along its length. The cantonment's Neo-Classical St John's Church (1822), where British residents had gathered for refuge when the revolt broke out, was the scene of a bloody massacre that fateful May day.

About 22 km (14 miles) to the west is the town of Sardhana, founded by French explorer Walter Reinhardt in the late 1700s. His wife, Begum Yohanna Samru, built two churches here: the Basilica of Our Lady of Grace, inspired by St Peter's in Rome, and the Roman Catholic Church, where she is buried.

↓ The charming Basilica of Our Lady of Grace in Sardhana, near Meerut

EAT

Haveli Hari Ganga

This palatial hotel has regal rooms and delicious food inspired by the flavours of India, Southeast Asia and Europe, plus a rooftop café with river views.

AE2 **Q**21 Pilibhit House, Ram Ghat, Haridwar **W**havelihariganga.com

₹₹₹

Ramana's Garden Organic Café

Try international dishes made with organic veg from the café's own garden. Proceeds fund a children's home.

AE2 **Q**Lakshman Jhula Rd, Tapovan, Rishikesh **Ø**Mid-Oct–mid-March: 11am–4pm Tue–Sun & 6–9pm Sat **W**ramanas. org/about/our-cafe

₹₹₹

 7

Rajaji National Park

AE2 **Q**Haridwar, Dehradun and Pauri Garhwal districts, Uttarakhand; 6 km (4 miles) NE of Haridwar and 21 km (13 miles) SE of Rishikesh **Ø**15 Nov–15 Jun: sunrise–sunset daily (entry: 6–9am or 3–6pm) **W**uttarakhand. gov.in

Found east and west of the Ganges between Haridwar and Rishikesh, and covering 820 sq km (317 sq miles), Rajaji National Park features a diverse range of habitats, including several types of forest and grassland.

The park is home to more than 50 species of mammals. These include tigers, of which there are over a dozen, and around 250 leopards, although these animals are notoriously elusive. The park's herd of 500 elephants represent the biggest population of any national park in India. Huge numbers of chital deer can also be seen here, along with sambar and barking deer, and sloth bears. The bird population, which counts more than 300 species, includes hornbills, kingfishers and peafowl. The park has accommodation, plus Jeep safaris and whitewater rafting. Firms such as **Mohan's Adventure Tours** in Haridwar can arrange packages.

Mohan's Adventure Tours

QNear railway station, Upper Road **W**mohans adventure.com

8

Rishikesh

AE2 **Q**Dehradun district, Uttarakhand; 228 km (142 miles) NE of Delhi **i**GMVN Office, Shail Vihar; www. uttarakhandtourism.gov.in

Situated at the confluence of the Chandrabhaga and the Ganges, Rishikesh marks the start of the holy Char Dham pilgrim route to the Himalayas. Muni ki Reti (literally "sand of the sages") lies upstream from the Triveni Ghat and is believed to be a blessed site since ancient sages meditated here. North of Muni ki Reti, two suspension bridges span the Ganges: Ram Jhula and Lakshman Jhula. The area around Ram Jhula bridge is home to several famous ashrams offering yoga courses. The dramatic Lakshman Jhula bridge, built in 1929, is Rishikesh's most iconic sight.

INSIDER TIP
Be More Yogi

Parmarth Niketan, Rishikesh's largest and most venerable ashram, offers relaxing yoga, meditation and ayurveda courses (www.parmarth.org).

The neighbourhood around it is popular with backpackers, and on its eastern side, the imposing 13-storey Kailash Niketan Temple contains a number of shrines dedicated to different gods.

Rishikesh has become India's adventure sports capital, an increasingly popular destination for activities such as rappelling, kayaking and mountain biking, and especially for rafting on the Ganges. Be sure to go with an organized tour run by certified experts, though; unofficial rafting camps upstream from the town have been criticized for littering and polluting the river. If you prefer to keep your feet dry, you can also hire a car and follow the road that snakes next to the river, following its flow.

↑ Pilgrims on the steps at Har ki Pauri ghat during the Kumbh Mela, Haridwar

 9

Haridwar

E2 **Haridwar district, Uttarakhand; 214 km (133 miles) NE of Delhi** **Railway Rd** **GMVN Office, Rahi Motel; www. uttarakhandtourism.gov.in**

The Ganges, India's holiest river, descends from the Himalayas to the plains at Haridwar, giving the town a unique status as a pilgrimage site. Haridwar is famous for the temples and ghats lining its river. At the main ghat, Har ki Pauri, hundreds attend the daily evening *arti*, when leaf boats, filled with flowers and lit lamps, are set adrift. Further south, the 11th-century Maya Devi Temple is one of the town's oldest.

A ropeway links the town to Mansa Devi Temple, which offers views of Haridwar; another hilltop temple with a ropeway lies 4 km (2 miles) south at Chandi Devi. North of town, the Bharat Mata (Mother India) Temple, inaugurated by Indira Gandhi in 1983, has statues of different Indian gods and heroes on each of its eight floors.

←

Ram Jhula suspension bridge spanning the Ganges at Rishikesh

A good way to experience Haridwar's ambience is to stroll along the riverside bazaar, lined with stalls full of ritual paraphernalia – small mounds of vermilion powder, coconuts wrapped in red and gold cloth, and brass idols. The most popular items with the pilgrims, however, are the jars and canisters sold here. These are used for a vital part of Hindu worship – to carry backwater from the Ganges *(Gangajal)*, which, the faithful believe, remains ever fresh.

KUMBH MELA

According to Hindu mythology, four drops of the immortal nectar *(amrit)* wrested by the gods from the demons, spilled over Haridwar, Allahabad, Ujjain and Nasik. A Kumbh Mela is held once every 12 years by rotation at these venues in Magh (Feburary–March). Hindus believe that they can imbibe the immortal *amrit* and wash away their sins by bathing in the Ganges at this propitious time. Haridwar's last Kumbh Mela, held in 2010, attracted over ten million people.

AGRA AND AROUND

Agra was founded in 1504 by the penultimate Delhi sultan Sikandar Lodi to act as his capital. The city remained the imperial capital of the Mughal court under both Babur and Humayun, before their successor Akbar moved the court to Fatehpur Sikri in 1571. This new city was abandoned after only 14 years; Shah Jahan later moved the court to the newly established Shahjahanabad (Old Delhi) in 1639. The Mughals, who were prolific builders, played a key role in developing the area directly around Agra. Under their rule, this picturesque riverine region surrounding the Yamuna river became peppered with palaces, tombs, forts and gardens. The main axis of the Mughal empire was the section of the Grand Trunk Road that links Agra to Delhi, passing through the rich pastoral and agricultural land around the holy towns of Vrindavan and Mathura, believed to be the homeland of Krishna.

The region south of Agra was initially dominated by Rajput rulers, although Delhi's Sultanate and Mughal dynasties conquered large parts of the area, including the spectacular fort city of Gwalior; other parts of the region managed to remain under Rajput control, including Orchha, founded in 1531 by the Bundelas clan. In the 18th century, the Mathuras took control of Gwalior and the surrounding area, although during British rule many cities – including Orchha and Gwalior – were left as semi-independent princely states.

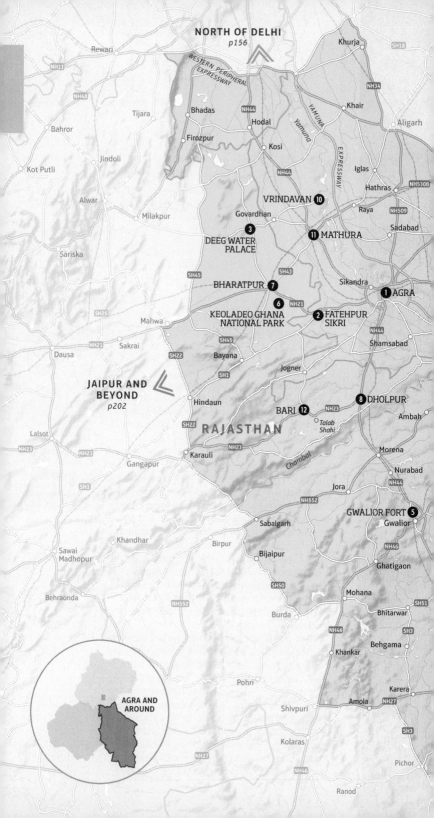

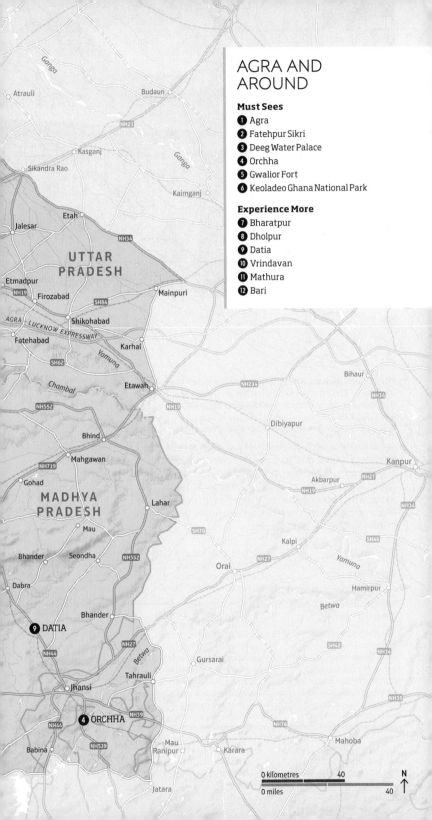

AGRA AND AROUND

Must Sees

① Agra
② Fatehpur Sikri
③ Deeg Water Palace
④ Orchha
⑤ Gwalior Fort
⑥ Keoladeo Ghana National Park

Experience More

⑦ Bharatpur
⑧ Dholpur
⑨ Datia
⑩ Vrindavan
⑪ Mathura
⑫ Bari

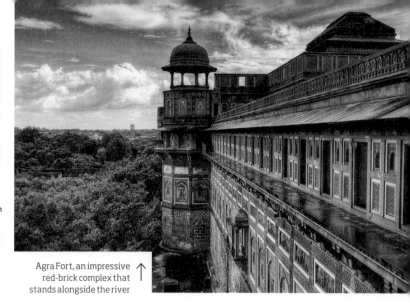

Agra Fort, an impressive red-brick complex that stands alongside the river ↑

❶

AGRA

🅰E5 🏛Agra district, Uttar Pradesh; 201 km (125 miles) SE of Delhi ✈Kheria, 8 km (5 miles) SW of city 🚉Agra Cantonment, Raja ki Mandi, Fort 🚌Idgah ℹUPSTDC, 64 Taj Rd; UPSTDC, Agra Cantt; ITDC, 191 Mall Rd; www.uptourism.gov.in/article/Agra-Fatehpur-Sikri

Agra was the seat of the imperial Mughal court during the 16th and 17th centuries, before the capital was shifted to Delhi. The city flourished under the patronage of the emperors Akbar, Jahangir and Shah Jahan. With the decline of the Mughals, Agra was captured by the Jats, the Marathas and finally the British, early in the 19th century.

Agra Fort

🕐Fort: 6am–6pm daily; Son et Lumière: 7pm daily
🌐agrafort.gov.in

Situated on the west bank of the Yamuna, Agra Fort was built by Emperor Akbar between 1565 and 1573. Its imposing red sandstone ramparts form a crescent along the riverfront, and encompass an enormous complex of courtly buildings, ranging in style from the early eclecticism of Akbar to the sublime elegance of Shah Jahan. The barracks to the north are 19th-century British additions. A deep moat, once filled with water from the Yamuna, surrounds the fort.

The impressive Amar Singh Gate, to the south, leads into the fort. To its right is the so-called Jahangir Mahal, the only major palace in the fort that dates back to Akbar's reign. This complex arrangement of halls, courtyards and galleries was the zenana or main harem. Along the riverfront are the Khas Mahal, an elegant marble hall with a vividly painted ceiling, characteristic of Shah Jahan's style of architecture, and two golden pavilions with *bangaldar* roofs

(curved roofs derived from Bengali huts). The Sheesh Mahal and royal baths are to the northeast, near Musamman Burj, a double-storeyed octagonal tower with clear views of the Taj, where Shah Jahan, imprisoned by his son Aurangzeb, spent the last years of his life. Mina Masjid, probably the smallest mosque in the world and intended for the emperor only, is nearby.

❷

St John's College

🏛Mahatma Gandhi Rd
🕐Mon–Sat 🚫Public hols
🌐stjohnscollegeagra.in

St John's College consists of a group of red sandstone

buildings, including a hall and library, arranged around a quadrangle, all designed in a quasi-Fatehpur Sikri (p182) style by Sir Samuel Swinton Jacob, who perfected the Indo-Saracenic style of architecture. Started by the Church Missionary Society in 1850, the college is now affiliated to Agra University and continues to be one of Agra's most prestigious institutions.

③ Roman Catholic Cemetery

🏠 Opp Civil Courts ⏱ Daily

Towards the north of the town stands the Roman Catholic Cemetery – the oldest European graveyard in North India – established in the 17th century by an Armenian merchant, Khoja Mortenepus. A number of Islamic-style gravestones, with inscriptions in Armenian, survive today; they include those of the cannon expert, Shah Nazar Khan, and Khoja Mortenepus himself. There are also tombs of European missionaries, traders and adventurers such as the 18th-century French freebooter Walter Reinhardt. The largest tomb is that of John William Hessing, a British commander in the army of the Scindias, the rulers of Gwalior (p192). Hessing's red sandstone tomb, built after his death in 1803, is modelled on the lines of the Taj Mahal. One of the oldest tombs belongs to the English merchant John Mildenhall, envoy of Elizabeth I, who arrived at the Mughal court in 1603 seeking permission to trade.

STAY

The Oberoi
Stylish and elegant, this hotel has a bar that offers picture perfect views of the Taj Mahal.

🏠 Taj East Gate Road, Paktola
🌐 oberoihotels.com

Hotel Taj Plaza
The best rooms here have good views of the Taj.

🏠 23-24 Taj East Gate Road, Paktola
🌐 hoteltajplazaagra.com

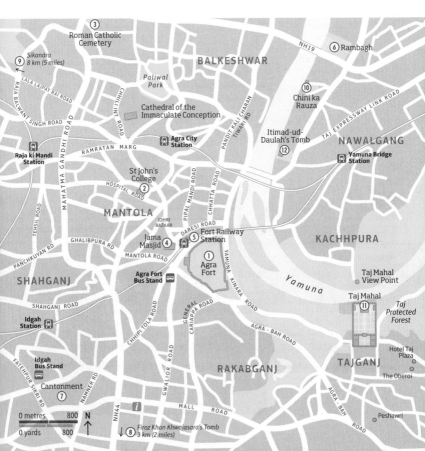

Jama Masjid

🕐 Sunrise–sunset daily
🕐 To non-Muslims during prayer times

A magnificently proportioned building in the heart of the historic town, the "Friday Mosque" was sponsored by Shah Jahan's favourite daughter, Jahanara Begum, who also commissioned several other buildings and gardens, including the canal that once ran down Chandni Chowk (p112) in Delhi. Built in 1648, the mosque's sandstone and marble domes with their distinctive zigzag chevron pattern dominate this section of the town. The eastern courtyard

---

INSIDER TIP
Explore Agra

To get a real insight into Agra's history and life, take one of Agrawalks' fascinating three-hour guided culture tours, or learn about local cuisine with their food tour (www.agrawalks.com).

---

wing was demolished by the British in 1857. Of interest are the tank with its *shahi chirag* (royal stove) for heating water within the courtyard, and the separate prayer chamber for ladies.

The area around Jama Masjid was once a vibrant meeting place, famous for its kebab houses and lively bazaars. A stroll through the narrow alleys offers glimpses of an older way of life, reminiscent of Mughal Agra. This is also the city's crafts and trade centre where a vast array of products such as jewellery, *zari* embroidery, inlaid marble objects, durries, dried fruit, sweets, shoes and kites are available. Quieter lanes such as Panni Gali have many fine buildings, with imposing gateways leading into secluded courtyards, where the thriving workshops of master craftsmen still exist.

Fort Railway Station

This memorable Raj building was constructed in 1891 as a stopping-off point for colonial tourists visiting Agra's many monuments. The octagonal bazaar chowk that originally connected the Delhi Gate and Agra Fort to the old city and the Jama Masjid was demolished, and this station, with its French château-style slate-roofed platforms, was built. It is still in use today. Agra's two other railway stations are located in the cantonment and at Raja ki Mandi.

Rambagh

📍 3 km (2 miles) N of Itimad-ud-Daulah's Tomb 🕐 Daily

Further upriver from Agra Fort, the quiet, tree-shaded Rambagh or Aram Bagh ("Garden of Rest") is thought to be the earliest Mughal garden, laid out by Babur, the first Mughal emperor, in 1526. The garden also served as his temporary burial place, before his body was moved to Kabul. The large walled garden, divided by walkways that lead to a raised terrace with open pavilions overlooking the river, was further developed by the empress Nur Jahan.

The red sandstone Jama Masjid, built in 1648, with its spacious courtyard ↑

GOLD THREAD AND BEAD ZARDOZI

Agra's flourishing traditional craft of elaborate gold thread *(zari)* and bead embroidery is called *zardozi*. Central Asian in origin, the technique came to the region with the Mughal emperors. Local craftsmen in the old city developed refinements and complex new patterns to make garments and accessories for the imperial court. With the decline of court patronage, the skill almost vanished. It owes its revival to encouragement from modern fashion designers.

(7) Cantonment

📍 Enclosed by Mahatma Gandhi Rd, Grand Parade Rd & Mall Rd

The pleasant, tree-shaded army cantonment area, with its own railway station and orderly avenues, has many interesting public buildings, churches, cemeteries and bungalows in a medley of styles dating from colonial times. St George's Church (1826) is a plastered ochre-coloured building designed by Colonel J T Boileau, architect of Shimla's famous Christ Church. Havelock Memorial Church, constructed in 1873 in a "trim Classical style", commemorates one of the British generals involved in the War of Independence of 1857.

(8) Firoz Khan Khwajasara's Tomb

📍 S of Agra, on Gwalior Rd
🕐 Daily

A signpost on the Gwalior Road indicates the turning to this unusual 17th-century octagonal structure, standing on the edge of a lake. This marks the spot where Firoz Khan Khwajasara, a eunuch and the custodian of Shah Jahan's palace harem, is buried. The red sandstone edifice stands on a high plinth and has a gateway attached to the main building. Steps lead to the upper storey where a central pavilion containing the grave is located. If the tomb is closed, the watchman from the village will open the gate.

Sikandra

📍 Agra district; 8 km (5 miles) NW of Agra 🚌🚗

The Mughal Emperor Akbar is buried in this small village on the outskirts of Agra. It is believed that Akbar designed and started the construction of his own **mausoleum** (free on Fridays), which was modified and completed by his son, Jahangir. The result is this impressive, perfectly symmetrical complex with the tomb located in the centre of a vast, walled garden. On each corner are four graceful marble minarets, considered to be forerunners of those of the Taj Mahal *(p176)*.

The large enclosed garden, where monkeys frolic, is in the *charbagh* style – divided in four (representing the four quarters of life) by a system of raised walkways, sunken groves and water channels.

The main tomb is a distinct departure from the conventional domed structure of the tomb of Akbar's father, Humayun, in Delhi *(p70)*. The first three storeys of its majestic four tiers consist of red sandstone pavilions.

Mausoleum
🏛 ☎ (0562) 264 1230 (for permission to go to the tomb terrace) 🕐 Sunrise–sunset daily (free on Fri)

↑ The magnificent, colourfully tiled ceiling of Chini ka Rauza

(10) Chini ka Rauza

📍 1 km (0.6 miles) N of Itimad-ud-Daulah's Tomb
🕐 10am–5pm daily

Chini ka Rauza (literally, "China tomb" after its tiled exterior) was built by Afzal Khan, a poet-scholar from Shiraz (Persia). The surface of this Persian-style square structure was once covered with tiles from Lahore and Multan, interspersed with calligraphic panels.

⑪ ⊗ Ⓜ 🛍

TAJ MAHAL

🏠 Tajganj 🚇🚌 🕐 Taj Mahal: 6am–7pm Sat–Thu; museum:
10am–5pm Sat–Thu 🚫 Taj Mahal: Fri; museum: public hols
🌐 tajmahal.gov.in

One of the world's most famous buildings, the Taj Mahal ("Crown of Palaces") was built by the Mughal emperor Shah Jahan in memory of his wife, Mumtaz Mahal. Its perfect proportions and exquisite craftsmanship have been described as "a vision, a dream, a poem, a wonder."

This sublime garden-tomb, an image of the Islamic garden of paradise, took 20,000 labourers around 15 years to build and was completed in 1648. Its four minarets, each 40 m (131 ft) high and crowned by a *chhatri* (an open octagonal pavilion), frame the tomb, highlighting the perfect symmetry of the complex. Inside the mausoleum, the octagonal chamber in the centre houses Mumtaz Mahal's cenotaph, which is raised on a platform and placed next to Shah Jahan's. The actual graves, in a dark crypt below, are closed to the public.

THE TAJ GETS A FACIAL

Over the years, the Taj's marble surface has been ravaged by pollution and grubby insects, and by the turn of the 21st century it was looking quite yellow. The fix has been a natural treatment long used by Indian women: a *multani mitti* mudpack, which has left the treated areas looking cleaner, younger and healthier.

Pietra Dura
Semiprecious and precious stone inlays, often in the form of ornate flowers.

Jali Screens
Filigree screens carved from stone slabs, casting mosaic-like shadows on the tomb.

Carved Reliefs
Intricate floral bas-reliefs, expertly carved out of polished marble or sandstone.

Calligraphy
Arabic verses and passages from the Qur'an, typically inlaid using black marble.

Incised Painting
Carved incisions filled with thick paint or stucco plaster, which is then delicately scraped off to leave the design.

← The perfectly proportioned Taj Mahal in the morning, as captured by a drone

Rs 15 million

The eventual cost of building the Taj Mahal, equivalent to nearly £600 million today.

1 Panels of exquisite Arabic calligraphy reach up and over the entrance arches to the mausoleum. The text increases in size as it gets higher, creating the optical illusion of uniform script.

2 Much of the red sandstone of the mosque is carved with rich, delicate reliefs representing a variety of flowers.

3 Inspired by the paradise garden, intricately carved floral designs inlaid with precious stones embellish the austere white marble surface to give it the look of a bejewelled casket.

DECORATIVE ELEMENTS OF THE TAJ

It is widely believed that the Taj Mahal was designed to represent an earthly replica of one of the houses of paradise. The mausoleum's impeccable marble facing, embellished by a remarkable use of exquisite surface design, is a splendid showcase for the refined aesthetic that reached its height during Shah Jahan's reign. Described as "one of the most elegant and harmonious buildings in the world", the Taj indeed manifests the wealth and luxury of Mughal art as seen in architecture and garden design, painting, jewellery, calligraphy, textiles, carpet-weaving and furniture.

PIETRA DURA

The Mughals were great naturalists who believed that flowers were the "symbols of the divine realm". In the Taj, *pietra dura* has been extensively used to translate naturalistic forms into decorative patterns that beautifully complement the majesty of its architecture. Flowers such as the tulip, lily, iris, poppy and narcissus were depicted as sprays or arabesque patterns. Stones of varying degrees of colour were used to create the shaded effects.

CARVED RELIEF WORK

Decorative panels of flowering plants, foliage and vases are realistically carved on the lower portions of the walls. While

↑ *Pietra dura* and carved reliefs decorating the Taj's interior

The Taj's exquisite exterior and *(inset)* calligraphic decoration ↑

the *pietra dura* adds colour to the pristine white marble these carvings highlight the texture of the polished marble and sandstone surface. Floral sprays carved in relief on the marble and sandstone lower levels, are framed with *pietra dura* and stone inlay borders. The profusion of floral motifs in the Taj symbolizes the central paradise theme. *Jali* patterns on the octagonal perforated screen surrounding the cenotaphs are a complex combination of the floral and geometric; the light filtering through them captures their intricate designs and casts mosaic-like shadows on the tombs.

CALLIGRAPHY

Inlaid calligraphy in black marble was used as a form of ornamentation on undecorated surfaces. The exquisitely detailed panels of inscriptions of Qur'anic passages, which line the recessed arches, were designed by the Persian calligrapher Amanat Khan.

PIETRA DURA CRAFTSMANSHIP

The Florentine technique of *pietra dura* is said to have been imported by Jahangir and developed in Agra as *pachikari*. Minute slivers of precious and semiprecious stones, such as carnelian, lapis lazuli, turquoise and malachite, were arranged in complex stylized floral designs into a marble base. Even today, artisans in the old city maintain pattern books containing the intricate motifs used on the Taj and can still re-create 17th-century designs in contemporary pieces.

Exploring the Taj Mahal

Surrounded by landscaped gardens, the elegant towers and graceful domes of the Taj are an awe-inspiring sight. The interior, decorated with precious stones, calligraphic panels and intricate filigree screens, is just as spectacular.

The 44-m (144-ft) double dome is capped with a finial.

The marble filigree screen was meant to veil the area around the royal tombs.

Intricately carved pietra dura floral designs embellish the white marble surface.

Four minarets, each 40 m (131 ft) high, frame the tomb and highlight its perfect symmetry.

Calligraphic panels inscribed with Qur'anic verses decorate the arches.

Pishtaq (recessed arches) provide depth, while their inlaid panels reflect the changing light to give the tomb a mystical aura.

Tomb Chamber

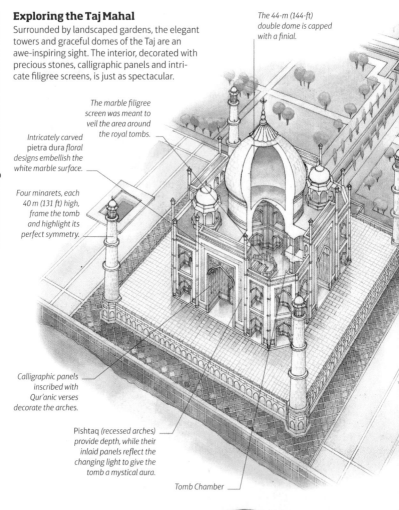

Timeline

1631

▽ Mumtaz Mahal, the favourite wife of Mughal Emperor Shah Jahan, dies in Burhanpur.

1632

Shah Jahan orders a mausoleum to be built along the Yumana's banks; work begins.

1648

The white marble mausoleum and many of the surrounding buildings are completed.

1666

△ Shah Jahan, who had been overthrown and imprisoned by his son, dies. He is interred next to Mumtaz Mahal in the Taj Mahal.

1908

▽ The Taj – after centuries of neglect – is restored under the orders of British Viceroy Lord Curzon.

The charbagh garden was irrigated with water from the Yamuna river.

← Illustration of the Taj Mahal, showing its interior and surrounds

12

ITIMAD-UD-DAULAH'S TOMB

E bank of Yamuna, 4 km (2 miles) upstream from the Taj Mahal Sunrise-sunset daily uptourism.gov.in

Lyrically described as a "jewel box in marble", the small yet elegant garden-tomb of Mirza Ghiyas Beg, titled Itimad-ud-Daulah, a Grand Vizier in the Mughal court, was built by his daughter Nur Jahan, the favourite wife of Mughal emperor Jahangir.

Begun in 1622, it took six years to complete this tomb, which is beautifully made of white marble, coloured mosaic, stone inlay and lattice work. The most stylistically innovative Mughal building of this era, it marks the transition in Mughal architecture from robust, red sandstone structures to more intricate and delicate buildings – of which the most famous example is the Taj Mahal. Itimad-ud-Daulah's square two-storeyed tomb stands in the centre of a *charbagh (p195)*. At the corners of the platform on which the tomb sits are four squat minarets. The polished marble exterior is covered in stone inlay, the first time the *pietra dura (p178)* technique had been extensively used. But the main glory of this tomb is its interior, covered in mosaics and painted-and-gilded stucco and stalactite patterns.

→ Mosaics and stuccowork lining the interior of Itimad-ud-Daulah's tomb

1983

▲ The building is named a UNESCO World Heritage Site for being "a jewel of Muslim art" and an internationally renowned masterpiece of the world's architectural heritage.

↑ The marble tomb, with its unusual square dome and surrounding gardens

2 ⬢ ⬢ ⬢ ⬢ ⬢

FATEHPUR SIKRI

🅐D5 🏠Agra district, Uttar Pradesh; 37 km (23 miles) W of Agra
🕐Sunrise-sunset daily 🌐fatehpursikri.gov.in

One of the greatest examples of Mughal architecture in India, Fatehpur Sikri is a well-preserved example of the might of this once-powerful empire – and so beautiful it could have fallen out of a storybook. Its immense yet elegant mosque, the Jama Masjid, is still a major site of pilgrimage.

Built by Emperor Akbar, one of the empire's most famous rulers, between 1571 and 1585, this sprawling city complex was the Mughal capital for 14 years. A magnificent example of a Mughal walled city, Fatehpur Sikri had defined private and public areas, and imposing gateways. Its architecture was a blend of Hindu and Islamic styles which reflected Akbar's secular vision as well as his style of governance.

After the city was abandoned, many of its treasures were plundered, until the British Viceroy, Lord Curzon (who also ordered the preservation of the Taj Mahal), a legendary conservationist, made efforts to preserve it. It is now a UNESCO World Heritage Site.

Did You Know?

The city was built on the site inhabited by the hermit who predicted that Akbar would have a son.

The lovely pool of Anoop Talao, outside Akbar's private chambers ↑

←

The soaring arches of the Jama Masjid, built in Akbar's favourite sandstone

→

The grand Diwan-i-Khas (Hall of Private Audience), showing the balcony where Akbar sat

THE GREAT AKBAR

The greatest of the Mughal emperors, Akbar (r 1556–1605) expanded his territory to stretch all the way from Afghanistan to Bengal and down to Maharashtra. A Sunni Muslim, Akbar was known for his religious tolerance. He had Hindu, Buddhist and Christian philosophers at court, and took a keen interest in the mystical Sufi side of Islam. He also permitted his Hindu wives to practise their religion. He died from an attack of dysentery, probably from drinking dirty water.

←
Buland Darwaza, the entrance to the grand Jama Masjid mosque

and Jain architecture with the elegant domes and arches of Islamic buildings, showing the diversity of Akbar's kingdom.

The gate opens into the cloistered courtyard of the Diwan-i-Aam, where Akbar would sit on a balcony and gave public audiences. A passage behind it leads into the inner citadel. This contains the Diwan-i-Khas, Khwabgah and Anoop Talao, along with the treasuries and the Abdar Khana where water and fruit for the royal household were stored.

The Haram Sara, or harem complex, was a maze of interconnected buildings. Its massive and austere exterior leads to a collection of palaces and a mosque, and form the outermost periphery of the palace complex. Beyond the royal complex, the most well-known building here is the Jama Masjid, the grand open mosque that contains the tomb of the Sufi mystic, Salim Chishti.

Exploring Fatehpur Sikri

Even today, access to the city is via a straight road built by the emperor, which was once lined with bazaars. It leads visitors through the Agra Gate to the triple-arched Naubat Khana, where the emperor's entry was announced by a roll of drums. Leading off from the Naubat Khana is the western entrance to the imperial palace complex. The principal buildings here are clustered on a series of terraces along the sandstone ridge, and formed the core of Akbar's capital. They merge pre-Islamic, Hindu

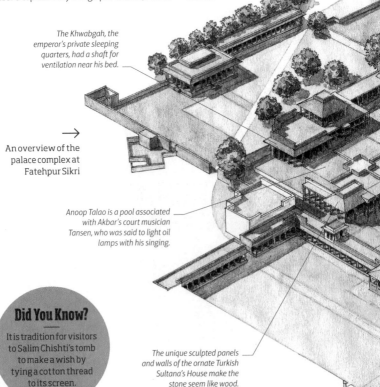

The Khwabgah, the emperor's private sleeping quarters, had a shaft for ventilation near his bed.

→
An overview of the palace complex at Fatehpur Sikri

Anoop Talao is a pool associated with Akbar's court musician Tansen, who was said to light oil lamps with his singing.

Did You Know?

It is tradition for visitors to Salim Chishti's tomb to make a wish by tying a cotton thread to its screen.

The unique sculpted panels and walls of the ornate Turkish Sultana's House make the stone seem like wood.

↑ The white marble tomb of Salim Chishti, within the Jama Masjid

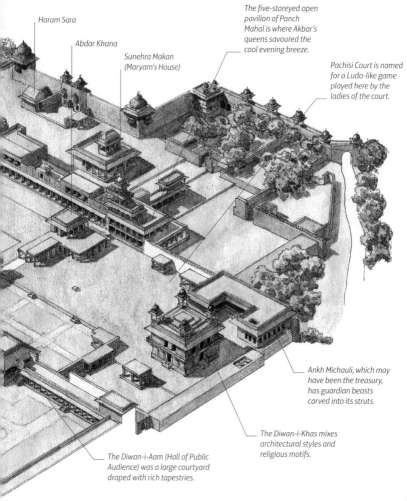

Haram Sara

Abdar Khana

Sunehra Makan (Maryam's House)

The five-storeyed open pavilion of Panch Mahal is where Akbar's queens savoured the cool evening breeze.

Pachisi Court is named for a Ludo-like game played here by the ladies of the court.

Ankh Michauli, which may have been the treasury, has guardian beasts carved into its struts.

The Diwan-i-Khas mixes architectural styles and religious motifs.

The Diwan-i-Aam (Hall of Public Audience) was a large courtyard draped with rich tapestries.

The tranquil Gopal Sagar Tank in front of the elegant Gopal Bhavan complex ↑

500

fountains are found in Deeg Palace, according to an Archaeological Survey of India estimate.

3

DEEG WATER PALACE

🅰 D5 🏠 Bharatpur district, Rajasthan; 95 km (59 miles) NW of Agra 🚌 🕐 9:30am–5:30pm Sat–Thu 🚫 Fri & the day after Holi (Mar) ℹ️ RTDC Hotel Saras, Bharatpur; (05664) 223 790

A lyrical composition of sandstone and marble pavilions, lush gardens and tranquil pools, this expansive palace complex is utterly spectacular.

The magic of the monsoon, and the traditions of music and dance associated with it, inspired the Bharatpur kings to build a romantic "water palace" at their summer capital, Deeg. This late-18th-century marvel, built by Raja Suraj Mal, used a number of innovative special effects that simulated monsoon showers, even producing rainbows. Dotted around the complex are a number of impressive bhavans, as well as charming *charbagh*-style gardens (*p195*). The palace's skilful cooling system drew water from a huge reservoir that originally took two days to fill. The coloured fountain-jets are now played only during festivals such as the Jawahar Mela.

> **This late-18th-century marvel, built by Raja Suraj Mal, used a number of innovative special effects that simulated monsoon showers.**

Gopal Sagar Tank ___

Sawan Pavilion ___
is shaped like an upturned boat; its ingenious water system created a semicircle of falling water.

Illustration of the many ↑ pavilions and pools of Deeg Water Palace

MONSOON ARCHITECTURE

In the dry areas of north India, architecture was guided by light and wind direction. Underground rooms, water channels, fountains, latticed screens, terrazzo floors and open courtyards were devices to keep homes cool before the advent of electricity. The Sawan-Bhadon pavilions at Deeg, named after the months of the monsoon (July-August), are an architectural style inspired by the rainy season. Built to savour the thunder and rain of the monsoon, such pavilions adorned forts and palaces.

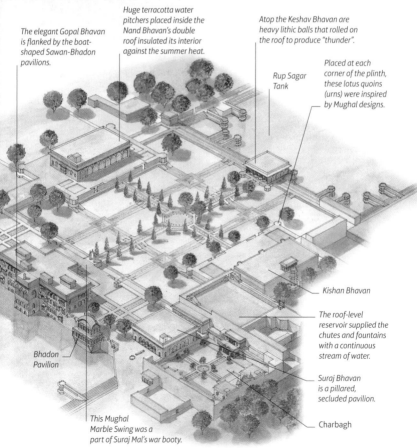

The elegant Gopal Bhavan is flanked by the boat-shaped Sawan-Bhadon pavilions.

Huge terracotta water pitchers placed inside the Nand Bhavan's double roof insulated its interior against the summer heat.

Atop the Keshav Bhavan are heavy lithic balls that rolled on the roof to produce "thunder".

Rup Sagar Tank

Placed at each corner of the plinth, these lotus quoins (urns) were inspired by Mughal designs.

Kishan Bhavan

The roof-level reservoir supplied the chutes and fountains with a continuous stream of water.

Bhadon Pavilion

Suraj Bhavan is a pillared, secluded pavilion.

This Mughal Marble Swing was a part of Suraj Mal's war booty.

Charbagh

4 🚶 🚲

ORCHHA

E7 ⬤ Tikamgarh district, Madhya Pradesh; 238 km (148 miles) S of Agra ⬤ Jhansi, 19 km (12 miles) NW of Orchha, then taxi or bus ⬤ Son et Lumière (Chaturbhuj, Jehangir Mahal & Raj Mahal): Mar-Oct: 7:30-8:30pm; Nov-Feb: 6:30-7:30pm 🅸 MP Tourism, Sheesh Mahal & Betwa Retreat; www.mptourism.com

Orchha is dramatically positioned on a rocky island, enclosed by a loop of the Betwa river. Founded in the 16th century, it was the capital of the Bundela kings until 1783, when it was abandoned for Tikamgarh. Crumbling palaces, pavilions, hamams, walls and gates, connected to the town by a 14-arched causeway, are all that remain today.

The most spectacular sights in the old town are the three main palaces: Raj Mahal, Jahangir Mahal and Rai Praveen Mahal (named after a royal paramour), all arranged together symmetrically. There are also three beautiful temples – the Ram Raja, the Lakshmi Narayan and the Chaturbhuj. A unique blend of palace, fort and temple styles, the Chaturbhuj Temple is dedicated to Vishnu (its name literally means "he who has four arms") and has huge arcaded halls for massed singing, plus a soaring spire.

Lying along the Betwa river, at the Kanchana Ghat stairs, are the 14 beautiful *chhatris* (cenotaphs) of the Orchha rulers. Built in the 17th century, they serve as reminders of Orchha's feudal history.

Jahangir Mahal

An excellent example of Rajput Bundela architecture, this palace was built by the Bundela king Bir Singh Deo, who commissioned and named it in honour of the Mughal emperor Jahangir, who spent one night here. The multilayered palace, a blend of Hindu and Islamic styles, has 132 chambers off and above the central courtyard and an almost equal number of subterranean rooms. The square sandstone palace is extravagantly embellished with lapis lazuli tiles, graceful *chhatris* and ornate *jali* screens. Its modest museum is worth a look, if only for the *sati* pillars – memorials to queens who sacrificed themselves (willingly or not) on their husband's funeral pyres.

→

Sunken baths in the central courtyard of Jahangir Mahal, overlooked by its domed pavilions

↑ The *chhatris* of Orchha reflected in the waters of the Betwa at sunset

1 Lakshmi Narayan Temple is dedicated to Lakshmi, the Hindu goddess of prosperity and consort of Vishnu.

2 The vibrant orange-and-pink Ram Raja Temple is the only temple where Rama is worshipped as a king – it was converted from a palace when an idol of Rama supposedly refused to be moved to the Chaturbhuj Temple.

3 Notable for the well-preserved and vibrant murals in its great halls, the Lakshmi Narayan Temple depicts a range of religious and secular life.

GWALIOR FORT

The massive Gwalior Fort stretches for nearly 3 km (2 miles) atop a 100-m- (328-ft-) high sandstone and basalt hill. Its formidable bastioned walls enclose a series of exquisite temples and palaces.

This spectacular fort has many and varied structures; of these, the Man Mandir Palace is the most worth visiting. Built between 1486 and 1516 by Raja Man Singh of the Tomar dynasty, the palace is regarded as one of the finest examples of Rajput secular architecture, embellished with superb stone carving and latticework. Brilliant blue, yellow and green tiles depicting parrots and peacocks, rows of ducks, elephants, banana trees and crocodiles decorate its façade.

Rounded bastions, topped with cupolas and decorated with tilework, and *(inset)* the Man Mandir's great hall

EXPERIENCE Agra and Around

Described by a 16th-century Persian chronicler as "the pearl in the necklace of castles of Hind", Gwalior Fort has had a turbulent history, beginning in the 8th century AD. It was successively ruled by Hindu dynasties, Delhi sultans, the Mughals and the Maratha Scindias, and was briefly in British hands in the 19th century.

The fort is best entered from the Urwahi Gate on its western side, where 21 colossal Jain sculptures (7th–15th century AD) depicting the *tirthankaras* are carved into the rock face. Lying to their left is the richly carved Teli ka Mandir, the tallest temple in the fort. To its north are two 11th-century Vishnu temples, the Saas-Bahu ("Mother-in-Law and Daughter-in-Law") Temples, whose *shikharas* were destroyed by Sultan Qutbuddin Aibak in the 12th century.

At the northeastern edge of the fort is the Archaeological Museum containing a fine collection of Jain and Hindu sculpture.

> **Described by a 16th-century Persian chronicler as "the pearl in the necklace of castles of Hind", Gwalior Fort has had a turbulent history.**

↑ Jain sculptures depicting the *tirthankaras* carved into the cliff on the approach to Gwalior Fort

WHAT ELSE TO SEE IN GWALIOR

Apart from its fort, Gwalior's main attraction is the 19th-century Jai Vilas Palace, whose magnificent Durbar Hall holds two of the world's largest chandeliers. Before they were hung, the roof was tested by having elephants stand on it. North of the fort is the old town, which has two striking Islamic monuments - the Tomb of Muhammad Ghaus, a Mughal nobleman, and the Tomb of Tansen, a famous singer and one of the "nine jewels" of the Mughal emperor Akbar's court.

TOP 3 ANIMALS TO SPOT

Cormorants
With the arrival of the monsoon, thousands of birds, such as greater cormorants, set up nesting colonies. As many as 60 noisy nests on one tree may be seen during this season.

Painted Storks
These birds can usually be seen between July and October, when the trees become nesting sites for nearly 5,000 pairs of storks.

Nilgai (Blue Bull)
The largest of all Asiatic antelopes, these avid crop grazers are protected against hunting because of their resemblance to the holy cow.

6

KEOLADEO GHANA NATIONAL PARK

🅐 D5 🏠 Bharatpur district, Rajasthan; 55 km (34 miles) W of Agra 🚉🚌 Bharatpur ⏰ Summer: 6am–6pm daily; winter: 6:30am–5pm daily 🛈 Deputy Chief Wildlife Warden, (05644) 222 777; RTDC Hotel Saras, Bharatpur, www.tourism.rajasthan. gov.in/keoladeo-ghana-national-park.html

This UNESCO World Heritage Site, one of the world's most important animal sanctuaries, is a mosaic of wetlands, woodlands, grass and scrub. It is most known for its incredibly diverse bird population; there are 375 species in the park, which include birds such as the world's tallest stork.

Keoladeo Ghana derives its name from a temple to the Hindu god Shiva (Keoladeo) within a dense forest *(ghana)*. This once-arid scrubland was first developed by Bharatpur's rulers in the mid-18th century by diverting the waters of a nearby irrigation canal to create a private duck reserve. Today, the park spreads over 29 sq km (11 sq miles) and attracts a wide variety of migrant and water birds, which fly in each winter from as far away as Siberia. Expert boatmen will navigate the wetlands for you, and bicycles and cycle rickshaws are available for the forest paths. The park is also home to nilgai (blue bull), whose broad backs offer comfortable resting places for birds.

Did You Know?

The Sarus crane attracts its partner with an elaborate dance and mates for life.

↑ A flamboyant flock of flamingos wading through the wetlands

Lucky onlookers spotting nilgai slipping gracefully into the water ↑

→

A pair of spotted owls nestling up against each together in the safety of a tree

STAY

The Bagh
Luxurious rooms with stunning gardens; perfect for visiting nearby Keoladeo National Park.

⌂ Bharatpur
⊞ thebagh.com

₹₹₹

Sunbird
Just a few hundred metres from the gates of Keoladeo Ghana National Park, with comfortable rooms and a great restaurant.

⌂ Bharatpur
⊞ hotelsunbird.com

₹₹₹

EXPERIENCE MORE

⑦

Bharatpur

▲D5 **◙**Bharatpur district,
Rajasthan; 55 km (34 miles)
W of Agra **ℹ**Opp RTDC
Hotel, Saras Circle, Agra Rd;
www.tourism.rajasthan.
gov.in/bharatpur.html

Most famous for the nearby
Keoladeo Ghana National
Park *(p192)*, the kingdom of
Bharatpur came into prominence during the final years
of the Mughal empire. It was
founded by the fearless Jats,
a community of landowners.
Their remarkable leader was
Raja Suraj Mal (r 1724–63), who
in 1755 captured and fortified
the city of Bharatpur, thereby
laying the foundations of his
capital. This powerful ruler
defied the reigning Mughal
emperor, stormed Delhi and
Agra and brought home the
massive gates of Agra Fort
and installed them at his own
fort at Deeg's Water Palace

↓ Bharatpur's Government
Museum, housed in a
former palace

> **Their remarkable leader was Raja Suraj
> Mal (r 1724-63), who in 1755 captured and
> fortified the city of Bharatpur, thereby
> laying the foundations of his capital.**

(p186), near Bharatpur. Also
a prolific builder, he used the
loot from Mughal buildings,
including a swing (now in
Deeg), to embellish the forts
and palaces he built throughout his kingdom.

In the centre of Bharatpur
is Lohagarh ("iron fort"), which
withstood repeated attacks
first by the Marathas and then
by the British until it was
finally captured by Lord Lake
in 1805. When built, it was a
masterpiece of construction
with massive double ramparts
made of solid packed mud
and rubble that were sur-
rounded by impressive moats.
Most of the outermost ramparts have disintegrated, but
the inner ones are intact and
are distinguished by two
towers, the Jawahar Burj and
Fateh Burj, built to mark
successive Jat victories over
the Mughals and the British.
The Victory Column at Jawahar

Burj carries an inscription with
the genealogy of the Jat kings.
Both its north and south gates
were part of the loot from the
imperial Mughal capital at
Delhi. Three palaces were built
in the fort by the rustic Jats in
a surprisingly fine mix of
Mughal and Rajput stylistic
detail. Two of the palaces,
located around the Katcheri
(court) Bagh, now house the
Government Museum, where
a rare collection of 1st- and
2nd-century stone carvings
and terracotta toys from
nearby excavations can be
seen. An interesting sunken
hamam is close by. In 1818,
Bharatpur became the first
Rajput state to sign a treaty
of alliance with the British
East India Company.

Government Museum
⊛ **◙**Near Nehru Park
◖(05644) 22 8185
◷9:45am–5:15pm Tue–Sun

Datia Palace, built on the order of Bir Singh Deo in the 17th century

Dholpur

🅰E5 🅿Dholpur district, Rajasthan; 54 km (34 miles) S of Agra 🚐 ℹwww.tourism.rajasthan.gov.in/dholpur.html

Situated on the banks of the River Chambal, the small town of Dholpur was strategically located on the route from Delhi to the Deccan, making it the target of invading armies. In 1504, Sikandar Lodi set up camp here for a month on his march against Gwalior. Some 20 years later, Babur made this a royal domain of his new empire. The ruined Shergarh Fort, said to be 1,000 years old, is in Dholpur, as is a modest 19th-century palace (closed to the public) which can only be seen through an ironwork railing. The palace has a number of Art Deco rooms covered with European tiles. Dholpur is today associated with the beige-coloured sandstone quarried nearby, used in buildings all over Rajasthan and made famous by Lutyens, who used it for the building of New Delhi (p70).

Dholpur town is a convenient base to explore a number of fascinating neighbouring sites. Machkund (3 km/2 miles west) has over 100 temples along its lake. Its waters are said to heal all skin diseases. Damoh, a popular picnic spot, has several waterfalls, while Talab Shahi (40 km/25 miles) has the remains of hunting lodges developed by the Jat rulers of Dholpur for their European guests. Off the beaten track is Jhor (16 km/10 miles), where in 1978 Babur's 400-year-old Lotus Garden was discovered.

PARADISE GARDEN

The concept of the Paradise Garden was introduced by the first great Mughal, Babur. Yearning for the natural beauty of Ferghana, his homeland in Central Asia, he re-created the Persian paradise garden based on Islamic geometric and metaphysical design concepts. The *charbagh* was an enclosed garden quartered by walkways, sunken groves and water channels. The Jhor garden of paradise, often referred to as the Lotus Garden, was laid out in 1527, barely a year after Babur invaded India.

Datia

🅰E7 🅿Datia district, Madhya Pradesh; 187 km (116 miles) S of Agra 🚐 ℹwww.mptourism.com

The main focus of this ghostly town is the five-storeyed Datia Palace, an outstanding building of great structural complexity that was commissioned by the Bundela king Bir Singh Deo in 1620.

Another important historic building is the later Rajgarh Palace, which offers a panoramic view of the entire walled town.

The Pitambara Peeth temple complex, situated at the southern end of town, is a favourite among pilgrims. The complex is dedicated to the ten Tantric forms of the goddess Parvati. An older Shiva temple inside the complex contains a *lingam* (a phallic representation of the god) that is believed to date back to the time of the *Mahabharata* epic (p163).

Did You Know?

Datia is known as "Laghu Vrindavan" (small Vrindavan) due to its many temples.

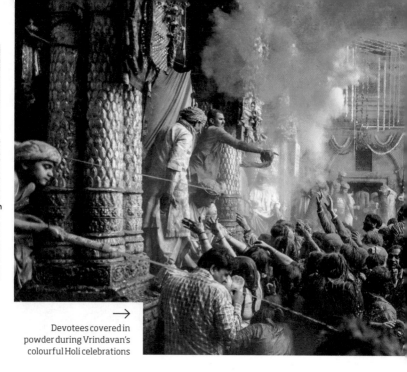

→
Devotees covered in
powder during Vrindavan's
colourful Holi celebrations

Vrindavan

🗺 D5 🏛 Mathura district,
Uttar Pradesh; 68 km
(42 miles) NW of Agra
🚌 ℹ www.uptourism.
gov.in/post/mathura-
vrindavan-explore

Positioned on the edge of the
River Yamuna, Vrindavan, or
Brindavan (literally, "forest
of fragrant basil"), became a
pilgrim centre following the
Krishna cult revival in the 16th
century. Krishna is believed to
have lived here as a young
cowherd. "His" cows have the
run of the streets, his name is
continuously chanted in prayer
halls and stalls outside temples
sell *peda* sweets, said to have
been his favourite.

Vrindavan's riverfront is
lined by temples and ghats,
built by the Hindu kings of
Amber, Bharatpur and Orchha,
and by rich merchants. On the
edge of the old town, Govind
Dev Temple, originally seven
storeys high, was endowed in
1590 by Raja Man Singh I of
Amber. Its presiding deity is

> ### THE KRISHNA CULT
>
> A peacock feather, a flute and the colour blue announce
> the presence of Krishna. Named after his dark skin,
> this most human of gods still haunts the glades and
> forests along the Yamuna. A naughty child who was
> passionately fond of milk and butter, Krishna is also
> the charming flute-player whose flirtatious dalliance
> with Radha is a metaphor for the complex metaphysics
> of temporal and spiritual love, widely celebrated in
> art and literature.

now in Jaipur's temple of the
same name (*p206*). Opposite is
the 19th-century Dravidian-
style Rangaji Temple, with a
gold-plated ritual pillar and a
museum of temple treasures.

On a hill by the river, Madan
Mohan Temple, built in 1580
with local red sandstone, is the
town's oldest temple, elegant
in its simplicity. Nearby, the
popular Banke Bihari Temple
forms the centre of the town's
Holi celebrations. The curtain
in front of its image of Krishna
is opened and closed at inter-
vals – it is believed that anyone
gazing too long at the image
will be overpowered by it.

On the Mathura Road,
the gleaming white Pagal

Baha Temple is worth a visit
to see its outrageously kitsch
moving puppet tableaux of
scenes from the life of Krishna.

At Janmashtami (*p54*) and
Holi (*p55*), Vrindavan becomes
a riot of colour and dance.

Mathura

🗺 D5 🏛 Mathura district,
Uttar Pradesh; 62 km
(39 miles) NW of Agra 🚆🚌
ℹ www.uptourism.gov.in/
post/mathura-vrindavan-
explore

Mathura, on the west bank of
the Yamuna, is the birthplace

EAT

Status Restaurant

An excellent veggie restaurant with a cool ambience, good *thalis* and a choice of north Indian, south Indian and Chinese dishes.

 🅐D5 🏠 Hotel Brijwasi Royal, SBI Crossing, Station Road, Mathura 🌐 brijwasihotels.com/dining-royal.htm

₹₹₹

Sri Krishna Janmasthan Temple

🏠 Mathura-Vrindavan Road 🕐 Summer: 5am-noon & 4-9:30pm daily; winter: 5:30am-noon & 3-8:30pm daily 🌐 shrikrishnajanmasthan.net

Government Museum

♿ 🏠 Dampier Nagar 📞 (0565) 250 0847 🕐 10:30am-4:30pm Tue-Sun 🚫 Mon, 2nd Sat of month & public hols

---

12

Bari

🅐D6 🏠 Dholpur district, Rajasthan; 84 km (68 miles) SW of Agra 🚌 ℹ www.tourism.rajasthan.gov.in

The site of an old 100-acre (40-ha) garden that was once so dense that sunlight could not reach the ground, Bari was where Emperor Shah Jahan built a number of pleasure pavilions. Located nearby is the Vana Vihar Ram Sagar Wildlife Reserve, home to crocodiles, sambhar, wild boar and several species of migratory bird. Remains of an old fort built by Feroz Shah Tughlaq can also be seen here.

of Krishna. The exact spot is said to be in a room at the **Sri Krishna Janmasthan Temple**. A 1960s complex, it was built to replace the original that was demolished by Mughal emperor Aurangzeb in 1660 to erect the Katra Masjid mosque nearby. This topic remains a source of tension between Hindus and Muslims, something which explains the heavy army presence. The mosque is closed to visitors, but the temple is open and worth seeing (though you can't enter with a phone or camera).

Along the tree-lined riverfront, the city's 25 ghats form a splendid network of temples, pavilions and steps leading to the water. The evening arti, when small oil lamps are floated on the river, is performed at Vishram Ghat, where legend says Krishna rested after he killed the tyrant Kamsa. Close by are the Sati Burj, a red sandstone pavilion built in the 1570s, and Kans Qila, the site of the old fort where Sawai Jai Singh II of Jaipur constructed one of his five observatories *(p212)*.

The Jama Masjid (main mosque), with its striking tile-work, plus a number of other buildings with carved façades, lie behind the riverfront. A charming oddity is the 1860 Church of the Sacred Heart, which combines Western elements with features from local temple architecture.

The **Government Museum** collection highlights the Mathura School of Art, which flourished in the 1st–6th centuries AD. It has some exquisite pieces, including a perfectly preserved standing Buddha, and a famous headless statue of the great Kushana king Kanishka.

 💬 INSIDER TIP
River Boat Trip

There's no better way to experience Vishram Ghat than by boat. Head out as evening draws in to see the water illuminated by glowing lamps, placed on the river by devotees. Haggle to get a fair price on the boat.

Visitors exploring
one of Vrindavan's
many temples ↑

A DRIVING TOUR
BRAJBHUMI

Locator Map
For more detail see p170

Length 105 km (65 miles) **Stopping-off points**
Vrindavan, Radhakund, Barsana **Terrain** Flat plains;
roads in small towns may be narrow and unpaved

Devotees believe that the Braj region is composed of
sacred *mandalas* (circuits) that map the idyllic pastoral
landscape of Krishna's early life. Divided by the Yamuna,
this tour partly follows the *chaurasi kos ki yatra*, a traditional pilgrimage of about 300 km (186 miles), undertaken
around Janmashtami *(p54)*, Krishna's birthday.

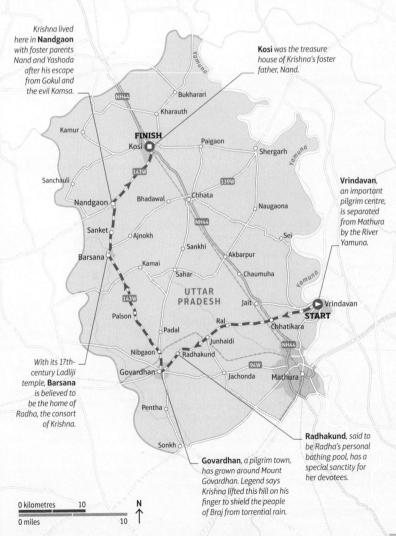

*Krishna lived
here in* **Nandgaon**
*with foster parents
Nand and Yashoda
after his escape
from Gokul and
the evil Kamsa.*

Kosi *was the treasure
house of Krishna's foster
father, Nand.*

Vrindavan,
*an important
pilgrim centre,
is separated
from Mathura
by the River
Yamuna.*

*With its 17th-
century Ladliji
temple,* **Barsana**
*is believed to
be the home of
Radha, the consort
of Krishna.*

Radhakund, *said to
be Radha's personal
bathing pool, has a
special sanctity for
her devotees.*

Govardhan, *a pilgrim town,
has grown around Mount
Govardhan. Legend says
Krishna lifted this hill on his
finger to shield the people
of Braj from torrential rain.*

0 kilometres   10

0 miles   10

N ↑

A DRIVING TOUR
BUNDELKHAND

Length 120 km (75 miles) **Stopping-off points** Gwalior, Sonagiri, Datia, Jhansi, Taragram, Orchha **Terrain** Undulating plains; roads in small towns may be narrow and unpaved

Gwalior *(p190)* and the adjoining region of Bundelkhand, named after the Bundela Rajputs, make up a culturally distinctive area in central India. Innumerable forts and monuments, situated in a boulder-strewn landscape, still echo with stories of the valour and pageantry of the Bundela courts, and of warriors such as the Rani of Jhansi, an important leader in the War of Independence in 1857. The area's rich history and cultural traditions are seen in the archi-tectural treasures of Gwalior and the medieval town of Orchha *(p188)*.

Locator Map
For more detail see p170

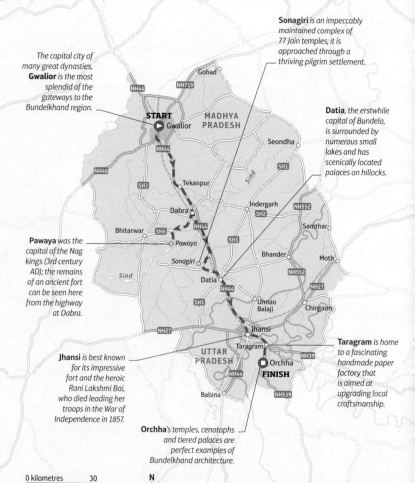

Sonagiri is an impeccably maintained complex of 77 Jain temples; it is approached through a thriving pilgrim settlement.

The capital city of many great dynasties, **Gwalior** is the most splendid of the gateways to the Bundelkhand region.

Datia, the erstwhile capital of Bundela, is surrounded by numerous small lakes and has scenically located palaces on hillocks.

Pawaya was the capital of the Nag kings (3rd century AD); the remains of an ancient fort can be seen here from the highway at Dabra.

Taragram is home to a fascinating handmade paper factory that is aimed at upgrading local craftsmanship.

Jhansi is best known for its impressive fort and the heroic Rani Lakshmi Bai, who died leading her troops in the War of Independence in 1857.

Orchha's temples, cenotaphs and tiered palaces are perfect examples of Bundelkhand architecture.

One of Orchha's
royal *chhatris*
(cenotaphs)

Women visiting Chand Baori, a stepwell near Jaipur

JAIPUR AND BEYOND

At the end of the 11th century, the Kachhawahas of Jaipur established their kingdom at Amber. In the region around it lay other Rajput kingdoms – the Chauhan stronghold of Ajmer that would soon fall to Muslim forces, and the massive Rathore jungle fort of Ranthambhore, which would later become a Mughal preserve. By the 18th century the fierce feudal lords of Shekhawati would become vassals of Amber-Jaipur, while Jat kings would rule over Bharatpur, the only non-Rajput kingdom in the area. The early Rajput states engaged in bitter internecine clan wars, but with the rise of the Delhi sultans, their energies were directed at keeping their lands safe from the marauding Muslim troops. Finally, under the Mughal emperor Akbar, military and matrimonial alliances paved the way for peace in the region. The result was a cultural and social synthesis which produced some outstanding art and architecture. The British also followed this policy of appeasement and offered the princes military protection in return for their loyalty. Following Indian independence in 1947, the rule of the princely states ended when they were incorporated into the modern state of Rajasthan, with Jaipur as the administrative capital. But despite the introduction of democracy, the Rajput feudal tradition, with its code of loyalty to the local chieftain, and immense pride in the past, remains alive.

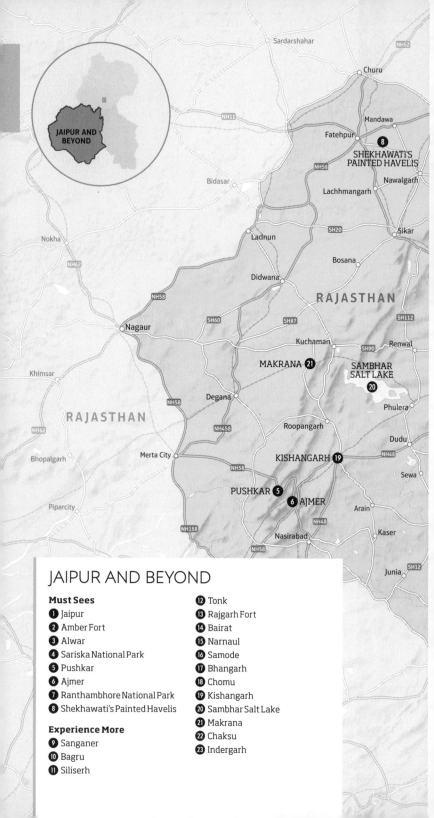

JAIPUR AND BEYOND

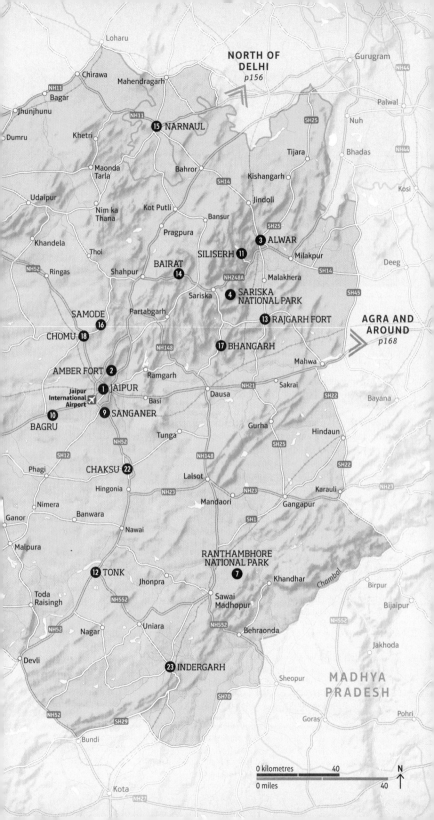

JAIPUR

🔺C5 🏠Jaipur district; 270 km (170 miles) S of Delhi
✈15 km (9 miles) S of city centre 🚌🚐 ℹ️Paryatan Bhawan,
Mirza Ismail Rd; www.tourism.rajasthan.gov.in/jaipur.html

A labyrinth of bazaars, opulent palaces and historic sights, Jaipur is known as the "Pink City" because of the rosy hue of its buildings. One of the most popular destinations in Rajasthan, its old walled city contains jewels such as the City Palace and the Hawa Mahal.

① Govind Dev Temple

🏠Jaleb Chowk (at City Palace) 🕐4:30am-9:30pm daily 🌐govinddevji.net

The flute-playing Lord Krishna (also known as Govind Dev) is worshiped at this unusual temple. The image of this god originally came from the Govindeoji Temple in Vrindavan (p196), but was brought to Amber (p222), then the capital of Jaipur's ruling family, in the late 17th century to save it from the zeal of the Mughal emperor Aurangzeb, who was known for his religious intolerance.

It is believed this temple was once a garden pavilion called Suraj Mahal, where Sawai Jai Singh II lived while his dream-city, Jaipur, was being built. Legend has it that one night the king awoke from his sleep to find himself in the presence of Krishna who asked that his *devasthan* ("divine residence") be returned to him, so Jai Singh moved to the Chandra Mahal, at the opposite end of the garden, and installed the image in the temple as the guardian deity of Jaipur's rulers. The temple has seven artis throughout the day where pilgrims can worship this incarnation of Krishna.

Just behind the temple is the 18th-century Jai Niwas Bagh, a Mughal-style garden with fountains and water channels. Towards the north is the Badal Mahal, an enchanting hunting pavilion.

② Hawa Mahal

🏠Hawa Mahal Rd 📞(0141) 261 8862 🕐9am-5pm daily
🕐Public hols

The pink façade of the fanciful Hawa Mahal ("Palace of Winds") has become the icon of Jaipur. Erected in 1799 by Sawai Pratap Singh (r 1778– 1803), the five-storey-high structure is only one room deep, with walls not more than 20 cm (8 inches) thick, designed to enable the ladies of the harem to watch the lively streets below while remaining unseen. Dedicated to Lord Krishna, the tiered Baroque-like structure was meant, when seen from afar, to look like the crown that often adorns the god's head.

> INSIDER TIP
> **Find Hidden Jaipur**
>
> Explore Jaipur on a wonderful walking tour with Virasat Experiences (www.virasatexperiences.com), who take visitors to see hidden temples, taste the best samosas and meet skilled crafts-men and jewellers.

← Hawa Mahal, a whimsical addition to the state's architectural vocabulary

from *chaugan*, a Persian form of polo played with a curved stick. The area, once used for festival processions and wrestling matches, still hosts major festivals.

 (4)

Albert Hall Museum

🏛 Ram Niwas Bagh 🕐 9am–5pm & 7-10pm daily 🚫 Public hols 🌐 alberthall jaipur.gov.in

The most imposing treasure at this grand museum is one of the world's largest Persian garden carpets (dating from 1632), which can be viewed on request in the Durbar Hall. The museum also has an extensive collection of paintings dating back to the 1500s.

(3)

Chaugan Stadium

🏛 Gangori Bazaar Road, Tripolia Bazaar

This large open area near the City Palace derives its name

Must See

EAT

Palladio
With an opulent interior reminiscent of a maharaja's palace, Palladio serves food and drinks inspired by Italy.

🏛 Narain Niwas Palace Hotel, Kanota Bagh
🌐 bar-palladio.com

₹₹₹

Peacock
This popular rooftop restaurant has great views and serves dishes from around the world.

🏛 Hotel Pearl Palace, 51 Hathroi Fort, Ajmer Rd 🌐 hotelpearl palace.com

₹₹₹

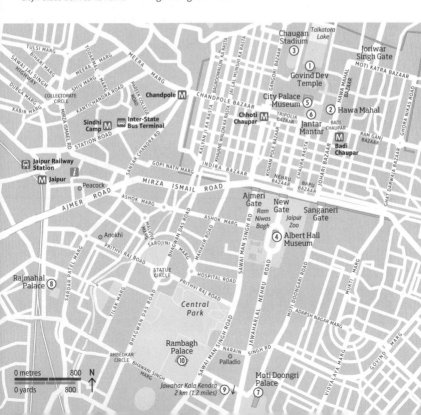

⑤ 🏛 🏛 🏛

CITY PALACE MUSEUM

🏛 **City Palace Complex** 🕐 **9:30am–5:30pm daily** 📅 **Second day of Holi** 🌐 **royaljaipur.in**

The Maharaja Sawai Man Singh II Museum, popularly known as the City Palace Museum, occupies Jaipur's City Palace. Built between 1729 and 1732 during the reign of Maharaja Sawai Jai Singh II, the palace lies at the heart of the city and has been home to the rulers of Jaipur since the 19th century. The sprawling complex is a superb blend of Rajput and Mughal architecture, with open, airy Mughal-style public buildings leading to private apartments.

The City Palace Museum's treasures are divided across five galleries – the Textile Gallery, Sabha Niwas (also called the Diwan-i-Aam), Sarvato Bhadra, Sileh Khana, and the Painting and Photography gallery – and provide a splendid introduction to Jaipur's princely past, and its fascinating arts and crafts. In the Textile Gallery are ornate garments, including extragavant medieval saris. The former ceremonial hall, Sabha Niwas, displays rare Mughal and Rajput miniature paintings, while Sarvato Bhadra is home to two giant, Guinness-World-Record-breaking silver urns. Sileh Khana houses a fine collection of antique weapons. In the Painting and Photography gallery, the illustrated manuscripts detailing the famous Hindu story of the Durga Saptashati and Bhagvata Puran are the stars of the show. Also within the complex is the wonderfully opulent Chandra Mahal palace.

The palace's brightly coloured, arcaded courtyard, accessed via the *(inset)* Rajendra Pol gateway ↑

RAJASTHANI MINIATURES

The vivid, intricate paintings of Rajasthan's princely states grew out of illustrated Jain and Hindu sacred texts. Originally, they depicted mainly religious themes, in bold lines and bright primary colours. During the 17th and 18th centuries, the lines became more delicate, and the range of colours and themes wider. Several distinctive schools of style evolved, usually showing human figures in profile and in different colours, while seasons, flowers and animals are used symbolically to express moods.

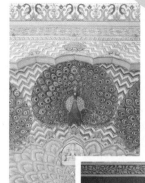

← The finely painted Peacock Gate, representing autumn and dedicated to Lord Vishnu

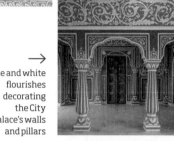

→ Blue and white flourishes decorating the City Palace's walls and pillars

Did You Know?

The descendents of maharajas of Jaipur still reside in the seven-storey Chandra Mahal.

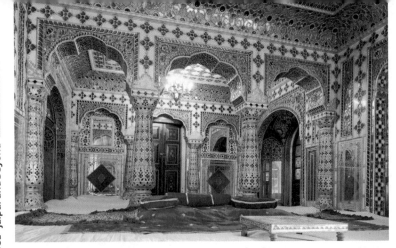

CHANDRA MAHAL

The beautiful seven-storeyed Chandra Mahal (Moon Palace) is located in the northwest of the vast City Palace. Built for Maharaja Sawai Jai Singh II, it was completed in 1734 and each of the seven floors is luxuriously decorated. The ground and first floors of the palace house the extensive art collection of the City Palace Museum. The second floor, Suhk Niwas (Hall of Pleasure),

has an open terrace decorated with colourful floral designs and Mughal miniatures. Rang Mandir (Temple of Colour), the third floor, is embellished with mirrors in the walls, pillars and ceilings, as is the fourth floor, Shobha Niwas (House of Beauty), which also has exquisite blue tiles and gold leaf. The fifth floor, Chhavi Niwas (Hall of Images), is decorated with blue-and-white painted

↑ The opulently gilded Shobha Niwas in the Chandra Mahal

floral designs. Both the sixth floor, Sri Niwas (Shining Hall), with its mirrored ceilings, and the top-floor, Mukut Niwas (House of the Crown), an open marble pavilion, offer magnificent views of the walled city and surrounding hills.

SILEH KHANA

This gallery, located near the Mubarak Mahal, is dedicated to arms and armour. Some of the exhibits, displayed under exuberantly painted ceilings, are reputed to be the finest examples of weaponry used in medieval India, and are a tribute to the Rajput warrior's worship of arms. Whether specially commissioned, or acquired by the maharajas, the weapons in the royal armoury were both lethal and exquisitely crafted. On view are a range of swords, daggers and katars, a dual-edged blade with a grip handle, which would have been worn hitched to the waistband. Some are of green or white jade and are carved, while others are studded with jewels. Hilts are engraved with hunting scenes,

images of deities, or topped with the heads of exotic birds and animals. Among the swords on display is one belonging to Raja Man Singh I (r 1590–1619) weighing about 5 kg (11 lbs). There are two swords of Jahangir and Shah Jahan and also Akbar's gold-encrusted helmet, shaped like a turban. A fascinating section displays gunpowder containers, some made of ivory, others decorated with mother-of-pearl inlay on shell. There's also a lotus-shaped steel mace belonging to Jai Singh I, used to disembowel his enemies.

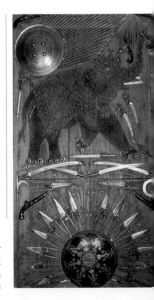

→ An array of arms and armour on display in the Sileh Khana

PAINTING AND PHOTOGRAPHY

Unveiled back in 2015, this relatively new exhibition showcases the museum's incredible collection of painting and photography, which spans the 18th to 20th centuries. Standouts of the collection include photographs by Maharaja Ram Singh II – around 2,000 glass negatives of images he took were recently discovered in the Madho Nivas wing of the museum. The prince's atmospheric shots of the city, the palace and his court include photographs of his doctor and – at the time controversial – portraits of the women of his household. All the images help to give a real flavour of what life was like in 19th-century Jaipur. The gallery also contains the illustrated manuscripts of a number of Hindu religious texts, such as the Durga Saptashati and Bhagavata Purana. In addition, there is a selection of fascinating portraits. The Painting and Photography gallery also houses a number of important manuscripts, maps and carpets, although these are not currently on display.

↑ The richly decorated and colourful interior of the Sabha Niwas

SABHA NIWAS (DURBAR HALL)

Leading from the Mubarak Mahal is a magnificent gateway with a brass door that opens into a stately courtyard and the fascinating Sabha Niwas (Hall of Public Audience). Also sometimes referred to as Diwan-e-Aam, it was built during the reign of Maharaja Sawai Pratap Singh (1778–1803), a period that saw great development in local architectural and building skills. The spacious, richly decorated assembly hall is built on a raised platform supported by artistically dressed marble columns. It was used by the maharajas for formal durbars (royal courts), ceremonies and receptions. The hall housed an art gallery for many years, but a conservation programme has restored its former status and sparkling decor. Visitors now have the sense of a real durbar as it used to be when Sawai Man Singh II, Jaipur's last maharajah, would hold his public audiences here. The last durbar took place in March 1949.

TEXTILES GALLERY

A glittering array of textiles and costumes from the royal *toshakhana* (treasure house) is displayed on the ground floor of Mubarak Mahal (Welcome Palace). Representing India's great textile tradition, the collection on view here covers everything from rich brocades, known as *kimkhabs*, from Aurangabad, Varanasi and Surat, to exquisitely embroidered and hand-loom-woven shawls from Kashmir. The expert and refined craftsmanship that existed in Jaipur almost three centuries ago is visible in the wide variety of blockprinted textiles from nearby Sanganer *(p240)* and tie-dye *(bandhini)* pieces produced by the palace workshops. Equally breath-taking is the range of royal garments. Dazzling gathered skirts and long, flowing veils *(odhnis)*, decorated with *zari* (gold thread embroidery) and *gota* (gold or silver frill), worn by the ladies of the court, vie for attention with the brocaded robes, waist-bands (patkas), pyjamas and turbans worn by the men.

⑥ ⊗ ⊗

JANTAR MANTAR

🏛 Chandni Chowk, outside City Palace 🕐 9am–4:30pm daily
🚫 Public hols 🌐 tourism.rajasthan.gov.in/jantar-mantar.html

A strange collection of circles, walls and stairs, Jantar Mantar is an early observatory. It was built by Sawai Jai Singh II in the early 18th century in order to predict the movements of the sun, moon and planets; he had five of these structures built across his kingdom, but the one in Jaipur is the largest and best preserved.

Built between 1728 and 1734, this impressive Jantar Mantar observatory has been described as "the most realistic and logical landscape in stone", its 19 instruments, or *yantas* (meaning a machine for calculating), resembling a giant sculptural composition. It was constructed on the orders of Sawai Jai Singh II, a keen astronomer who kept abreast of the latest astronomical studies around the world. Some of the instruments are still used to forecast how hot the summer months will be, as well as the expected date of arrival, duration and intensity of the monsoon, and the possibility of floods and famine.

→

The Krantivrtta, which measured the longitude and latitude of objects in the sky

TOP 5 **CALCULATION INSTRUMENTS**

Rashivalaya Yantra
This *yantra* is composed of 12 pieces, one for each zodiac sign, and is used by astrologers to draw up horoscopes. It is the only one of its kind.

Ram Yantra
This instrument's readings determine the celestial arc from horizon to zenith, as well as the altitude of the sun.

Laghu Samrat Yantra
This "small sundial" calculates local time to within 20 seconds.

Samrat Yantra
The largest machine on site, this 27-m- (89-ft-) high sundial forecasts the year's crop prospects.

Chakra Yantra
These two circular metal instruments can be used to calculate the angles of stars and planets from the equator.

↑ Rashivalaya Yantra's 12 pieces set in front of the tall Samrat Yantra

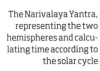

← Illustration of Leo, one of the signs of the zodiac, found at Jantar Mantar

→ The Narivalaya Yantra, representing the two hemispheres and calculating time according to the solar cycle

⑦

Moti Doongri Palace

🏠 Jawaharlal Nehru Marg
🚫 To the public

A large walled fort astride a hill, Moti Doongri owes its exterior, which resembles a British castle, to Sawai Man Singh II (r 1922–49), who converted the old fort here into a palace. In 1940 he married Princess Gayatri Devi of Cooch Behar, and this palace became the venue for the couple's glittering parties. At the foot of the

SHOP

Anokhi

The best place to shop for fair trade textiles, beautiful clothes and homewares, with a great on-site café.

🏠 KK Square, Prithviraj Rd, Panch Batti, C Scheme
🕐 10am–8pm

hill is Lakshmi Narayan Temple, with its elaborate carvings.

⑧

Rajmahal Palace

🏠 Sardar Patel Marg
🌐 sujanluxury.com

Now a grand hotel, this palace was built in 1739 for Sawai Jai Singh II's favourite queen, Chandra Kumari Ranawatji, and used as a summer resort by the ladies of the court. In 1821, it became the official home of the British Resident in Jaipur – but the most memorable phase of its history came when Jaipur's last maharaja, Man Singh II, and his wife Gayatri Devi moved here in 1956. Among the celebrities they entertained were Prince Philip and Jackie Kennedy.

⑨

Jawahar Kala Kendra

🏠 Nehru Marg   🕐 Daily
🌐 jawaharkalakendra.rajasthan.gov.in

Designed by the noted Indian architect Charles Correa, this

arts centre is a remarkable example of contemporary Indian architecture. The building is split into nine squares to reflect Jaipur's famous grid system, with eight connecting buildings, surrounding a central courtyard. The gallery displays a range of textiles, handicrafts and weaponry. In the centre, the open-air plaza is used for performances of traditional Rajasthani music.

⑩

Rambagh Palace

🏠 Bhawani Singh Rd
🌐 tajhotels.com

The Rambagh Palace, now a splendid hotel, was built in 1835 as a small garden pavilion for Ram Singh II's wet nurse. Later, Madho Singh II, Ram Singh II's son, transformed it into a royal playground with a polo field and indoor pool, surrounded by lush gardens. In 1933, it became the official residence of Madho Singh's heir, Man Singh II, who added a red-and-gold Chinese room, black marble bathrooms and Lalique crystal chandeliers. It became a hotel in 1957.

The splendid lobby of the Rambagh Palace, now a heritage hotel

JAIPUR JEWELLERY

Be it the fabulous rubies and emeralds sported by former maharajas and their queens or the splendid silver and bone ornaments worn by peasants, jewellery is an integral part of Rajasthani culture. Even camels, horses and elephants have specially designed anklets and necklaces. Jaipur is one of the largest ornament-making centres in India, and *meenakari* (enamel work) and *kundankari* (inlay work with gems) are the two traditional techniques for which it is most famous.

STONE CUTTING

Jaipur is a centre of lapidary, specializing in cutting emeralds and diamonds from Africa, South America and various regions of India, which are used in refined *kundankari* work. Gem-cutters learn their skill by cutting garnets.

STONE SETTERS

The skill of stone-setting can be seen in the crowded alleys of Haldiyon ka Rasta, Jadiyon ka Rasta and Gopalji ka Rasta. An inherited art, the jewellery trade is in the hands of artisans' guilds.

STYLES OF JEWELLERY

Kundankari uses highly refined gold as a base, inlaid with lac and set with precious and semiprecious stones to provide colour and design. *Meenakari* is the art of enamelling gold and can be used to embellish the obverse side of *kundan* jewellery.

AMRAPALI MUSEUM

Showcasing over 4,000 pieces of jewellery collected over 50 years, Jaipur's privately owned Amrapali Museum *(www. amrapalimuseum.com)* aims to preserve and educate about Indian craftsmanship. While the pieces on display come from all over India, the museum highlights those of Rajput and Jaipur artisans.

Pieces of Jewellery

Chandbali Earrings

Known for the crescent moon design style, these earrings originated in Rajasthan, but became popular across India.

Sarpech

A cypress-shaped turban ornament, the *sarpech* was introduced by the Mughal emperors in the early 17th century and used to display their finest gems. Rajput rulers sported dazzling pieces such as this one, enamelled with gold.

Kundan Pendant

This pendant was made with diamonds and gold, using the intricate, traditional *kundankari* technique.

A SHORT WALK
BADI CHAUPAR

Distance 2 km (1 mile) **Nearest Bus Station** Badi Chaupar
Time 30 minutes

Near Jaipur's biggest attractions of the City Palace and Hawa Mahal, the Badi Chaupar ("Large Square") sits at one end of the colourful Tripolia Bazaar. The area is a hub of activity, rich with pungent smells and vibrant colours, with temple bells adding to the cacophony of street sounds, and narrow pedestrian lanes

branching out from the main streets. Wander down these to find artisans fashioning handicrafts in tiny workshops, and the *havelis* of former eminent citizens, now used as schools and shops. As few changes have been made to the original 18th-century street plan, walking these streets is a stroll through history.

Did You Know?

Jaipur was the first planned city in India, organized into nine square grids that still remain.

*Constructed in 1734, the impressive **Tripolia Gate** was once the main entrance to the City Palace.*

*Ishwari Singh built the **Isar Lat** tower in 1749 to commemorate his victory over his step-brother, Madho Singh I.*

Marigolds and other flowers, sold here, are made into garlands and used as offerings to beloved deities in temples and roadside shrines.

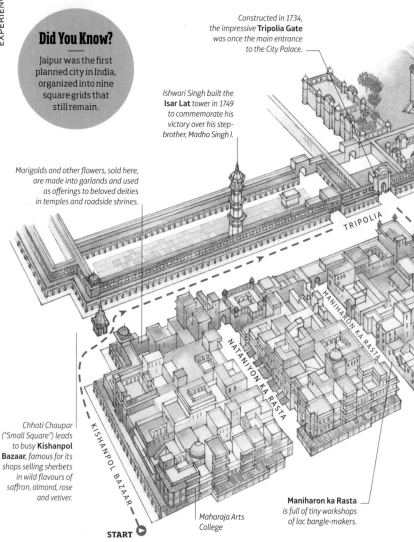

TRIPOLIA

MANIHARON KA RASTA

NATANIYON KA RASTA

*Chhoti Chaupar ("Small Square") leads to busy **Kishanpol Bazaar**, famous for its shops selling sherbets in wild flavours of saffron, almond, rose and vetiver.*

KISHANPOL BAZAAR

Maniharon ka Rasta *is full of tiny workshops of lac bangle-makers.*

Maharaja Arts College

START

←
Bustling and colourful Tripolia Bazaar, one of the most popular sights in Badi Chaupar

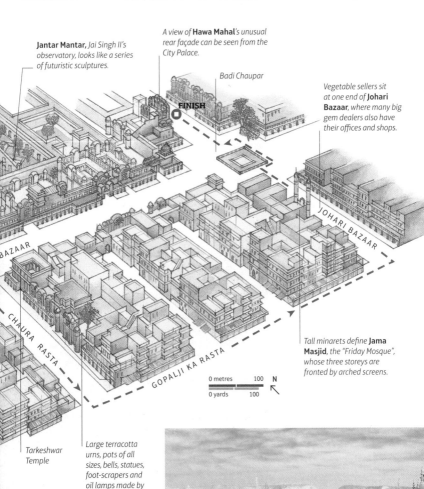

Jantar Mantar, *Jai Singh II's observatory, looks like a series of futuristic sculptures.*

A view of **Hawa Mahal***'s unusual rear façade can be seen from the City Palace.*

Badi Chaupar

FINISH

Vegetable sellers sit at one end of **Johari Bazaar,** *where many big gem dealers also have their offices and shops.*

BAZAAR

CHAURA RASTA

GOPALJI KA RASTA

JOHARI BAZAAR

Tall minarets define **Jama Masjid,** *the "Friday Mosque", whose three storeys are fronted by arched screens.*

| 0 metres | 100 |
| 0 yards | 100 |

N

Tarkeshwar Temple

Large terracotta urns, pots of all sizes, bells, statues, foot-scrapers and oil lamps made by craftsmen are sold at this excellent **pottery shop.**

→
Looking over the rooftops of Badi Chaupar from Hawa Mahal

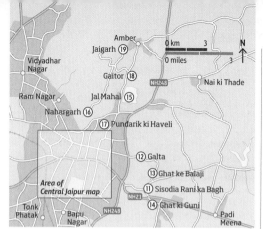

Area of
Central Jaipur map

AROUND JAIPUR

Sisodia Rani ka Bagh

📍 Jaipur district; 6 km
(4 miles) E of Jaipur
📞 (0141) 261 8862
🕐 8am–5pm daily

This elegant and beautiful palace, surrounded by spectacular terraced gardens, was laid out in the 18th century for Sawai Jai Singh II's second wife, a Sisodia princess from Udaipur. The marriage was one of convenience, to foster better relations between the two powerful princely states, and one of the conditions was that the new queen's son would succeed to the Jaipur throne. To escape the ensuing and inevitable palace intrigues, the queen decided to shift to a more private home outside the walled city.

The interiors of this little double-storeyed palace are decorated with lively murals depicting episodes from Krishna's life, hunting scenes and polo matches, mythical beasts and heroic events. The palace is surrounded by beautiful gardens artfully planted with fragrant bushes of jasmine, where peacocks wander amid the spray of fountains and gurgling water channels. Behind the gardens, temples coated in the yellow wash, which is used throughout the compound, are open for worship at midday and in the early evening. Not surprisingly, this enchanting place has become a popular set location for Indian films.

Opposite the palace is Vidyadhar ka Bagh, a small and beautiful 18th-century garden laid out in the valley between two hills. Designed along the lines of a Mughal garden with fountains, shady trees and flowerbeds, it is dedicated to the courtier traditionally credited with designing Jaipur.

---

⑫
Galta

📍 Jaipur district; 10 km
(6 miles) E of Jaipur

The picturesque Galta gorge plunges down the hillside to join the Jaipur–Agra road. A great sage, called Galav, is supposed to have lived and performed penance here. Deep within the gorge is Galta Kund, an 18th-century religious site with two main temples dedicated to Ram and Vishnu; the Achariyon ki Haveli; and a number of smaller shrines. High on the ridge is the Surya Temple.

At different levels are sacred tanks, fed by natural spring water flowing from a rock resembling a cow's mouth. The water is said to have curative powers. The two *baradaris* (pavilions with 12 pilars) on either side of the complex have well-preserved frescoes depicting legends from Krishna's life, including a ceiling painted with gorgeous lotus blooms.

From the summit there are spectacular views of Jaipur, but do beware of monkeys in search of food here; more than 5,000 live here, attracting tourists who watch them splash about in the water tanks. While peanuts are sold at the temple gate as food for the monkeys, it is best not to feed them as they can sometimes become bold and aggressive.

Galta Kund and *(inset)* the interior of one of the temples ↓

Ghat ke Balaji

🏠 Jaipur district; 6 km (4 miles) E of Jaipur
📞 (0141) 268 0964

Behind Sisodia gardens, a double flight of steps ends in a pair of tall gateways leading to a small temple dedicated to the popular monkey-god Hanuman (also known as Balaji). This endearing deity is cherished by the local people who treat him with tender care, and in winter wrap his image in a muffler and quilt to keep him warm. The monkeys that inhabit the area are equally well looked after. Every day

at 4pm, a charming ritual takes place when, to the call of the priests, hordes of silver grey langurs with black faces and long tails descend on the temple for a meal specially cooked for them. Then, swishing their tails, they head back to the valley.

Ghat ki Guni

🏠 Jaipur district; 6 km (4 miles) E of Jaipur

In the 18th and 19th centuries the ministers and dignitaries of the Jaipur court created a tranquil summer retreat in this valley, when the area would bustle with the constant comings and goings of the aristocracy. Now, the deserted *havelis* (mansions), temples and bathing ghats are all that remain of this once exclusive resort. On either side of the road are dense rows of niched façades perforated by tiny windows and arched *chhatris*, elegant eaves and domes. While among the ruins and winding alleys, a number of tea-stalls and little shops selling trinkets and souvenirs have sprung up.

HANUMAN - THE MONKEY GOD

A much loved figure in the pantheon of Hindu gods *(p140)*, Hanuman appears wherever Rama is worshipped. In the *Ramayana*, this loyal trouper and his monkey army play a crucial role in Ravana's defeat and Sita's rescue. The cult of Hanuman as a martial god and protector is so widespread that even a simple stone daubed with orange vermilion paste *(sindoor)* signals his presence.

Looking out towards the Jal Mahal palace, rising out of Man Sagar lake

⑮ Jal Mahal

 Jaipur district; 8 km (5 miles) NE of Jaipur

During the monsoon when water fills the Man Sagar lake, the Jal Mahal or "water palace" seems to float serenely on the calm waters of the lake. Built in the mid-18th century by Madho Singh I, it was based on the Lake Palace at Udaipur where the king spent his childhood. Later it was used as a lodge for duck shooting parties and, even today, a large number of waterbirds can be sighted here. A terrace garden is enclosed by arched passages, and at each corner is a semi-octagonal tower capped by an elegant cupola. The palace is not open to visitors.

Sawai Jai Singh II performed a number of Vedic *yagnas* (a type of Hindu sacrafice) on the western banks of Man Sagar. Dating to that period are traces of a Yagna Stambha ("pillar") where he performed a horse sacrifice, and the Kala Hanumanji, a temple dedicated to the popular monkey god.

To the north of Jal Mahal is the splendidly restored Kanak Vrindavan Temple, dedicated to Krishna, where the image of Govind Dev was lodged before it was taken to the City Palace.

This picturesque complex, with its well-landscaped gardens, fountains and pavilions, makes a popular picnic spot.

⑯ Nahargarh

 Jaipur district; 9 km (6 miles) N of Jaipur **(** (0141) 513 4038 **◷** 10am–5:30pm daily **◷** Public hols

The forbidding hill-top fort of Nahargarh ("tiger fort") stands in what was once a densely forested area. The fierce Meena community ruled this region until they were defeated by the Kachhawahas. Legend says that this was the site of the cenotaph of Nahar Singh, a martyred Rathore warrior, and when Sawai Jai Singh II ordered that its fortifications be strengthened to defend the newly built Jaipur,

---

 HIDDEN GEM
Sculpted Sights

The elegant rooms and grand courtyards of Madhavendra Bhavan house India's first public Sculpture Park *(www.thesculpturepark.in)*, which showcases an amazing array of contemporary sculptures.

---

the warrior's spirit resisted all construction until a priest performed tantric rites. Successive rulers further expanded the fort. Madho Singh II added a lavish palace called Madhavendra Bhavan for his nine queens. Laid out in a maze of terraces and courtyards, it has a cool, airy upper chamber from which the ladies of the court could view the city. Its walls and pillars are an outstanding example of *arayish*, a plaster-work technique that is hand-polished with a piece of agate to produce a marble finish.

---

⑰ Pundarik ki Haveli

 Shastri Chowk, Brahmpuri **(** (0141) 513 4038 **◷** 8am–5pm daily

Lying to the east of Nahargarh, on the way to Gaitor, is the Brahmpuri area where the grand *havelis* (mansions) of the pundits and scholars of the Jaipur court once stood. One mansion was the residence of Pandit Ratnakar Pundarik, a Brahmin courtier during the reign of Sawai Jai Singh II who, it is said, conducted the *puja* (ritual prayer) that appeased the spirit of Nahar Singh. Fortunately, this *haveli* has survived the ravages of time and is partly occupied. A portion is now a protected monument to preserve the superb frescoes decorating the walls and ceilings of the living rooms. These lively and colourful paintings depict an array of different things, including gods and goddesses, courtly scenes and festival processions. One also portrays life on the different floors of the seven-storeyed Chandra Mahal *(p210)*.

Gaitor

Jaipur district; 8 km (5 miles) NE of Jaipur
10am–5:30pm daily
Public hols

The marble cenotaphs of the Kachhawaha kings are enclosed in a walled garden just below Nahargarh. Sawai Jai Singh II chose this to be the new cremation site after Amber *(p222)* was abandoned. Ornate, carved pillars support the marble *chhatris* (open pavilions) erected over the platforms where the maharajas were cremated. One of the most impressive cenotaphs is that of Sawai Jai Singh II himself. It has 20 marble pillars, carved with mythological scenes and topped by a white marble dome. Another is that of Sawai Ram Singh II, with stone pillars and dome panels carved with images of Hindu deities and scenes from Krishna's life. There is another sandstone and marble *chhatri* in memory of Sawai Madho Singh II.

The most recent cenotaph was erected in 1997 in memory of Jagat Singh, the only son of Sawai Man Singh II and Gayatri Devi.

The *chhatris* of the official wives of the Jaipur kings are located in a separate enclosure called **Maharani ki Chhatri**, outside the Jorawar Singh Gate of the walled city, on the road to Amber. Set in a pleasant garden, the complex with its cupolas and carved pillars was restored in 1995.

Maharani ki Chhatri

 Amber Rd 9am–4:30pm daily Public hols

---

(19)

Jaigarh

Jaipur district; 12 km (7 miles) NE of Jaipur
(0141) 267 1848 9am–4:30pm Public hols

Legendary Jaigarh, the "victory fort", watches over the old capital of Amber *(p222)*, found just north of Jaipur. The fort's great, crenellated outer walls delineate the edge of a sharp ridge for 3 km (2 miles) from north to south. Located within the fort is one of the world's few

surviving cannon foundries; its most prized possession is the huge Jai Van, cast in 1720 and believed to be the world's largest cannon on wheels. Its 6-m- (20-ft-) long barrel has carvings of elephants, birds and flowers. Ironically, despite its impressive size, the cannon was never actually fired.

An interesting sight is the massive Diva Burj, a tower. Until the top two storeys were struck down by lightning, a huge oil lamp would be lit at the top of the tower on the king's birthday and during Diwali. The fort has two temples and a large palace complex built over 200 years by different rulers. Located here are the Subhat Niwas (audience hall), the profusely painted Aram Mandir (an airy pleasure pavilion), the residential Laxmi Niwas with baths, and a small theatre for music, dance and puppet shows. The fort's intricate system of collecting and storing rainwater in huge tanks located in the courtyard is unique. Legend has it that Man Singh I's vast treasure, amassed during his military campaigns, was hidden within these tanks. In 1976, the government carried out a massive but unsuccessful hunt, to the extent of draining the water tanks in hope of locating this legendary trove.

The imposing battlements of Jaigarh Fort at sunset ↓

2

AMBER FORT

C5 📍 Jaipur district, Rajasthan; 11 km (7 miles) N of Jaipur ⏱ 8am–5:30pm & 6:30–9pm daily 🚫 Public hols 🌐 tourism.rajasthan.gov.in/amber-palace.html

A grandiose and dramatic reminder of a time when Rajasthan was split into different kingdoms ruled by maharajas, Amber Fort – pronounced "Amer" – was the centre of what became the Jaipur state from 1037 until 1727, when the capital moved to Jaipur.

Located in the Aravalli Hills, Amber Fort was a monument to the power of the Kachhawaha Rajputs and was home to the maharajas and their families. The complex is spectacularly opulent, with splendid mosaics and frescoes, halls decorated with inlaid mirrors, and a particularly glorious set of moulded silver doors.

The existing citadel was established in 1592 by Man Singh I, one of the members of the ruling Kachwaha dynasty, on the remains of an 11th-century fort – but the numerous buildings added by Jai Singh I (r 1621–67) form the most magnificent part of the palace.

Looming above Amber Fort, but connected to it by an underground tunnel, is Jaigarh Fort (*p129*); this heavily fortified building housed the state treasury and was also where the rulers would retreat when Amber came under attack.

In 1727, the capital moved from Amber to nearby Jaipur, but successive rulers continued to come here on important occasions to seek the blessings of the family deity, Shila Devi. An epic structure, Amber Fort is recognized as one of the finest examples of a hill fort in Jaipur, and, along with five other forts in Rajasthan, is protected as a UNESCO World Heritage Site.

→
The imposing walls of Amber Fort, protecting palaces and gardens

↑ Kesar Kyari Bagh, a garden of saffron in Maota Lake, sprawling under the fort

→ The elegant arches and light and airy courtyard of Amber Fort

BLOCK PRINTING IN JAIPUR

India has been exporting cloth since the 6th century BC, and its fabric is notable for its hand-printed block designs. Most states have their own distinctive style. In Rajasthan, the centre of the textile trade has always been around Jaipur. Here, artisans dye cotton and use different blocks to create hundreds of unique patterns. The Anokhi Museum in Amber *(Chanwar Palkiwon ki Haveli, near the fort)* showcases both local and country-wide textile traditions.

The Fort Complex

A steep hike from the town below is Amber Fort's main entrance, the imposing Suraj Pol ("Sun Gate"), so called because it faces the direction of the rising sun, the Kachwaha family emblem. The gate leads into a huge courtyard, Jaleb Chowk, lined on three sides with shops. From here, a flight of steps leads to the Shila Devi Temple, which has silver doors, silver oil lamps and grand pillars carved to look like banana trees, and contains the Kachwaha family deity, a stone *(shila)* image of the goddess Kali. The next courtyard is the Diwan-i-Aam, the space for public audiences. Near it is the Sattais Katcheri, a colonnade of 27 *sattais* (pillars), where scribes once sat to record revenue petitions. Magnificent Ganesh Pol is the gateway to three graceful pleasure palaces, each with special features, built around a Mughal-style garden. The oldest end of the fort was converted into the women's quarters, with screens and covered balconies for the seclusion of the royal ladies in purdah. Faint traces of frescoes are still visible on the walls here. In the centre of the courtyard is the Baradavi Pavilion, which has 12 *sattais*.

On Maotha Lake below the palace, the Kesar Kyari Bagh has star-shaped flower beds once planted with saffron flowers; Dilaram Bagh, also on the lake, was built in 1568 as a resting place for Emperor Akbar on his way to Ajmer.

WHAT ELSE TO SEE IN AMBER

The Chand Pol ("Moon Gate"), directly opposite Suraj Pol, leads to the old town outside the fort. The beautiful Jagat Shiromani Temple, with its remarkable *torana* (gateway), is one of the many temples that lie along this route. To the east lies Sagar, a popular picnic spot with two lakes. The Jaipur-Delhi Highway cuts across the town, and Amber's main market and bus stand are located on this road. Further north is the Akbari Mosque, built in 1569, while towards the east is Bharmal ki Chhatri, a walled enclosure containing a group of memorials.

Jas Mandir, the Hall of Private audience, has latticed windows and an elegant alabaster-and-glass ceiling.

Aram Bagh was the palace's pleasure garden.

The flame of a single candle, reflected in the tiny mirrors embedded in the Sheesh Mahal (Hall of Mirrors), transforms the chamber into a starlit sky.

↑ Aram Bagh, Amber Fort's famous pleasure garden, with its pool

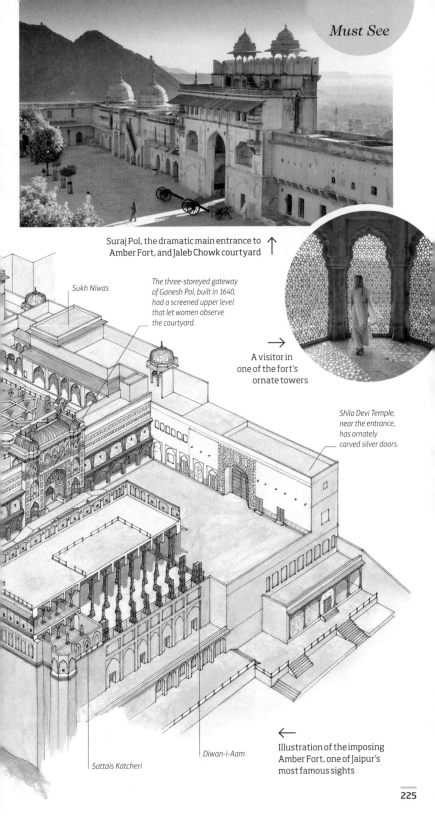

Suraj Pol, the dramatic main entrance to Amber Fort, and Jaleb Chowk courtyard ↑

Sukh Niwas

The three-storeyed gateway of Ganesh Pol, built in 1640, had a screened upper level that let women observe the courtyard.

→ A visitor in one of the fort's ornate towers

Shila Devi Temple, near the entrance, has ornately carved silver doors.

Sattais Katcheri

Diwan-i-Aam

← Illustration of the imposing Amber Fort, one of Jaipur's most famous sights

← The emerald waters of the
pool found next to Alwar's
City Palace

③

ALWAR

 C5 Alwar district, Rajasthan; 150 km (93 miles) NE
of Jaipur *i* Nehru Marg, opposite railway station;
www.tourism.rajasthan.gov.in/alwar.html

Situated between Mughal and Rajput territories, Alwar
grew from a vassal state of the Kachhawaha kings to
a significant Rajput state after Pratap Singh captured
the fort of Bala Qila in 1775. Today, this provincial
town is home to some remarkable monuments.

①
City Palace

Mohalla Ladiya, near
Collectorate 10am–
4:30pm Sat-Thu

A stunning profusion of architectural features marks this
eye-catching palace, with
Rajput *bangaldar* eaves and
chhatris (open pavilions) alongside Mughal floral tracery and
jalis. Built in 1793, the palace
is now largely occupied by the
District Collectorate and Police
Headquarters, so it is best
viewed from the large central
courtyard; a stairway flanked
by two marble kiosks leads
from here to the Durbar Hall
and Sheesh Mahal (special permission is required to enter).

A door on the right of the
courtyard leads to the **City
Palace Museum**, spread over
three halls of the upper storey.
It contains some treasures of
the erstwhile rulers, such as
their famed collection of miniature paintings of the Alwar,
Jaipur and Mughal schools.
The 7,000 rare manuscripts
in Persian, Arabic, Urdu and
Sanskrit include an illuminated Qur'an, a version of the
rare and precious *Gulistan* of
the great Persian poet Sa'adi,
as well as the *Babur Nama* or
"Memoirs of Babur" (1530).
The armoury display includes
the swords of Muhammad
Ghori, Akbar and Aurangzeb,
and a macabre coil called a
nagphas, used for strangling
enemies. The first room

contains a silver dining table
with dividers, through which
moving metal shoals of swimming fish can be seen.

Behind the palace, across
a magnificent *kund* (pool),
is the cenotaph of Maharaja
Bakhtawar Singh (r 1791–
1815). It is locally known as
Moosi Maharani ki Chhatri
after his mistress who performed *sati* here when he
died. One of Rajasthan's
most elegant monuments,
blending brown sandstone
and white marble, its carved
pavilion has domed arches
with exquisite floral tracery,
and ceilings adorned with
fading gold leaf paintings of
mythological characters and
courtly scenes.

City Palace Museum
 (0144) 233 1122
 10am–5pm Tue-Sun

> INSIDER TIP
> **Get Festive**
>
> Alwar is bursting with
> festivals, from the
> three-day-long tourist
> festival in February to
> the spectacular Sawan
> Teej monsoon festival in
> early August and a
> sprawling Mega Trade
> Fair in October.

Moosi Maharani ki Chhatri
 ⏱ 10am–4:30pm 🚫 Fri & public hols; shoes not allowed

---

②
Bala Qila

🕐 Daily (written permission is needed from the office of the Superintendent of Police, City Palace)

Perched on a steep hill above the city, easily accessible by car, the Bala Qila was originally a 10th-century mud fort. Several additions were made to it by the Jats and Mughals until it was finally captured in 1775 by Pratap Singh of Alwar. The frescoed palace within, the Nikumbh Mahal, was named after its first occupants, the Nikumbh Rajputs. Now a police wireless station, much of the fort is not open to the public; however, visitors can still access the fort's extensive ramparts to admire a spectacular panorama of the city stretched out below.

---

③
Company Bagh

📍 Vivekanand Marg
🕐 Sunrise-sunset daily

A lovely garden when it was laid out in 1868, the Company Bagh – while admittedly not as splendid as it once was – is still a welcome pocket of green. It was originally named after Alwar's British ally and protector, the East India Company, but was then later christened Purjan Vihar by Maharaja Jai Singh. An enchanting greenhouse was later added to the garden – it is named "Simla", because it reminded the maharaja of the British summer capital in North India. An incredible 3-km- (2-mile-) long aqueduct, made of solid stone masonry, brought water all the way from a reservoir at Siliserh to this garden.

---

④
Fateh Jang's Tomb

📍 Near Alwar Railway Station 🕐 Sunrise-sunset daily

The tomb of Fateh Jang, one of Shah Jahan's ministers, is a five-storeyed monument, constructed in 1647. Dominated by an enormous dome, its walls and ceiling have raised plaster reliefs, while on the first floor there are some fine calligraphic inscriptions. A school now occupies the tomb's compound.

To the north of Alwar, located at the edge of Vijay

Must See

SHOP

Baba Thakur Das & Sons

Alwar is known for its local version of a milk-cake sweet called *kalakand*, invented at this shop – it is without a doubt the best place to try a slice or two.

📍 Ghanta Ghar, Main Market, Hope Circus 🌐 babathakur daskalakand.com

Sagar Lake, is the utterly spectacular 105-roomed Vijay Mandir Palace, built to look like an anchored ship by Jai Singh (r 1892–1937). A great builder of palaces, the eccentric Jai Singh had the famous 100-roomed Moti Doongri palace-fortress to the south of the Company Bagh blown up because it offended his sensibilities. Vijay Mandir was his last official residence and he lived here for many years. The former ruling family still occupies the palace and they continue to reserve the right of admission to it.

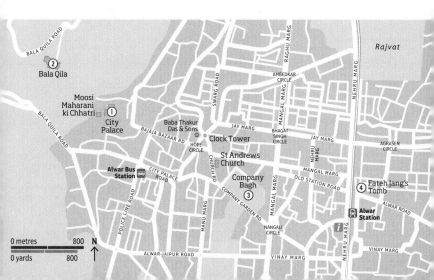

SARISKA NATIONAL PARK

C5 ⬛ Alwar district, Rajasthan; 37 km (23 miles) SW of Alwar
🚌 Alwar ⏰ 6-10am & 3-6pm daily; limited access Jul-Sep ℹ️ Field
Director, Project Tiger Sanctuary, Sariska; (0144) 284 1333

Encircled by the undulating Aravalli Hills, this wild national park is home to a wealth of wildlife, including dainty cheetals (spotted deer), cheeky langur monkeys and endangered tigers.

Designated a tiger reserve under Project Tiger *(p160)* in 1979, the Sariska National Park sprawls over 800 sq km (308 sq miles) with a core area of 480 sq km (185 sq miles). The Aravallis branch out at Sariska, forming low plateaus and valleys that harbour a wide range of wildlife in the dry jungles. Formerly the private hunting ground of Alwar State, Sariska owes a debt to the strict game and protection laws laid down by its conservation-conscious rulers, which preserved its natural habitat and wildlife. As of September 2018, the park's tiger population has increased to 17. A 17th-century fortress and several ancient temple ruins, such as the Pandupol Temple, also lie within the park.

TOP 5 ANIMALS TO SPOT

Tiger
These majestic yet elusive animals are the park's most endangered species.

Leopard
There are around 40 of these stealthy big cats in Sariska National Park.

Langur monkeys
These highly social monkeys can often be spotted resting in the park's trees.

Crested Serpent Eagle
This huge eagle is Sariska's biggest bird of prey.

Indian Horned Owl
This distinguished-looking owl is the region's rarest bird.

Did You Know?

Langur monkeys are known as "leaf-eating monkeys" as they primarily feed on leaves.

→
A group of langur monkeys resting in a tree in the park

The Aravallis branch out at Sariska, forming low plateaus and valleys that harbour a wide spectrum of wildlife in the dry jungles.

Two of the park's multicoloured White-Throated Kingfishers ↑

→ The impressive 17th-century Kankwari Fort, overlooking a lake

5
PUSHKAR

🅰A6 📍Ajmer district, Rajasthan; 144 km (89 miles) SW of Jaipur 🚌 🛈RTDC, Hotel Khadim, Civil Lines, Ajmer; www.tourism.rajasthan.gov.in/pushkar.html

A peaceful pilgrim town of lakes and temples, Pushkar derives its name from *pushpa* (flower) and *kar* (hand) after a legend that tells its lakes were created from the petals that fell from the divine hands of Brahma, the Creator. Today, life revolves around its lakeside ghats, temples and vibrant bazaars – it is this harmonious mix that draws people to Pushkar.

EAT

Pink Floyd Café
Run by ardent Pink Floyd fans, this quirky rooftop restaurant has beautiful river views.

📍Chotti Basti 📞(0145) 277 2317

₹₹₹

①
Brahma Temple

📍Brahma Temple Road, Ganahera
🕐Sunrise–sunset daily
🕐1:30–3:30pm daily

This is one of the few temples in India dedicated to Brahma who, as myth says, was cursed by his wife Savitri when, in her absence, he invited Gayatri, a tribal girl, to take her place in an important ritual. Made of marble with a distinctive red *shikara* (steeple), the temple originally dates from the 14th century. Its inner shrine, off-limits to all but priests, contains a venerable image of the four-faced god. Entry to the temple is free, but beware of hustlers.Note also that photography is prohibited.

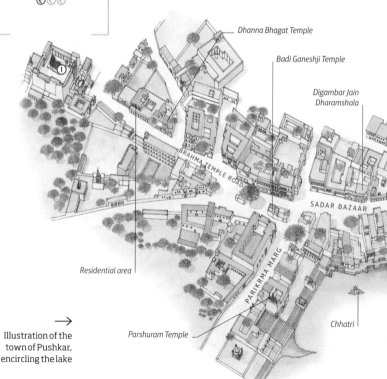

Dhanna Bhagat Temple
Badi Ganeshji Temple
Digambar Jain Dharamshala
BRAHMA TEMPLE ROAD
SADAR BAZAAR
PARIKRMA MARG
Residential area
Parshuram Temple
Chhatri

→ Illustration of the town of Pushkar, encircling the lake

↑ Pushkar's temple-lined lake, bathed in late-afternoon sunshine

② Old Rangaji Temple

🏠 Chhoti Basti 🕐 To Hindus only

This temple, built in 1644, is conspicuous for its South Indian style of architecture, combined with Rajasthani elements. Its *gopuram* (south Indian-style pagoda) towers over the area. The temple is dedicated to Ranganath, a form of Vishnu popularly worshipped in the south,

and contains an image of him reclining on the serpent king Shesha. The temple is open to Hindus only, but the exterior is beautifully carved and worth seeing.

③ Pushkar Lake

This peaceful lake is believed to have sprung from the spot where a petal from Brahma's sacred lotus fell when he was battling a demon. The lake, mentioned in the *Ramayana* and *Mahabharata* (p163) epics, is a major pilgrimage site.

Surrounding the lake are 52 ghats. Devout Hindus make at least one pilgrimage here to bathe at the holy ghats and wash away their sins. The main ghat is Gau Ghat, on the lake's north side, considered the most sacred. Others include Brahma Ghat, near the

Brahma Temple, and Varaha Ghat, the most central, off the main square. Priests may approach you and ask for a donation to enter the ghats, but beware of people posing as priests. Atop the hills surrounding the lake are the temples of Savitri and Gayatri.

At one time, the lake was infested with crocodiles, a real danger to pilgrims bathing in its waters, but they were removed to a nearby reservoir in the 1950s.

> ### Did You Know?
>
> Pushkar is a vegetarian town, with no meat products sold – its omelettes are also egg-free.

Mosque

SADAR BAZAAR

PUSHKAR MELA

Ten days after Diwali, this quiet town comes alive as the much-anticipated annual cattle fair gets going. Pushkar has always been the region's main cattle market for local herdsmen and farmers, and over the years the Mela has become one of Asia's largest cattle fairs. It has also taken on a carnival-like atmosphere, with thousands of people coming here to enjoy the giant ferris wheels, open-air theatres, and food and souvenir stalls that pop up. The fair reaches a crescendo on the night of the full moon *(purnima)*, when pilgrims take a dip in the holy lake. At dusk, during the magical *deepdan* ceremony, hundreds of clay lamps on leaf boats are lit and set afloat on the lake.

 6

AJMER

 A6 Ajmer district, Rajasthan; 135 km (84 miles SW of Jaipur) ⓘ RTDC Hotel Khadim, Civil Lines; www.tourism.rajasthan.gov.in/ajmer.html

Ajmer is framed by undulating hillocks dotted with evocative ruins. It is famous as the holiest Muslim pilgrim centre after Mecca, due to the fact it contains the dargah of Sufi saint Khwaja Moinuddin Chishti (p234).

 ①

Taragarh Fort

⌂ Taragarh Rd ⏰ Sunrise-sunset daily

The rugged, sprawling 7th-century "Star Fort" occupies the summit of Beetli Hill. A series of five gateways lead

into this once-impregnable citadel, said to be the earliest hill fort in the country. Many ruined buildings lie within it, among which are a mosque, still in use, and the shrine of Miran Sayyid Hussain, a 12th-century governor of the fort. Further structures were added by the British who occupied the fort in the 19th century.

> GREAT VIEW
> **Fortuitous View**
>
> The once-mighty Taragarh Fort may now lie in ruins, but the epic views it affords remain undiminished - head up to the battlements for a 360-degree panorama over Ajmer and the surrounding landscape.

---

②

Adhai Din ka Jhonpra

⌂ N of Dargah Sharif, Nalla Bazaar ⏰ 10am–4:30pm daily

This impressive complex of pillared cloisters is all that remains of a mosque built around AD 1198 by the ruler of

the Slave dynasty, Qutbuddin Aibak. Like the Quwwat-ul-Islam mosque at Delhi's Qutb complex (p128), also built at the same time, pillars and fragments from nearby Hindu and Jain temples were used for its construction. The mosque itself, said to have been built over a demolished Jain college, stands on a platform cut out of the hillside, with ten domes supported by 124 columns. The glory of the structure is an exquisite seven-arched screen in front of the many-pillared hall – every column is ornamented with delicate engravings and calligraphic inscriptions in both Kufic and Tughra (early Arabic scripts). The first Director-General of the Archaeological Survey of India, Alexander Cunningham described it as "one of the noblest buildings the world has produced".

---

③

Government Museum Ajmer

⌂ Near bus stand ☎ (0145) 262 0637 ⏰ 9:30am-5:30pm Sat-Thu

Akbar's fort and palace was the first seat of Mughal power

ten avatars of Vishnu. Other displays include antique coins, paintings and weapons.

← Two women promenade at dawn along the bank of Anasagar Lake

④

Nasiyan Temple

🏠 Anok Chowk, Prithviraj Marg 🚫 To non-Jains

Built in the 19th century, the "Red Temple" in the heart of Ajmer is a fine example of a Jain religious building. Just behind the main temple is the double-storeyed Svarna Nagari Hall. It is elaborately decorated with coloured glass mosaics, and large gilded wooden figures re-create scenes from Jain mythology.

⑤

Anasagar Lake

🏠 Circular Rd 🕗 8am–8pm daily

This tranquil lake to the north of the city is named after Anaji (r 1135–50), the grandfather of Prithviraj Chauhan. Charmed by its scenic beauty, Jahangir laid out a garden, Daulat Bagh, and Shah Jahan built the marble pleasure pavilions.

AN ISLAND OF THE RAJ

After long being the object of rivalry between the neighbouring kingdoms of Mewar (Udaipur) and Marwar (Jodhpur), Ajmer fell to first the Mughals and then the Marathas, who sold it to the East India Company in 1818. As a result, during the Raj, Ajmer was a little Muslim enclave of British India surrounded by Hindu-ruled Rajput states.

---

⑥

Mayo College

🏠 Srinagar Rd 🕗 Can visit with the principal's permission 🌐 mayocollege.com

Set up in 1875 by Lord Mayo as an "Eton of the East" for Rajput princes, the school's main building is a jewel of Indo-Saracenic architecture. Today, it is rated as one of India's best public schools.

---

in Rajasthan and was later used by the British as an arsenal. On the orders of Viceroy Lord Curzon, it was converted into a museum in 1908. Its varied collection highlights sculpture and other antiquities gathered from sites all over Rajasthan. The most impressive exhibits are the sculptures dating from the 4th to 12th centuries, of which the most remarkable is a doorframe from the ancient site of Baghera, depicting the

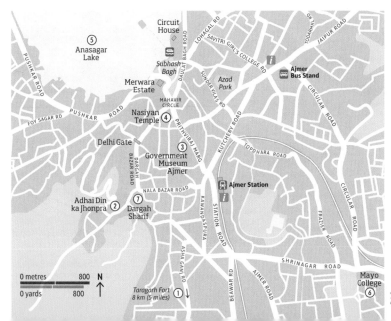

⑦

DARGAH SHARIF

🏠 Khadim Mohalla, Diggi Bazaar 🕐 Sunrise–sunset daily

A revered Muslim pilgrim centre since the 12th century, the Dargah Sharif is an extensive complex containing the simple tomb of the celebrated Sufi saint Khwaja Moinuddin Chishti. The shrine draws a crowd of around 150,000 pilgrims every year.

Popularly called Garib Nawaz, or "protector of the poor", Chishti (1143–1236) was reputed to possess miraculous powers. The saint continues to draw people of every faith to his dargah to seek favours and blessings. It is said that the saint entered his cell to pray in seclusion until his death on the sixth day. Each year, six days in the seventh lunar month (October) are marked as his *Urs* (death anniversary celebrations). Over the years, the saint's royal devotees built grand extensions to the tomb, so that today the dargah complex, teeming with pilgrims and tourists, is virtually a township in itself.

Did You Know?

The 99 sacred names of Allah and 33 Qur'anic verses are beautifully inscribed on the Shahjahani Masjid.

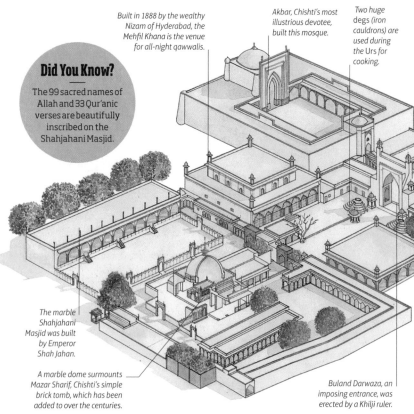

Built in 1888 by the wealthy Nizam of Hyderabad, the Mehfil Khana is the venue for all-night qawwalis.

Akbar, Chishti's most illustrious devotee, built this mosque.

Two huge degs (iron cauldrons) are used during the Urs for cooking.

The marble Shahjahani Masjid was built by Emperor Shah Jahan.

A marble dome surmounts Mazar Sharif, Chishti's simple brick tomb, which has been added to over the centuries.

Buland Darwaza, an imposing entrance, was erected by a Khilji ruler.

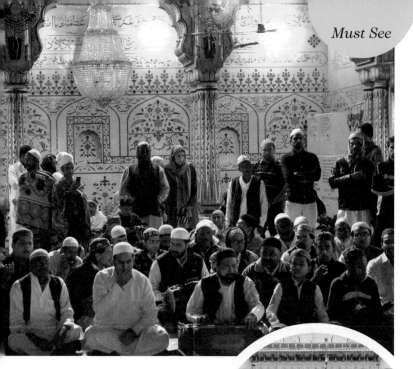

↑ Followers of Chishti gathering to celebrate the saint and sing qawwalis

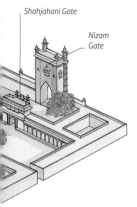

Shahjahani Gate

Nizam Gate

→ Nizam Gate, the towering main entrance to the complex

↑ Illustration of the expansive Dargah Sharif complex in Ajmer

QAWWALIS

Qawwalis are poetic devotional songs that go back to medieval Sufi (mystical Islamic) groups. Sung intensely to lead listeners into a state of religious ecstasy, they celebrate the power of divine love. The songs are usually performed by a large group, with a lead vocalist supported by several other singers, whose voices harmoniously weave different melodies together. The vocalists are usually supported by a harmonium (a small organ), and percussion in the form of hand clapping and drums. These ethereal songs are often performed on Thursdays, when those who have already passed are remembered, while special performances of qawwalis also take place at shrines annually, typically on the anniversary of the death of the saint that the shrine is dedicated to.

7 ⬡ ⬡ ⬡

RANTHAMBHORE NATIONAL PARK

🅰C6 🏠Sawai Madhopur district, Rajasthan; 150 km (93 miles) SE of Jaipur 🚌🚖 ⏱Oct–Jun ℹ️Project Tiger, (07462) 220 479; RTDC Hotel Vinayak, Sawai Madhopur; www.tourism.rajasthan.gov.in/ranthambore.html

Once a hunting ground for the royals of Jaipur, Ranthambhore is now one of India's most beloved national parks. It is a haven for an array of wildlife, but most people visit here seeking a glimpse of a tiger.

The park lies in the shadow of the Aravalli and Vindhya mountain ranges and covers a core area of 392 sq km (151 sq miles). Its jagged ridges, deep gorges, lakes and jungles are the habitat of carnivores such as panthers and hyenas, as well as many species of deer and a rich variety of birds. The most famous resident, however, is the endangered tiger – the park was established to protect this predator. Their numbers have recently increased to around 70 thanks to conservation efforts. Only Jeeps hired from the Project Tiger office are allowed in the park.

STAY

Khem Villas
Get intimate with nature in this stylish wilderness camp, where you can watch an abundance of birds from your veranda.

🏠Sherpur Khiljipur
🌐khemvillas.com

₹₹₹

A majestic Bengal tiger prowling through the tall grass by a lake ↑

↑ The cenotaph of Hamir Dev
Chauhan, one of many historic
buildings in the park

→

A proud peacock putting on a
fine-feathered display for
the park's peahens

TIGER WATCH

Set up by the former
director of the national
park, Tiger Watch
exists to monitor and
help protect the park's
tigers. It warns that
villagers pose as much
of a threat as poachers,
as locals graze cows
during monsoon season,
which degrades the
vegetation. However,
tiger numbers are on the
up; some have even been
taken to repopulate
nearby Sariska, which
lost all of its tigers to
poaching in the 2000s.

Did You Know?

Thanks to
conservation efforts,
there are now over
2,500 Bengal tigers
across the world.

→
The spectacularly frescoed
Chokhani Double Haveli in
the town of Mandawa

8

SHEKHAWATI'S PAINTED HAVELIS

**⛰ B4 🏠 Sikar & Jhunjhunu districts, Rajasthan; Nawalgarh, 140 km
(87 miles) NW of Jaipur ℹ www.tourism.rajasthan.gov.in/shekhawati.html**

Spectacularly decorated *havelis* (mansions) cover the historic region
of Shekhawati. These beautifully painted houses stand in ghostly
splendour, adorning the landscape with pops of colourful opulence.

Situated along the old camel caravan trade route, Shekhawati,
or the "garden of Shekha", was named after Rao Shekha, a
fiercely independent ruler who consolidated the region in
the 15th century. Between the late 18th and early 20th centuries,
local Marwari merchants – who had migrated to the port cities
of Bombay and Calcutta to seek their fortunes – began building
opulent *havelis* with exuberantly frescoed walls. Their inter-
action with the British and exposure to modern urban and
industrial trends influenced their lifestyles and their homes.
In fact, the style and content of the Shekhawati frescoes are a
telling comment on the urbanization of a traditional genre.

←

A colourful fresco at the exquistely decorated
Podar *haveli* in the town of Nawalgarh

←
One of the richly decorated mansions found in the town of Fatehpur

> **The style and content of the Shekhawati frescoes are a telling comment on the urbanization of a traditional genre.**

Local artists still followed the one-dimensional realism of traditional Indian painting, but juxtaposed among the gods, martial heroes and goddesses are images from a changing world – frescoes of top-hatted gentlemen, brass bands and soldiers, trains, motor cars, aeroplanes and gramophones, symbolize the emerging industrial society of the late 19th century.

Today, the region resembles a vast open-air museum full of these beautifully frescoed mansions, with some of the best *havelis* found in the towns of Nawalgarh, Mandawa, Fatephur and Lachhmangarh. A network of excellent roads through semiarid scrubland connects most towns and villages containing the painted *havelis*.

EXPERIENCE MORE

9 Sanganer

 C5 Jaipur district, Rajasthan; 15 km (9 miles) S of Jaipur Paryatan Bhawan, Mirza Ismail Rd, Jaipur; www.tourism.rajasthan.gov.in/jaipur.html

Two ornate triple-arched gateways lead into Sanganer, a colourful town renowned for its blockprinted cotton textiles. According to local lore, this tradition of block-printing goes back to the 16th century when Sanga, one of the 18 sons of Prithviraj, the Kachhawaha ruler of Amber, re-established the town. Printers from nearby villages were asked to migrate to this new settlement to develop a range of textiles or the Jaipur court. It was Sanganer's river, whose mineral powers help fix the colours of the dyes, that gave this printing village its fame and wealth. Today, the town resounds with the thud of printing, as craftsmen work in their sheds amid bolts of cloth, dye-soaked pads and wooden blocks. Most of the printers and dyers in the town belong to a guild with retail outlets that sell reasonably priced fabric, tailored linen and accessories.

Sanganer is also a centre of handmade paper, a spin-off from textile printing, and Jaipur's famous Blue Pottery. Raja Man Singh I of Amber set up the first workshops here to produce this special type of hand-painted pottery, inspired by Persian and Chinese blue and white tiles, so popular at the Mughal court. Blue pottery was revived after the 1950s under the patronage of Rajmata (queen mother) Gayatri Devi.

Tucked away in the old walled town is an impressive 11th-century Jain temple. The Sanghiji Temple was probably built by a Jain trader with additional donations from the town's other wealthy merchants. Like other Jain temples found elsewhere in Rajasthan, this too is lavishly decorated with ornate stone carvings that include images of all the 24 Jain *tirthankaras* (saints) and a beautiful statue of Mahavira, the founder of Jainism, in the innermost sanctuary.

Sanganer is now a busy suburb of Jaipur city and the location of its airport.

10 Bagru

 B5 Jaipur district; 28 km (17 miles) SW of Jaipur past Sanganer on Ajmer Rd Paryatan Bhawan, Mirza Ismail Rd, Jaipur; www.tourism.rajasthan.gov.in/jaipur.html

Bagru is another textile printing centre, with a fabric printers' quarter called Chippa Mohalla. Bagru's prints are bolder and more earthy than those of Sanganer, and they were originally just red and black – the indigo, yellow and green that we see today being later additions. Bagru's rather run-down fort is privately owned and open to the public only for certain festivals.

> **INSIDER TIP**
> **Blocks of Colour**
>
> Learn about Bagru's blockprinting heritage with a tour of one of its printing studios. Vedic Walks *(www.vedicwalks.com)* offers the chance to meet local craftspeople and try your hand at the art.

→ Freshly printed cotton textiles drying in a workshop in Sanganer

A craftsperson printing a floral design onto cloth using *(inset)* traditional wooden blocks ↑

BLOCKPRINTED TEXTILES

The ancient art of blockprinting is still practised in Sanganer and Bagru. In the workshops of the Chhipa Mohalla (printers' quarters) each stage of this ancient technique, from chiselling intricate patterns on wooden blocks to dyeing the fabric, is all done by hand.

BLOCKPRINTING PROCESS

Colourful blockprinted textiles are created using wooden blocks that have been carved by hand with popular design motifs. These are dipped in dye to print the cloth, which has been stretched across a low stool. Previously, colours were extracted from vegetable and mineral matter, such as pomegranate rinds, saffron, madder root, turmeric and the indigo plant. Chemicals have now replaced some natural dyes. In the more complex designs, a single motif may use up to ten different colours with as many blocks, each with a different design. In the final stage of the process, the swathes of printed cloth are spread on riverbanks or hung on huge frames to dry under the sky.

TRADITIONAL MOTIFS

Motifs differ between areas. Delicate flowers and foliage, paisleys, birds and animals on a white background are typical of Sanganer; handed down the generations, these designs were inspired by the flower studies of miniature paintings and Mughal pietra dura motifs. In Bagru, floral, figurative and geometric motifs are popular and are printed on a coarse cotton cloth that is made into blouses and skirts. Today, traditional designs have been reimagined by modern Indian designers.

HANDMADE PAPER

In Sanganer the Kagazi Mohalla, the colony of papermakers, recycles scraps of cloth and silk thread to produce an impressive range of decorative and functional paper products. Fabric is first converted into pulp and then flattened on a wire mesh. The thin sheets of paper are finally peeled off and hung up to dry. These craftspeople jealously guard their trade secrets.

⑪ Siliserh

🅐C5 🏠 Alwar district, Rajasthan; 13 km (8 miles) SW of Alwar 🚌 ℹ️ Nehru Marg, opposite railway station, Alwar; www. tourism.rajasthan.gov.in/ alwar.html

This enchanting spot is found midway between Alwar and Sariska National Park (p228). The 10.5-sq-km (4-sq-mile) Siliserh Lake, in a valley surrounded by low forested hills, is still the main reservoir supplying water to Alwar and the surrounding area. On a hillock overlooking the lake is the water palace built in 1845 by the king of Alwar, Vinay Singh. Now a hotel, this is an ideal place for a quiet getaway, as the only sounds you hear are those made by cormorants, ducks and other waterbirds.

⑫ Tonk

🅐C6 🏠 Tonk district, Rajasthan; 96 km (60 miles) S of Jaipur on NH12 🚌 ℹ️ www.tourism.rajasthan. gov.in/tonk.html

The small principality of Tonk, the only Muslim kingdom in Rajasthan, was established

↑ Elegant arches decorated with gilded stucco in the Sunehri Kothi mansion at Tonk

in 1818 under the terms of a treaty after the Third Anglo-Maratha War, with the British granting the Pathan warlord Amir Khan the title of nawab.

The legacy of its nawabs is evident throughout the old city. They constructed the imposing Jama Masjid and a number of fine painted mansions, such as the **Sunehri Kothi** ("golden mansion"), built in 1824 by Amir Khan in the old palace complex. Magnificent enamelled mirror-work and gilded stucco cover the walls and ceilings of its jewel-like interior, the windows are fitted with stained-glass, and the floors beautifully painted.

The nawabs were dedicated patrons of art and literature. In the late 19th century, the third ruler established a grand centre of Islamic art, now known as the **Maulana Abul Kalam Azad Arabic and Persian Research Institute**. Its collection of rare Arabic and Persian manuscripts includes several illuminated Qur'ans, such as Aurangzeb's *Alamgiri Koran Sharif* and the *Koran-e-Kamal,* prepared on the orders of Shah Jahan. There are also translations of the epics, the *Ramayana* and the *Mahabharata (p163),* inscribed in exquisite Persian as well as Arabic calligraphy.

Sunehri Kothi

 Najar Bagh Rd ⏰ Hours vary, enquire at the Maulana Abul Kalam Azad Arabic and Persian Research Institute

Maulana Abul Kalam Azad Arabic and Persian Research Institute

📍 Near new bus stand
⏰ 10am–5pm Mon–Sat
🌐 maapritonk.nic.in

---

13 Rajgarh Fort

🗺 C5 📍 Alwar district, Rajasthan; 35 km (22 miles) S of Alwar 🚌 Miter Vihar Colony 🚉 Sadulpur ℹ Nehru Marg, opposite railway station, Alwar; www.tourism.rajasthan.gov.in/alwar.html

Overlooking a picturesque valley is the grand hilltop fort of Rajgarh, the old capital of the Alwar rulers. Built by the founder of the dynasty, Pratap Singh, in the mid-18th century, its status as the capital was brief, and in 1775, when Pratap Singh captured Bala Qila, the court moved to Alwar. The fort, with its once beautiful Sheesh Mahal, frescoed walls and secret passages, was maintained as a summer residence, but over time it fell into disuse until finally it was abandoned. The town, too, at the foot of the hill, wears a desolate look.

---

14 Bairat

🗺 C5 📍 Alwar district, Rajasthan; 64 km (40 miles) SW of Alwar 🚌 ℹ Nehru Marg, opposite railway station, Alwar; www.tourism.rajasthan.gov.in/alwar.html

The striking topography of the Aravalli Hills provides a dramatic backdrop for Bairat, an excavated archaeological site that dates back to the 3rd century BC. One of the cities along the main north-south trade route, this was a major Buddhist centre. A rock edict of Emperor Ashoka (273–232 BC) was found here, and at one end of the village, high on a hillock

← Siliserh's 19th-century palace overlooking the tranquil lake

known as Bijak ki Pahadi, are the remnants of a Buddhist monastery and circular temple. It is believed to be India's oldest free-standing structure. Historians have identified it as a *chaitya* hall or chapel which was once supported by 26 octagonal wooden columns.

Bairat's history, however, goes back to the time of the *Mahabharata (p163)* (around the 9th century BC), when this land formed part of a kingdom comprising much of eastern Rajasthan, and was ruled by King Virat from his capital of Viratnagar (present Bairat). It was here that the Pandavas spent the 13th year of their exile. Locals believe that one of the Pandava brothers, the mighty Bhim, lived at Bhim ki Doongri ("Bhim's hillock"), and that Arjuna created the River Banganga when he struck an arrow into the earth. King Virat joined the Pandavas in the battle at Kurukshetra.

On the other side of town, near the rock edict, is an early 17th-century garden mansion. Within the compound is a Jain temple, and just outside is the charming 16th-century hunting lodge where Akbar camped on his way to Ajmer.

THE PANDAVAS IN EXILE

The *Mahabharata (p163)*, describes how, after losing the Pandava kingdom and his wife Draupadi to his cousins the Kauravas at a game of dice, Prince Yudhishthira and his brothers Bhim, Arjuna, Nakul and Sahdev were banished to 13 years of exile. The last year was the most crucial and had to be spent in complete anonymity for, if recognized, it meant another 12 years of exile. Forced to accept these rigid terms, the Pandavas roamed the country, spending their 13th year in disguise at the court of King Virat in Bairat. The story of the Pandavas, their exile and the final battle are key components of the land's folklore, while sites such as Kurukshetra *(see p162)*, associated with their adventures, are venerated pilgrim spots.

 15

Narnaul

C4 Narnaul district, Haryana; 132 km (82 miles) SW of Delhi ☐☐☐ ⓘ www. haryanatourism.gov.in

The town of Narnaul is home to the magnificent Afghan-style mausoleum of Ibrahim Shah Suri, grandfather of the great ruler Sher Shah Suri (p58).

The Jal Mahal ("water palace"), situated in what was once an artificial lake built by Shah Quli Khan in 1591, is a Mughal-style structure; so is

the Birbal ka Chatta, with its projecting balconies and pavilions. In the town's old section are some magnificent, but neglected, *havelis* with murals in the Shekhawati style (p238).

 16

Samode

C5 Jaipur district, Rajasthan; 42 km (26 miles) NW of Jaipur ☐ samode.com

Samode's romantic palace, immortalized in films such as *The Far Pavilions*, is the main reason why this minor Rajput hamlet is now a luxurious tourist destination. Erected in the late 19th century by a powerful noble of the Jaipur state, this jewel-like palace nestles among the hills below an older hill fort. A flight of stairs leads up to a massive gateway and into the palace.

The Mughal architecture of the Jal Mahal, situated in a now dry lake in Narnaul

Its simple exterior is deceptive for, surrounding the vast central courtyard, are spacious rooms on three levels. Of these, the chambers on the uppermost level are the most opulent. The Durbar Hall, Sheesh Mahal and Sultan Mahal are embellished with dazzling mirror work and elaborate murals that depict courtly life, hunting scenes and religious themes, along with floral and geometric motifs. The murals represent the best of the Jaipur style and are said to rival those at Jaipur's Chandra Mahal (p210) and Tonk's Sunehri Kothi (p242). The palace is now a luxury hotel, but non-guests can pay an entry fee to see it.

A short distance away is Samode Bagh, where the more adventurous can stay in one of the 50 deluxe tents pitched in the formal garden. Other points of interest are the abandoned old fort at the end of a strenuous walk up 376 steps, and the quaint little village where a wide variety of local handicrafts such as Lac bangles and *jootis* (slippers) are available.

← One of the Samode Palace's beautifully decorated rooms and *(inset)* the exterior of the palace

as the "City of Ten Thousand Homes". A stone pathway lined with market kiosks, stables or residences leads to the inner sanctum at the foot of the hills, where the ruined Randiyon ka Mahal ("palace of the prostitutes") remains, overlooking the Someshwar Temple, still in use. Three other temples dot the site, of which the Mangala Devi Temple, with a corbelled dome and finely carved exterior, is the most imposing.

Bhangarh

🅰C5 🏛Alwar district, Rajasthan; 56 km (35 miles) S of Sariska via Thana Gazi 🚌 ℹNehru Marg, opposite railway station, Alwar; www.tourism.rajasthan. gov.in/alwar.html

A bumpy ride from Sariska will take you to the abandoned city of Bhangarh, a fascinating site said to be a Kachhawaha clan citadel before Amber *(p222)*. Local legend says that the place was deserted when cursed by an evil magician.

Built in the early 1600s by Madho Singh, the younger brother of Amber's Raja Man Singh I, Bhangarh is also known

Did You Know?

Bhangarh Fort is famous for its ghosts, and it is said to be the most haunted place in Asia.

Chomu

🅰C5 🏛Jaipur district, Rajasthan; 32 km (20 miles) NW of Jaipur ℹParyatan Bhawan, Mirza Ismail Rd, Jaipur; www. tourism.rajasthan.gov.in/ jaipur.html

The small town of Chomu links Jaipur with the Shekhawati region *(p238)*. Traces of a grander past are visible in its fort, *havelis* and stepwells. But Chomu's charm lies in its rural ambience, where bullocks and camels plough the fields, and a unique four-pillared well is the main source of water. In the market, tractor spare parts vie for attention with mounds of ber *(Zizyphus mauritiana)*, the region's famous berry.

STAY

Ramgarh Lodge

This former 1920s hunting lodge is now a smart heritage hotel.

🅰C5 🏛Ramgarh Lake, Jamwa Ramgarh 🌐tajhotels.com

₹₹₹

Phool Mahal Palace

This historic palace near Kishangarh Fort has striking frescoes and comfortable rooms.

🅰D4 🏛Old City Road, Deshwali Mohalla, Kishangarh 🌐royalkishangarh.com

₹₹₹

Samode Palace

An Indo-Saracenic palace that blends traditional decor with modern luxury.

🅰C5 🏛Samode Village, Tehsil Chomu 🌐samode.com/ samodepalace

₹₹₹

Sambhar Heritage Resort

Sleep in a historic lodge or in deluxe tents at this lakeside hotel.

🅰B5 🏛Shakhambri Temple Road, Jhapok, Sambhar Lake 🌐sambharheritage.com

₹₹₹

Hill Fort Kesroli

Spectacularly perched on a rocky outcrop, this 14th-century fort offers elegant rooms.

🅰C5 🏛Kesroli, Bahala, Alwar 🌐neemrana hotels.com

₹₹₹

Kishangarh

B6 **Ajmer district, Rajasthan; 30 km (19 miles) NE of Ajmer on NH 8** **RTDC Hotel Khadim, Ajmer; www. tourism.rajasthan.gov.in/ajmer.html**

Of all Rajputana's princely states, this was the smallest. It was established in 1609 by Kishan Singh, a Rathore prince from Jodhpur, on lands near Ajmer. The king's sister is believed to have been one of Jahangir's wives, a privilege that gave him a special status at the Mughal court. An obvious outcome of this proximity was that the Kishangarh kings tried to emulate the cultured lifestyle of the Mughal emperors, and when the arts lost imperial patronage under the leadership of the austere Aurangzeb, this tiny state became a haven for several migrant miniature painters.

The old city remains much as it was in the past. The narrow streets are lined with *havelis*, some of which have been converted into shops, and on the pavements are vendors selling all kinds of merchandise, including red chillies for which the region is famous. The **Phool Mahal Palace**, a privately owned palace that is now a heritage

hotel *(p245)*, has an idyllic setting on the banks of a lake that attracts a variety of waterbirds. Shady balconies, courtyard gardens and brass doors flanked by paintings hint at its past glory.

The 17th-century Roopangarh Fort, 25 km (15 miles) from Kishangarh, was once the capital of the state. Among the riches of this splendid heritage hotel is a rare collection of the famous Kishangarh miniatures.

Sambhar Salt Lake

B5 **Jaipur district, Rajasthan; 70 km (44 miles) NE of Ajmer**

Sambhar Lake is one of six sites in India designated by the World Wide Fund for Nature (WWF) as a wetland of international importance. This vast inland saline lake spreads over an area of roughly 230 sq km (89 sq miles) and is fed by four river streams. During November and December, several species of migratory bird, especially flamingos, can be seen here.

THE THAR DESERT

Stretching from the Aravalli Hills to the Indus Valley, the Thar Desert takes up much of Rajasthan. The town of Pushkar *(p230)* and the Sambhar Salt Lake lie on its eastern edge. Most of the area is covered by sand dunes, but parts of the Thar Desert have arid vegetation, inhabited by animals such as blackbuck, chinkara gazelle and Bengal foxes, not to mention wild peafowl. The camel was introduced around the 8th century and is still an important pack animal in the Thar.

A number of local legends are connected with the lake's origin, and a Shiva temple and two sacred tanks dedicated to mythological princesses are an indication of the lake's antiquity. The place, however, came into prominence after it was noticed by Babur in the 16th century. Since then, it has been a major source of salt for the country. One of the reasons

↑ People working amid the expansive and famous salt pans of Sambhar Salt Lake

for this is that after a good monsoon, the water level can rise by up to 1 m (3 ft), but over winter, the lake turns brackish due to capillary action caused by evaporation, drawing up salt from underground deposits. Nearby, the Shakhambari Devi Temple is an important pilgrimage sight.

The little township that has grown around the lake survives on the extraction and packaging of salt. Locals can be seen working at the many trenches and mounds that are spread across the ghostly-white terrain. This has now become a highly commercial business. Many *bunds* (small dams) have been illegally constructed in the catchment area to retain rainwater for small-scale operations. This has affected the flow of water into the lake and has also put a considerable strain on its ecosystem.

Tourism has also been on the rise here, with old properties being converted into resorts and bungalows from where guests can enjoy the clear skies and vivid colours of the salt lake. The ecofriendly Sambhar Heritage Resort (*p245*) runs tours of the lake and birdwatching expeditions.

←
Birds perching on a dome of the Phool Mahal, a lakeside hotel in Kishangarh

small white temple dedicated to Shitala Mata, the goddess who wards off disease, in particular smallpox. Shitala Mata is much venerated in parts of rural Rajasthan. A hundred steps lead to the shrine, around which devotees gather for a gossip session after propitiating the deity. Every year in March or April a fair held here attracts a large number of pilgrims. Food is cooked a day before Ashtami, the eighth and most auspicious day after the new moon, and offered cold to the goddess to ensure her protection.

㉑

Makrana

B5 ⧉ Nagaur district, Rajasthan; 80 km (50 miles) N of Ajmer 🛈 RTDC Hotel Khadim, Ajmer; www.tourism.rajasthan.gov.in/ajmer.html

Makrana is a highly commercial stone-quarrying centre. The quarries stretch over a distance of 20 km (12 miles) and produce the luminous white marble that was used to build the Taj Mahal (*p176*). Quarrying began several centuries ago, and traditional open-pit methods are still used to excavate the stone. The demand for good quality marble has not lessened, and nearly 50,000 tons are mined annually and transported throughout the country.

Many small workshops have sprung up where artisans carve statues, pillars, vases, lamps and other objects for local sale and export.

㉒

Chaksu

C6 ⧉ Jaipur district, Rajasthan; 43 km (27 miles) S of Jaipur 🚌

This sleepy village on the road from Jaipur towards Sawai Madhopur is known for its

㉓

Indergarh

C7 ⧉ Kota district, Rajasthan; 52 km (33 miles) S of Sawai Madhopur

This small town, founded by Raja Indrasal in 1605, lies huddled beneath the imposing ramparts of the hilltop **Indergarh Fort**. This picturesque fort is clearly visible from the flat rooftops of the town's houses. Though dilapidated, some fort areas still bear traces of exquisite murals depicting colourful court scenes and legends. The town's two main temples, one dedicated to Bijasan Mata (a form of Durga) and the other to Kuanwalji (Lord Shiva), are popular places of worship for pilgrims.

Indergarh Fort

🕒 8am–5pm daily (on request to the caretaker who lives below the fort)

 PICTURE PERFECT
Pretty in Pink

A good time to visit Sambhar Salt Lake is between the months of June and November, when you can take a picture of flocks of pink flamingos reflected in the mirror-like waters of the lake.

NEED TO KNOW

Autorickshaws outside Agra Station

BEFORE
YOU GO

Forward planning is essential to any successful trip. Be prepared for all eventualities by considering the following points before you travel.

AT A GLANCE

CURRENCY
Indian rupee
(INR)

AVERAGE DAILY SPEND

SAVE	SPEND	SPLURGE
₹2,500	₹10,000	₹20,000

BOTTLED WATER	COFFEE	BEER	DINNER FOR TWO
₹50	₹75	₹300	₹1,000

ESSENTIAL PHRASES

Hello/ Goodbye	Namaste
Thank you	Dhanyavad
Good/agreed	Accha
Do you speak English?	Kya aap angrezi bolte hain?
I (female) don't understand	Main samjhi nahin
I (male) don't understand	Main samjha nahin

ELECTRICITY SUPPLY

Power sockets are type C, fitting two-pin plugs, or type D or M for three-pronged plugs. Standard voltage is 230 bolts.

Passports and Visas

Almost all nationalities require a visa. Tourist visas are valid for six months and may be single- or multiple-entry. Consult **India Visa Online** to find out where you can apply.
Indian Visa Online
🅦 indianvisaonline.gov.in

Travel Safety Advice

Visitors can get up-to-date travel safety information from the **UK Foreign and Commonwealth Office**, the **US Department of State**, and the **Australian Department of Foreign Affairs and Trade**.
Australia
🅦 smartraveller.gov.au
UK
🅦 gov.uk/foreign-travel-advice
US
🅦 travel.state.gov

Customs Information

An individual is permitted to carry the following within India for personal use:
Tobacco products 100 cigarettes, 25 cigars or 125g tobacco
Alcohol 2 litres of wine or spirits
Cash If you plan to enter or leave India with foreign currency over US$10,000 – or US$5,000 in cash – you must declare it to the customs authorities. Indian currency may not legally be imported or exported by non-residents.
Telephones Satellite phones are banned.

Insurance

It is wise to take out an insurance policy covering loss of belongings, medical problems, delays and cancellations.

Vaccinations

Visitors arriving from certain African and South American countries need a yellow fever vaccination certificate. No other inoculations are legally required, but it is highly advisable to make sure you are covered for tetanus, polio, typhoid, hepatitis A and meningococcal meningitis.

Mosquitos are not a problem in Delhi, Agra or Jaipur during the winter and the dry season, but become common during and after the monsoon. The region is low-risk for malaria and, unless you are travelling to other parts of the country, you do not need to take malaria pills. However, day-biting mosquitoes can spread diseases such as dengue and zika, so visitors in June–October should cover up, plus bring and use high-DEET or PMD mosquito repellent.

Money

ATMs are widely available, apart from in more remote areas. Major credit and debit cards are accepted in most hotels and in many upmarket shops and restaurants, but note that credit card fraud is quite common, especially in Agra – to avoid your card data being copied never let anyone swipe your card out of your sight. Be careful not to accept torn banknotes as these cannot be used.

Booking Accommodation

Delhi, Agra, Jaipur and the region surrounding these cities offers a variety of accommodation, including luxury five-star hotels, family-run guesthouses and budget hostels. Some of the best places to stay are heritage hotels.

Travellers with Specific Needs

India can be a challenge for people with limited mobility, but things are slowly changing. **Delhi Metro Rail** and **Jaipur Metro** are now wheelchair-accessible and have tactile paths for people with visual impairments. Ramps are becoming more and more common, and popular sites are making an effort to be more wheelchair friendly. Hotels are unlikely to have wheelchair-adapted rooms, and those that do will tend to be at the top of the market – some are listed on **Disabled Access Holidays**. Ginger and Ibis are two hotel chains who often cater for people with limited mobility. In the UK, **Disabled Holidays** offer package tours to the region for people with disabilities.
Delhi Metro Rail
W delhimetrorail.com/differentlyable.aspx

Disabled Access Holidays
W disabledaccessholidays.com/disabled-holidays/
Disabled Holidays
W disabledholidays.com
Jaipur Metro
W transport.rajasthan.gov.in/jmrc

Language

The main language in this region is Hindi, India's official language, which is written in Devangari script. Urdu, the language of India's Muslims, is very similar, but written in Arabic-type script. Most north Indian languages are related to Hindi and Urdu, including Punjabi, which is spoken by many people in Delhi, and also in places to its north and west, such as Chandigarh. Jaipur's local language is Rajasthani, which is very similar to Hindi. English is widely used in India, and many books, newspapers and magazines are published in it. Around one in three people know at least some English. Indian English is as distinctive as British, American or Australian, and has its own style, expressions and turns of phrase.

Closures

Sundays Some shops close.
Public holidays Each state has its own calendar of holidays. Only Republic Day, Independence Day and Gandhi Jayanti are national public holidays.

PUBLIC HOLIDAYS	
1 Jan	New Year's Day
26 Jan	Republic Day
Mar	Holi
1 May	Labour Day
May/Jun	Eid al-Fitr
Jul/Aug/Sep	Eid ul-Adha
Aug/Sep	Krishna Janmashtami
15 Aug	Independence Day
2 Oct	Gandhi Jayanti
Oct/Nov	Dussehra and Diwali
Nov	Guru Nanak's birthday
25 Dec	Christmas Day

GETTING AROUND

Whether you're visiting for a short city break or travelling around the region, discover how best to reach your destination and travel like a pro.

AT A GLANCE

PUBLIC TRANSPORT COSTS

DELHI

₹150

24-hour metro pass
(plus ₹50 deposit)

DELHI

₹450

3-day metro pass
(plus ₹50 deposit)

JAIPUR

₹50

24-hour metro pass
(plus ₹50 deposit)

SPEED LIMIT
Speed limits are not standardized in India, and vary from state to state, but they are generally as follows:

EXPRESSWAYS

120 km/h (75mph)

NATIONAL HIGHWAYS

100 km/h (60mph)

SECONDARY ROAD

70 km/h (40mph)

URBAN AREAS

50 km/h (30mph)

Arriving by Air

Most visitors travelling by air to the region will arrive at Delhi's Indira Gandhi International Airport, which serves both domestic (terminals one and two) and international (terminal three) flights. Terminal three offers such facilities as left luggage services, currency exchange counters, duty-free shops, restaurants and rest rooms with disabled access. In addition, there are counters for pre-paid taxis and car rentals.

Jaipur International Airport receives flights from local and Middle Eastern operators, while Agra Airport (also known as Kheria Airport) runs a domestic service only.

There are five daily flights between Delhi and Jaipur with Air India and the no-frills IndiGo, and four weekly between Jaipur and Agra with Air India. However, although these flights take under an hour, journeying by air saves very little time once travel to the airport and checking-in times are taken into account; travelling by train is also more ecofriendly. For information on getting to and from the region's main airports, see the table opposite.

Domestic Train Travel

The Indian rail network runs the length and breadth of the country and is one of the most scenic ways to get around.

Delhi has five main stations. Many intercity trains use Hazrat Nizamuddin station, but New Delhi station (between New Delhi and Old Dehi) is likely to be more convenient; there are also the Delhi Junction (Old Delhi), Sarai Rohilla and Anand Vihar Terminal railway stations. Agra has two stations, Cantonment and Agra Fort, while Jaipur has one, simply called Jaipur station.

Each train is known by its name and number. Trains have first- and second-class chair-cars, and two- and three-tiered sleeper coaches (berths fold back during daytime to provide seating). Air-conditioned express trains offered by **Indian Rail** – such as the Rajdhani Express or Shatabdi Express – have fewer stops and offer better facilities and services than ordinary trains, providing punctual connections between the

GETTING TO AND FROM THE AIRPORT

Airport	Fare	Public Transport	Journey Time
Delhi Indira Gandhi	500 INR	Taxi	45–60 mins
International (Terminal 3)	60 INR	Metro	20 mins
Agra Kheria airport	700 INR	Taxi	30 mins
Jaipur International Airport	450 INR	Taxi	40–50 mins

region's main cities. They are more expensive but meals and mineral water are included in your fare. Otherwise, food and drinks are sold by vendors at stations, and meals are offered by rail catering services.

Printed timetables ("Trains at a Glance") are available in most station bookshops, or you can check Indian Rail and **IRCTC**. Be aware that trains can often be hours late and stations are often very busy. Book well in advance as trains are always crowded. Buying rail tickets involves filling in a form, and giving your age and gender (which will appear on your ticket along with the coach and seat number). If reserved tickets are unavailable, you can get an RAC (Reservation Against Cancellation) ticket allowing you to board the train and find seating space; you may then get a berth (apply to the train's ticket collector), but there is no guarantee of this. It is possible to travel without a reservation, but not advisable for journeys of any length.

There are computerized ticket counters at railway stations, and most travel agents can get tickets. At New Delhi Railway Station, the International Tourist Bureau is located upstairs from the main hall – beware of touts trying to misdirect you to dubious travel agents posing as tourist bureaux. The real Tourist Bureau is open Monday to Saturday 8am–8pm and Sunday 8am–2pm. Here you can purchase tickets, payable in US dollars, euros or pounds sterling, or rupees backed by exchange certificates, and get priority reservations. Tickets are refundable, subject to cancellation charges. Booking centres and tourist counters are also located at other railway stations.

Indian Rail
W indianrail.gov.in
IRCTC
W irctc.co.in

Trains Between Delhi, Agra and Jaipur

Some 30 trains run daily between Delhi and Agra, and the journey can take anything from under two to over six hours. The best trains leave New Delhi station in the morning and include air-conditioned Shatabdi Express trains run by Indian Rail. There is also the high-speed Gatimaan Express, which takes only an hour and forty minutes from Delhi's Hazrat Nizamuddin to Agra.

There are nearly 30 daily services running between Delhi and Jaipur, taking from just under three hours to nearly seven. Most leave from Delhi Junction (Old Delhi) or Sarai Rohilla station, but the morning Shatabdi leaves from New Delhi, as does the evening Rajdhani service. The early-evening Shatabdi is the most convenient train for the return journey.

While most of Agra's intercity services use the city's main Agra Cantonment station, trains to Jaipur use Agra Fort station. There are more than a dozen daily services, including a speedy Shatabdi Express, which leaves Jaipur in the morning and Agra in the evening, although there are some almost equally fast non-air-conditioned services too.

Luxury Trains

For those that wish to travel in style, India has a range of luxury trains, including the **Palace on Wheels**, the **Royal Rajasthan on Wheels** or the **Maharajas' Express**. All are seasonal, and serve Delhi, Agra and Jaipur, plus other destinations, with quick excursions in each.

Maharajas' Express
W maharajas-express-india.com
Palace of Wheels
W thepalaceonwheels.com
Royal Rajasthan on Wheels
W royalindiantrains.com

Long-Distance Bus Travel

The region has an extensive bus and coach network. While neither are as fast nor as comfortable as trains, travelling by bus or coach means you often have a wider choice of timings, stops and itineraries; plus, buses can get to places that trains do not reach.

You don't need to book tickets for normal bus services, but may need to for certain routes on deluxe buses; you can reserve tickets through travel agencies such as **Redbus**. For Jaipur, the **Rajasthan State Road Transport Corporation** (RSRTC) provides deluxe bus services to and from Delhi and Agra. They have their own terminals, so avoid the chaotic interstate bus terminals used by most other long-distance buses.

Rajasthan State Road Transport Corporation
W transport.rajasthan.gov.in/rsrtc
Redbus
W redbus.in

Local Transport in Cities

Delhi, Agra and Jaipur are all home to reliable taxi, rickshaw and autorickshaw services. Delhi and Jaipur have metro systems too, and Delhi also has an extensive bus system. The anti-pollution drive has seen the introduction of vehicles run on Compressed Natural Gas (CNG); taxis and autos that have converted to CNG usage have a green band across the usual yellow-and-black body.

Metro

Delhi has an extensive and efficient metro system. Trains run daily from 6am to 11pm, at a frequency of about every 3 minutes in rush hour and every 12 minutes off-peak. Jaipur's metro system is much smaller than Delhi's but still useful. There is no metro in Agra, although it is due to get one around 2024.

In both Delhi and Jaipur, tickets, in the form of tokens, Tourist Cards or Smart Cards, are available to purchase from metro stations. A token is valid for a single trip, whereas Smart and Tourist Cards are top-up travel cards that allow multiple journeys. Top-up cards may offer discounts on daily or weekly fares. Day passes also exist in the form of 1- and 3-day tourist cards. Fares are so low, however, that saving money isn't an issue, but these do save queuing, which can take a long time at some stations during the rush hour. Large or heavy baggage is prohibited on the metro, except on Delhi's Airport Express. Try to avoid rush hour travel as serious overcrowding can occur.

Most metro systems and some suburban trains have "ladies only" compartments which women are advised to use, especially during commuting hours and at night.

Cycle Rickshaws

Cycle rickshaws are slow but cheap. They are excluded from most of central New Delhi, but are commonly seen in the walled city of Old Delhi, and are the most popular means of local transport in Jaipur, Agra and small towns. Agree the price before setting off, which will involve haggling, with foreigners usually paying more than local residents. Drivers ("rickshawwalas") are among the very poorest workers, and many tourists like to be generous with their fare and their tips. In Agra however, cycle rickshaws (and autorickshaws and taxis) touting for business can be a real nuisance. As a rule of thumb, avoid these drivers as they often seriously overcharge and operate commission scams – ignore them and flag one down yourself.

Autorickshaws

The ubiquitous autorickshaws (popularly called autos) are the most common mode of transport. They are essentially a motor-scooter with a couple of seats mounted on the back. Autos are cheaper than taxis, but be prepared for some hair-raising drives.

Most autos in Delhi have a meter, but drivers ("autowalas") are usually unwilling to use it, and are notorious for overcharging tourists – you should insist on paying by the meter or haggle for a good price before getting in.

Autos in Agra and Jaipur do not have meters and so fares should be negotiated in advance – ask hotel staff for an estimate cost for the route so you are better able to haggle.

Carry some small change, as drivers often claim not to have any. Extra charges for baggage are unusual, but may apply when you take a pre-pay auto from a railway station. Pre-paid auto booths with fixed prices exist at some transport terminals and spots in central Delhi (on the inner ring at Connaught Place, for example, by Palika Bazaar car park), as well as at Agra's Cantonment train station, Jaipur's train station and bus station, and Chandigarh's bus station.

Taxis

The black-and-yellow taxis in Delhi operate within the city limits. They can be hailed in the street or hired at local taxi stands, although it is always best to ask your hotel to organize a taxi for you. These vehicles are always well-maintained with the meters in good working order.

In Agra and Jaipur, taxis don't run by the meter but charge a pre-fixed rate according to distance or time period: half a day (4 hours or 40 km/25 miles) or a full day (8 hours or 80 km/50 miles). Your hotel or travel agent can tell you where to find reliable drivers and can give you estimates on what rates you should be paying. Taxis often charge a higher rate at night; in Delhi, for example, that applies from 11pm until 5am and is around 20 per cent. Adding extra charges for baggage are rare, but more likely when you take a pre-pay auto cab from a railway station. Airports may charge an access fee for motor-vehicles which cab passengers will have to pay.

Another popular alternative are the various radio taxi companies – such as **Mega Cabs** and **Meru Cabs** – which can be booked by phone or on line. Radio taxis are much more expensive than regular cabs, but they are more reliable, and are air-conditioned. Car-sharing services such as **Uber** and **Ola Cabs** can be accessed with a smartphone in Delhi, Jaipur and Chandigarh, with the latter also operating in Agra.

Mega Cabs
W megacabs.com
Meru Cabs
W meru.in
Ola Cabs
W olacabs.com
Uber
W uber.com

Things to Be Aware Of
Many drivers of taxis and rickshaws have agreements with certain shops and hotels to give them a commission if they bring customers who spend money, the commission being added to the price paid by the customer. Drivers may therefore try to divert you, unasked, to such places, even falsely telling you, in the case of hotels, that the one you want is closed. In such cases, be firm about where you want to go, and remember that tipping is discretionary.

Buses in Cities

Bus services are barely adequate for the large numbers who can afford only this cheap means of travel, and so buses are often crowded.

You buy tickets from a conductor once you have boarded the bus. However, if a bus is full, it will not stop, and so bus stops can get crowded with waiting commuters who often jump onto the bus while it is still moving.

Delhi has an extremely complex bus network that is often too difficult for visitors to make sense of. In addition, the city's bus drivers are notorious for their reckless driving. Even the so-called luxury buses move at a great speed. If you insist on travelling by bus ask at your hotel or the nearest tourist information centre for advice.

Driving

Driving in India is potentially hazardous. Cows, cyclists and pedestrians appear oblivious of traffic, while cars and motorcycles can behave unpredictably; they may turn or change lanes without indicating, overtake on the wrong side or drive at night with no lights. Road conditions

can also be poor and hazards may be unmarked. Accidents can attract an angry mob, especially if pedestrians or cows are involved, and it is advisable in such cases to leave the scene and go to the police to report the accident.

Car Rental
Most car rental firms offer a vehicle with a driver, and this is the option most tourists take – it is comparatively affordable if you are in a group. Remember to check if your driver speaks English and has a working knowledge of the region – try to meet them and inspect the car before you pay. Note that your driver will expect a tip at the end of each day.

If you are keen to self-drive, there are many reputable Indian companies you can choose from. **Hertz** also has representatives in India. Be aware that hire cars are not always licensed to drive beyond their origin state – travelling outside these boundaries can often add an extra charge.

Hertz
W hertz.com

Rules of the Road
Driving is on the left. There are no standard speed limits, even within individual states. On average, you may travel 100km/h (60 mph) on national highways and 50km/h (30 mph) on urban roads; however on more remote dirt tracks you may only reach around 10km/h (6 mph). Seat belts are compulsory for drivers and front-seat passengers; while this is rarely enforced (apart from in Delhi), it is extremely advisable for everybody in a car to use a seat belt. Avoid driving in the dark.

Bicycles and Motorbikes

One way to get about in and around Delhi, Agra and Jaipur is by bicycle or motorcycle. Motor-cycles are sometimes available for hire on a daily basis – it is possible to rent motorbikes from firms such as **Lalli Singh** in Delhi, who also offer organized tours. Cycling is a good way to travel, although it brings its own challenges. A tourist on a bicycle, for example, may attract a lot of attention in rural areas between the big cities, sometimes including unwanted attention from children or dogs. Some tourists bring bicycles from abroad, but be aware that spare parts may be hard to come by. It is easy to buy bicycles locally, and operators such as **Art of Bicycle Trips** offer cycling package tours in the region. **Delhi Metro Rail Corporation** also offers "rent a bicycle" service at select metro stations.

Art of Bicycle Trips
W artofbicycletrips.com/destinations/india
Delhi Metro Rail Corporation
W delhimetrorail.com/bicyclefacility.aspx
Lalli Singh
W lallisinghadventures.com

PRACTICAL
INFORMATION

A little local know-how goes a long way in this region. Here you will find all the essential advice and information you will need during your stay.

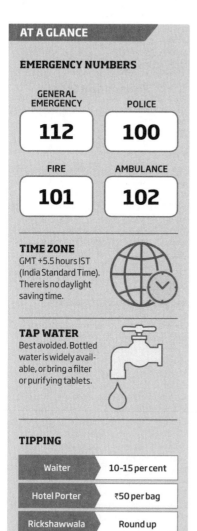

AT A GLANCE

EMERGENCY NUMBERS

GENERAL EMERGENCY	POLICE
112	**100**

FIRE	AMBULANCE
101	**102**

TIME ZONE
GMT +5.5 hours IST (India Standard Time). There is no daylight saving time.

TAP WATER
Best avoided. Bottled water is widely available, or bring a filter or purifying tablets.

TIPPING

Waiter	10-15 per cent
Hotel Porter	₹50 per bag
Rickshawwala	Round up
Concierge	₹200
Taxi Driver	10-15 per cent

Personal Security

Travelling in the region is relatively safe, but it is recommended that you follow a few simple precautions. Wear a money belt under your shirt and be discreet with your camera and phone. While shopping, ensure shopkeepers make out a bill and process your credit/debit card in front of you. Never accept food or drink from strangers, especially on public transport. Keep your baggage close at transport terminals and beware of staged distractions; always padlock your luggage to the chain beneath your seat during train journeys.

Female Travellers

Although sexual harassment ("eve-teasing") is a punishable offence, women – both Indian and foreign – face unwanted male attention on a daily basis, and there have been incidents of rape and violence against female travellers, not least in urban Delhi. Avoid walking alone in isolated places and in the rougher parts of cities, or taking buses at night. When hiring a car or taxi, ask your hotel to book it for you (or go to a cab rank) and note the licence plate number. When queuing for train or cinema tickets, use the "ladies' lines", and use the "ladies only" seats or compartments on buses and trains, if available.

LGBTQ+ Safety

Laws banning homosexuality have been overturned as unconstitutional, but same-sex marriages are not allowed. Hijras, who may be transwomen or intersex, are semi-accepted as a third sex, but face much discrimination. Public displays of affection are seen as taboo for everyone.

Health

Seek medical supplies and advice for minor ailments from pharmacies. Wash, dress and cover all cuts and grazes, even if you would not bother at home. Delhi, Agra and Jaipur have reasonably good hospitals, with 24-hour services equipped to handle casualty and emergency cases. Contact your embassy for a list of approved

hospitals, clinics, doctors and dentists. Avoid food that is not freshly cooked, even unpeeled fruit unless you can purify it. In case of stomach upsets, drink plenty of fluids and stick to plain boiled food until the sickness subsides, or consult a doctor.

Smoking, Alcohol and Drugs

Some religious sites and temple towns, such as Haridwar and Pushkar, are alcohol-free; alcohol is not legally sold in them. Even Delhi has numerous dry days. Smoking is banned in public places, and in temples and mosques. India produces hashish and marijuana bud, but both are illegal with harsh penalties in force for possession. Bhang (marijuana leaf) is legally sold in licensed shops in Mathura and parts of Rajasthan.

ID

There is no requirement to carry or show ID in India, and passports can usually be left in a hotel safe. It is nonetheless a good idea to keep a photo of your passport on your phone. You will need your passport to make train reservations.

Local Customs

Eat with your right hand only, as the left hand is reserved for practical usages, like going to the toilet. It is normal to take off shoes (with the left hand) before entering a house. Putting feet up on furniture will be considered bad manners, as is touching someone with your feet. If sitting on the floor, keep feet tucked underneath. Living in close quarters with family and neighbours gives Indians a different sense of "personal space" than many Westerners. If crowded or jostled be tolerant as space is often at a premium.

Indians tend to dress conservatively and keep the body well covered. Wearing shorts is considered uncouth, and women wearing clothes that display their legs, arms or stomachs will draw stares and unwanted male attention.

Visiting Temples and Mosques

When visiting a temple or mosque, you should be covered from below the elbow to below the knee (women preferably to the wrist and ankle). Remove shoes on entry and if sitting, keep feet facing away from the main shrine. Men and

women may be asked to cover their heads with a handkerchief or scarf. Jain temples do not allow leather items inside, even wallets and watch straps. A few Hindu temples also ban entry for non-Hindus. Women are sometimes banned from Jain and Hindu temples, although this is controversial and some of these restrictions are being challenged in court.

Mobile Phones and Wi-Fi

SIM cards for mobile phones are widely available, but you will need your passport to buy one. It is worth putting them on "do not disturb" mode to ban spam calls. Most hotels offer free Wi-Fi, but sometimes only in the lobby area. Many cafés, bars and restaurants also have free Wi-Fi, and Wi-Fi hotspots are found around many of the main cities, although these are still not widespread. Privately operated internet cafés with the latest facilities can be found in the shopping areas of most large cities and smaller towns.

Post

Mail sent abroad from India may take 1–3 weeks to arrive. Post offices are open Monday to Friday between 10am and 5pm, and on Saturdays until noon. Some services, such as Poste Restante (general delivery), may close earlier. Parcels sent overseas cannot exceed 20 kg (44 lb), and must be specially packed – check for details at the post office. Book Post is a cheaper option for printed material such as books and magazines.

Taxes and Refunds

GST (Goods and Services Tax) is levied on all goods and services, typically at 18 per cent for non-essential items. It is included in displayed prices. While GST on souvenirs should be refundable to foreign residents on leaving the country, no mechanism for this has yet been put in place.

WEBSITES AND APPS

www.incredibleindia.org
The official tourism website for India.
www.delhitourism.gov
The official tourism website for Delhi.

INDEX

Page numbers in **bold** refer to main entries

Index

GLOSSARY

ARCHITECTURE

ashram: hermitage

bagh: garden

baoli: underground stepwell

bangaldar: curved roof derived from Bengali hut

baradari: pavilion with 12 pillars

basti: settlement

burj: residential or fortificatory tower; also bastion

chajja: overhanging eaves or cornices to protect buildings from the sun and rain

charbagh: quadripartite garden

chhatri: open square or octagonal pavilion, literally an umbrella

Diwan-i-Aam: Hall of Public Audience

Diwan-i-Khas Hall of Private Audience

dharamshala: charitable rest house for pilgrims

gali: lane

ghar: house, *crypt*

gumbad/gumbaz: dome, often crowned with a finial; the term is also used for a mausoleum

jaali: carved lattice work on stone screens

jharokha: overhanging oriel window supported on brackets; some were used for the official appearances of the ruler

katra: side lane

khirkee: window

kotla: a citadel or fortified area within a city

kund: pool, tank

mahal: palace

mardana: men's quarters in a palace

maqbara: burial-palace, mausoleum, sepulchre

masjid: mosque

mehmankhana: guesthouse

mihrab: arched niche facing Mecca in a mosque

minar: freestanding tower

minaret: tower in mosque for calling the faithful to prayer

namazgah: space near mosque for celebration of major Muslim festivals

pol: gate

qila: castle, fortress, citadel

sheesh mahal: chamber profusely decorated with mirror mosaic; glass palace

stambha: stately pillar, post or column

stupa: tumulus, burial or reliquary mound

toshakhana: state treasury

zenana: women's quarters in a palace

CRAFT AND CULTURE

bandhini: tie-and-dye

dholak: drum

Dhrupad: style of North Indian classical music

ganjifa: set of playing cards

gharana: school of classical music or dance

ikat: tie-and-dye yarn woven in a pattern

katha: epic tale

matka: earthenware pot

mela: fair, fête

patachitra: painted scroll with mythological tales

phad: painted cloth scroll from Rajasthan

pichhwai: cloth painting depicting Krishna lore

qawwali: style of devotional Sufi music

raga: melodic structure with a fixed sequence of musical notes

rasa: mood; essence

shahtoosh: a fine shawl, now banned, that can pass through a ring. It is woven from the down of the endangered chiru antelope.

tala: rhythmic cycle of varying beats

thal-posh: dish cover

DRESS

burqa: concealing cloak worn by some Muslim women

chador: ceremonial pall of cloth or flowers placed over a Muslim tomb

dhoti: unstitched garment of Hindu men which covers the lower half of the body

gota: gold or silver frill

jootis: slippers

khadi: hand-woven, hand-spun cloth popularized by Gandhi

lehenga: flounced skirt

mukut: crown

zari: gold thread

RELIGION

arti: ritual of Hindu worship

ahimsa: non-violence

amrit: sacred nectar of the gods

Balaji: one of Hanuman's many names in North India

bhajan: devotional song

Chishtiyas: followers of the 12th-century Sufi saint, Moinuddin Chishti

dharma: duty, calling

kalasha: urn

lila: divine sport

linga: phallic emblem of Lord Shiva

madrasa: Islamic theological college

Mahabharata: famous Hindu epic

namaaz: ritual prayers of Muslims

pir: Muslim saint

puja: ritual prayer

Ramayana: epic on the legend of Lord Rama

samadhi: memorial platform over site of cremation

sati: practice of self-immolation by a widow on her husband's funeral pyre

Shaivite: followers of Shiva

tirthankara: Jain prophet

Upanishads: philosophical texts regarded as sacred scripture, dating to the later Vedic age

Vaishnavite: followers of Vishnu

Vedas: texts codifying Aryan beliefs and principles, these were orally transmitted until transcribed into Sanskrit as the *Rig Veda, Sama Veda, Yajur Veda* and *Atharva Veda*

yagna: vedic rite

MISCELLANEOUS

badal: cloud

bahi khatha: cloth bound account book

charpoy: string cot

chowkidar: watchman

Doctrine of Lapse: this gave the British the right to take direct control of princely states that did not have an undisputed heir

haat: open-air market

ikka: pony trap

jheel: shallow lake

katar: two-sided blade

loo: hot westerly wind that blows over North India from April to June

machan: look-out post

mohur: Mughal gold coin

nawab: a Muslim prince

pachisi: a ludo-like dice game

Raj: the period of British rule in India

Satyagraha: a form of moral protest started by Gandhi

thakur: Hindu chieftain

PHRASE BOOK

Hindi is the national language of India and even though it is not the mother tongue of a major proportion of the population, it is spoken widely in this region. All nouns are either masculine or feminine and the adjective agrees with the noun. Most masculine nouns end with -aa (as in rather), most feminine nouns end with -i (as in thin), while all plural nouns end in -e (as in hen). Verb endings also differ if it is a man or woman speaking. In the present tense, a man ends his verbs with -a, a woman ends hers with -i.

IN AN EMERGENCY

Help!	Bachão!
Stop!	Roko!
Call a doctor!	Doctor ko bulão!
Where is the nearest telephone?	Yahān phone kahān hai?

COMMUNICATION ESSENTIALS

Yes	Hān
No	Nā/Nahīn
Thank you	Dhanyavād/Shukriā
Please	Kripayā/ Meherbanī sé
Excuse me/Sorry	Kshamā karen/ Māf karen
Hello/Goodbye	Namasté
Stop	Rook jāo
Let's go	Chalo
Straight ahead	Sīdhā
Big/Small	Badā/Chhotā
This/That	Yeh/Voh
Near/Far	Pās/Door
Way	Rāstā
Road	Sadak
Yesterday	Kal
Today	Āj
Tomorrow	Kal
Here	Yahān
There	Wahān
What?	Kyā?
Where?	Kahān?
When?	Kab?
Why?	Kyon?
How?	Kaisé?
Up	Ūpar
Down	Nīché
More	Aur zyādā
A little	Thodā
Before	Pehlé
Opposite/Facing	Sāmné
Very	Bahut
Less	Kum
Louder/Harder	Zor sé
Softly/Gently	Dhīré sé
Go	Jāo
Come	Āo

USEFUL PHRASES

How are you?	Āp kaisé hain?
What is your name?	Āpkā nām kyā hai?
My name is...	Merā nām... hai
Do you speak English?	Kyā āp ko angrezi āti hai?
I understand	Samajh gayā (male)/ gayī (female)
I don't understand	Nahīn samjhā (m)/ samjhī (f)
What is the time?	Kyā bajā hai?
Where is...?	...Kahān hai?
What is this?	Yeh kyā hai?
Hurry up	Jaldi karo
How far is...?	...Kitnī door hai?
I don't know	Patā nahīn
All right	Achhā/Thīk hai
Now/Instantly	Abhī/Isi waqt
Well done!	Shābāsh!
See you	Phir milengé
Go away!	Hat jāo/Hato
I don't want it	Mujhe nahin chāhiyé
Not now	Abhī nahīn

USEFUL WORDS

Which?	Kaun sā?
Who?	Kaun?
Hot	Garam
Cold	Thandā
Good	Achhā
Bad	Kharāb
Enough	Bus/Kāfī hai
Open	Khulā
Closed	Bundh
Left	Bāyān
Right	Dāyān
Straight on	Sīdhā
Near	Pās/Nazdīk
Quickly	Jaldī
Late	Der sé
Later	Bād mein
Entrance	Pravesh
Exit	Nikās
Behind	Pīchhé
Full	Bharā
Empty	Khālī
Toilet	Shauchālaya
Free/No charge	Nihshulk/Muft
Direction	Dishā
Book	Kitāb
Newspaper	Samachār patra

SHOPPING

How much does this cost?	Iskā kyā dām hai?
I would like...	Mujhe... chāhiyé
Do you have...?	Kya āp ké pās... hai?
I am just looking	Bus dekh rahen hain
Does it come in other colours?	Yeh doosré rangon main bhī ātā hai kya?
This one	Yeh wālā
That one	Voh wālā
Black	Kālā
Blue	Nīlā
White	Safed
Red	Lāl
Yellow	Pīlā
Green	Harā
Brown	Bhurā
Cheap	Sastā
Expensive	Mehengā
Tailor	Darzī

BARGAINING

How much is this?	Yeh kitné kā hai?
How much will you take?	Kitnā logé?
That's a little expensive	Yeh to mehengā hai
Could you lower the price a bit?	Dām thodā kam kariyé
How about ...rupees?	...rupeye laingé?
I'll settle for ...rupees	...rupeye mein denā hai to dijiyé

STAYING IN A HOTEL

Do you have any vacant rooms?	Āpké hotel mein khāli kamré hain?
What is the charge per night?	Ek rāt ka kirāyā kyā hai?
Can I see the room first?	Kyā mein pehlé kamrā dekh saktā hoon?
Key	Chābī
Soap	Sābun
Towel	Tauliyā
Hot/Cold water	Garam/Thandā pānī

EATING OUT

Breakfast	Nāshtā
Food	Khāna
Water	Pānī
Ice	Baraf
Tea	Chai
Coffee	Coffee
Sugar	Chīnī
Salt	Namak
Milk	Doodh
Yoghurt	Dahī
Egg	Andā
Fruit	Phal
Vegetable	Subzī
Rice	Chāval
Pulses (lentil, split peas etc)	Dāl
Fixed price menu	Ek dām menu
Is it spicy?	Mirch-masālā tez hai kyā?
Make it less spicy please	Mirch-masala thodā kam
Knife	Chhurī
Fork	Kāntā
Spoon	Chammach
Finished	Khatam

NUMBERS

1	Ek
2	Do
3	Tīn
4	Chār
5	Pānch
6	Chhé
7	Sāt
8	Āth
9	Nau
10	Dus
11	Gyārah
12	Bārah
13	Terah
14	Chaudah
15	Pandrah
16	Solah
17	Satrah
18	Athārah
19	Unnīs
20	Bīs
30	Tīs
40	Chālīs
50	Pachās
60	Sāth
70	Sattar
80	Assī
90	Nabbé
100	Sau
1,000	Hazār
100,000	Lākh
10,000,000	Karod (crore)

TIME

One minute	Ek minute
One hour	Ek ghantā
Half an hour	Ādhā ghantā
Quarter hour	Paunā ghantā
Half past one	Derh
Half past two	Dhāi
A day	Ek din
A week	Ek haftāh
Monday	Somwār
Tuesday	Mangalwār
Wednesday	Budhwār
Thursday	Guruwār
Friday	Shukrawār
Saturday	Shaniwār
Sunday	Raviwār
Morning	Subah
Afternoon	Dopahar
Evening	Shām
Night	Rāt

ACKNOWLEDGMENTS

The publisher would like to thank the following for their kind permission to reproduce their photographs:

Key: a-above; b-below/bottom; c-centre; f-far; l-left; r-right; t-top

123RF.com: meinzahn 92clb.

4Corners: Reinhard Schmid 112-3t, 119tl; Luigi Vaccarella 230-1t.

akg-images: Heritage Images / Fine Art Images 57bl.

Alamy Stock Photo: AC Images 210t; age fotostock 25tl, 57tl, / Dinodia 148br; Leonid Andronov 222-3b; Antiqua Print Gallery 56t; Archimage 94-5b; Archive Pics 180br; Dheeraj Arora 132tc; Art Collection 3 75br; Arterra Picture Library 198; Sourabh Bharti 192-3t; BIOSPHOTO 161cla; Anders Blomqvist 75crb; Charles O. Cecil 174b; Classic Image 57cla, 59br; Matjaz Corel 48-9t; Anil Dave 42-3t; dbimages 61cra, 183cra, / Roy Johnson 98-9b; Design Pics Inc 108br, 209cra; Roop Dey 11t, 108crb; Dinodia Photos 26tl, 57tr, 59bl, 95tr, 152b, 163clb,177br, 183br, 186-7t, 188br, 210br, 215clb, 237br; Eagle Visions Photography / Craig Lovell 56br, 114t; ephotocorp 51tr; Bella Falk 139cr; Michele Falzone 11br, 20t; Jorge Fernandez 196-7t; FLPA 50-1t; Chris Fredriksson 193clb; Anil Ghawana 51crb, 161tl; Ankit Goyal 229tl; Granger Historical Picture Archive 60clb, 180bl; Martin Harvey 160bl; hemis.fr / Patrick Frilet 12-3b, 22cr, 26cla, 240b, / Franck Guiziou 130t, 194b, 246b, / Francis Leroy 189bc, / Ludovic Maisant 18crb, 43crb, / Collection and image courtesy of Ranjini Shettar's installation Sing Along, Kiran Nadar Museum of Art 47b, / Alain Schroeder 191br; Christina Hemsley 226t; The Historic Collection 58cb, 58bl; imageBROKER 51cl, 179tr, 213br, 214b; imageBROKER / Olaf Krüger 195tr; ImageDB 24cra; IndiaPicture 36b, 58tr; / Amit Pasricha 134b; INTERFOTO 12clb, 57crb; ITPhoto 22crb; Paul Kennedy 12t, 47tr; Andrey Khrobostov 78-9t; Joana Kruse 31tl; Abhishek Kumar 223tl; Guillem Lopez 177bc; Ingemar Magnusson 215cla; Don Mammoser 20cr; Saji Maramon 117bl, 128-9l; Maroš Markovic 184tl; Chris Mellor 103b; Franck Metos 247tl; Stelios Michael 52tr; PACIFIC PRESS 61crb; David Pearson 111tc, 180cb; The Picture Art Collection 115tr, 127tl, 163t; Leonid Plotkin 45crb; Graham Prentice 160-1b, 237cra; PRISMA ARCHIVO 59t; randomclicks 141b; John Rees 18cr; Juergen Ritterbach 181cr; robertharding 82b, 92b, 181clb, / Peter Barritt 117tr; Pep Roig 39clb; Grant Rooney 244-5t, 245tc; Ruby 241br; Oleksandr Rupeta 48bl; Alec Scaresbrook 38-9t; Sham 223c;

Mahesh Dutt Sharma 131crb, 131b; A G Shoosmith New Delhi 60tl; Sanjay Shrishrimal 161tr; Paulette Sinclair 96cr, 97t, 97cra; Aditya "Dicky" Singh 236-7b; Gurcharan Singh 150bl; michael smith 244bl; sondipon 31clb, 116-7t; Drew Stewart 248-9b; Petr Svarc 179clb; Travel Wild 25tr, 34-5b; United Archives GmbH 60-1t; Lucas Vallecillos 30tl, 52-3b, 67, 75clb, 76tl, 80tr, 88-9, 138-9b; Vibrant Pictures 37t; wayfarer 74br, 77cla; Westend61 GmbH 87tl; Jan Wlodarczyk 35tl, 225t; World History Archive 56cb; Xinhua 49tr.

Amrapali Museum: 215cra.

Anokhi Museum of Hand Printing: © S. Skidmore 46tr.

AWL Images: Michele Falzone 176-7t; Nigel Pavitt 109; Doug Pearson 217tl; Reza 234-5t; Alex Robinson 86bl.

Bridgeman Images: Victoria & Albert Museum, London / Colonel James Tod travelling by elephant through Rajasthan with his Cavalry and Sepoys Indian School, (18th century) 58cra / Ann & Bury Peerless Picture Library / The First Incarnation of Vishnu as Matsya 'The Fish': The Deluge (paint on paper), Indian School 141tr, Dinodia / Ganesh, the Elephant God (gouache on paper), Indian School, Mumbai, India 140bl.

Dorling Kindersley: Idris Ahmed 127c, 135cl, 136t, 137b; Akhil Bahkshi 243cra; Dinesh Khanna 42br; Aditya Patankar 215bc.

Dreamstime.com: Leonid Andronov 127cra, 206-7t; Swapan Banik 152t; Christophe Cappelli 238-9t; Lazar Adrian Catalin 211cl; Richie Chan 10clb; Anil Dave 215bl; Dbyjuhfl 154-5b; Donyanedomam 28tr, 135br, 181br; Euriico 153bl; Pablo Hidalgo 208cl; Kalcutta 241t; Fabio Lamanna 189cb; Pius Lee 34tl; Lindrik 212-3t; Mdsindia 69cb, 142, 162b, 235crb; Meinzahn 13cr, 24tl, 26-7t, 46b, 228-9b, 229cra; Dmitrii Melnikov 53cl, 82clb; Mvorobiev 20bl, 39ca, 132-3b; Noracarol 10-1b; Subhrajyoti Parida 20crb; Sanga Park 189bl; Marina Pissarova 22t, 148t; Pixelartistic 54cra; Pjhpix 22bl; Radiokafka 27tr; Dmitry Rukhlenko 188-9t, 190-1b, 201; S4sanchita 13br; Siempreverde22 212br; Silentgunman 29clb; Sundraw 53tr; Suronin 53br.

Getty Images: 500px / SKT Photography 208-9b; AFP / Christophe Archambault 40-1b, / Laurene Becquart 58tl, / Rebecca Conway 33bl, / Chandan Khanna 54cla, 74-5t, / Narinder Nanu 45br, 164t, / Raveendran 102t, / Manan Vatsyayana 29cl;

Main Contributers Daniel Jacobs, Victoria McCulloch, Anuradha Chaturvedi, Dharmendar Kanwar, Partho Datta, Premola Ghose, Ranjana Sengupta, Subhadra Sengupta

Senior Editor Ankita Awasthi Tröger

Senior Designers Tania Da Silva Gomes, Bess Daly

Project Editor Rachel Laidler

Project Art Editors Dan Bailey, Stuti Tiwari Bhatia, Hansa Babra, Jaileen Kaur, Bharti Karakoti, William Robinson

Designer Jordan Lambley

Factchecker Gaurav Joshi, Avanika

Editors Sylvia Tombesi-Walton, Emma Grundy Haigh, Lucy Sara-Kelly, Lucy Sienkowska, Lauren Whybrow

Proofreader Ben Ffrancon Davies

Indexer Helen Peters

Senior Picture Researcher Ellen Root

Picture Research Nimesh Agrawal, Sophie Basilevitch, Sumita Khatwani, Rituraj Singh, Harriet Whitaker

Illustrators Ajay Sethi, Ampersand, Ashok Sukumaran, Avinash, Dipankar Bhattacharya, Gautam Trivedi, Mark Warner

Senior Cartographic Editor Casper Morris

Cartography Uma Bhattacharya, Mohammad Hassan, Suresh Kumar

Jacket Designers Maxine Pedliham, Tania Da Silva Gomes,

Jacket Picture Research Susie Watters

Senior DTP Designer Jason Little

DTP Nand Kishor Acharya

Producer Samantha Cross

Managing Editor Hollie Teague

Art Director Maxine Pedliham

Publishing Director Georgina Dee

First edition 2000

Published in Great Britain by Dorling Kindersley Limited, 80 Strand, London, WC2R 0RL

Published in the United States by DK Publishing, 1450 Broadway, Suite 801, New York, NY 10018

Copyright © 2000, 2019 Dorling Kindersley Limited
A Penguin Random House Company
19 20 21 22 10 9 8 7 6 5 4 3 2 1

A CIP catalog record for this book is available from the British Library.

A catalog record for this book is available from the Library of Congress.

ISSN: 1542 1554
ISBN: 978 0 2413 6884 8

Printed and bound in Malaysia.

www.dk.com

MIX
Paper from responsible sources
FSC™ C018179
www.fsc.org

The information in this DK Eyewitness Travel Guide is checked regularly.

Every effort has been made to ensure that this book is as up-to-date as possible at the time of going to press. Some details, however, such as telephone numbers, opening hours, prices, gallery hanging arrangements and travel information, are liable to change. The publishers cannot accept responsibility for any consequences arising from the use of this book, nor for any material on third party websites, and cannot guarantee that any website address in this book will be a suitable source of travel information. We value the views and suggestions of our readers very highly. Please write to: Publisher, DK Eyewitness Travel Guides, Dorling Kindersley, 80 Strand, London, WC2R 0RL, UK, or email: travelguides@dk.com